THE
BATTLE
OF
SAVATE

Piet Nortje

28/10/2015

THE
BATTLE
OF
SAVATE

32 Battalion's Greatest Operation

PIET NORTJE

Published by Zebra Press
an imprint of Penguin Random House South Africa (Pty) Ltd
Reg. No. 1953/000441/07
The Estuaries No. 4, Oxbow Crescent, Century Avenue, Century City, 7441
PO Box 1144, Cape Town, 8000, South Africa

www.zebrapress.co.za

First published 2015

1 3 5 7 9 10 8 6 4 2

PUBLISHER: Marlene Fryer
MANAGING EDITOR: Robert Plummer
EDITOR: Bronwen Leak
PROOFREADER: Mark Ronan
COVER DESIGNER: Monique Cleghorn
TYPESETTER: Monique van den Berg
INDEXER: Sanet le Roux

Set in 11.5 pt on 16.5 pt Adobe Garamond

Printed and bound by Interpak Books, Pietermaritzburg

ISBN 978 1 77022 779 8 (print)
ISBN 978 1 77022 780 4 (ePub)
ISBN 978 1 77022 781 1 (PDF)

For those who fought in the Battle of Savate
In remembrance of those who fell

Contents

Acknowledgements

Compiling this book brought back many memories, especially when I read the recollections of the men and realised that I had been involved in some of the incidents they described. To everyone who contributed, even if it was only one sentence, your recollections appear in this book under your name. Please accept these simple references as my acknowledgement and gratitude to you, not only for helping me, but also for preserving the history of the Battle of Savate. I could list the names of the veterans who provided me with information and their personal experiences, but I prefer to use the space to tell the story of the battle.

Nevertheless, there are a few former 32 Battalion members who have made a tremendous effort to help me and whom I wish to thank individually:

Colonel Jan Breytenbach, for allowing me to include his opinion of the Battle of Savate in this book.

Justin Taylor, for unselfishly authorising me to use his personal memoir, *A Whisper in the Reeds*, which is the most complete memoir regarding service with 32 Battalion that I have ever read.

Kevin FitzGerald, for going to the effort of calling together former Reconnaissance Wing men to answer my questions and offer their recollections.

Frans 'F.L.' Smit, who was responsible for the declassification of the 32 Battalion files for my book *The Terrible Ones*. Not only did he answer my wish for a speedy declassification, but he also found the official Operation Tiro-Tiro war diary, which was not recorded on any index list and was hidden away between other files.

Stefanus van der Walt, for allowing me to use his 2010 Savate Day address, 'Let us remember', which appears in Chapter 10. He also supplied most of the material concerning the 2012 Savate battlefield tour. Without his help and support, this book would never have seen the light.

Peter Williams, who managed to convince a few guys – who, for years, had promised to give their recollections but never produced – to produce.

Anton Roets and Marius Scheepers, two former 32 Battalion men who do not feature in the book, but whose video recordings of the 2012 Savate tour added to my knowledge.

Several people who are not former 32 Battalion members also went to great lengths to help me and deserve my thanks:

Tinus de Klerk, who unselfishly sent me documents covering aspects of Operation Tiro-Tiro that he found in files other than the 32 Battalion ones, while researching his own Special Forces publication.

Angela McIntyre, for her work on the oral history project, *Missing Voices*, about the untold stories of the apartheid era. Some of the interviews she conducted with former 32 Battalion men, including a Portuguese-speaking soldier, have been incorporated into this book. Her work is available from the William Cullen Library at the University of the Witwatersrand. Michele Pickover and Gabriele Mohale from the library kindly provided me with copies of the *Missing Voices* interviews.

Linda de Jager, of Endgame Media, carried out extensive research for her own television production, and unselfishly allowed me to use her interview with one of the Battle of Savate veterans.

Louis Engelbrecht, for sharing his life story and amazing military career with me, and for allowing me to use his story in this book. Unfortunately, for security reasons, I am unable to write about his military achievements; however, I am sure that both his late parents would be extremely proud of him.

Because I do not live in South Africa, Lourens Etchell spent many hours at the Department of Defence Documentation Centre doing research on my behalf, working through thousands of documents and sending me photographs of document pages. If it were not for his dedication, this work would have taken much longer.

Eugenio Camacho, who graciously travelled to Cuangar to conduct interviews with Savate veterans. His efforts helped me to either confirm or contradict facts in my email correspondence with the FAPLA acting commander.

During the battle, only the Chief Staff Intelligence (CSI) operative was allowed to take photographs. The Battle of Savate images that appear in this book were taken by him and come from the official 32 Battalion operations photograph album and the Department of Defence Documentation Centre photograph library. These photographs are of poor quality because, due to the operation's security classification, the film was developed by CSI rather than professionals. The rest of the photographs were taken by various people, some of whom indicated that they had received them from some-one else, who had, in turn, got them from someone else, etc. Most of the 2012 battlefield tour photographs are from Justin Taylor and Stefanus van der Walt.

I owe much gratitude to Marlene Fryer and Robert Plummer of Zebra Press for agreeing to publish this book. By doing so, they have ensured that important South African military history is preserved for generations to come.

Special thanks go to my wife, Mariana, and our children, Ruanné and Mariné, who both followed in my footsteps to become soldiers in the British Army. Ruanné is a full-time soldier in the Royal Welsh Regiment and Mariné is part-time with the City of Edinburgh Universities Officers' Training Corps while she studies at Queen Margaret University, Edinburgh. My family's support has never wavered over the years, and they cheerfully tolerate my endless hours at the computer. Without your love and under-standing there would be no books. You are and always will be my most important concerns.

Preface

On 21 May 1980, under the codename Operation Tiro-Tiro, 32 Battalion attacked and routed, without air or artillery support, the FAPLA brigade at Savate, a small Angolan town in the Cuando Cubango Province 75 kilometres north of the border with South West Africa. Fifteen members of 32 Battalion were killed in the action and many more wounded. It was the highest South African casualty rate in a single skirmish since the start of the Border War. Overall, however, Savate was a significant victory for 32 Battalion. According to reports, FAPLA suffered heavy casualties and the invaders captured a great many vehicles, weapons, ammunition and other equipment, as more than a thousand FAPLA cadres fled the base.

Operation Tiro-Tiro, or the Battle of Savate, as it became known, was the first time the SADF had engaged FAPLA in battle since 1975. And, despite the record number of casualties, it was 32 Battalion's biggest victory since its formation in March 1976. Even though the Border War came to an end in 1989 and 32 Battalion was disbanded in March 1993, to this day a remembrance service and parade are held annually on the Sunday closest to 21 May to commemorate the Battle of Savate, and to remember 32 Battalion's victory and the price they paid.

Perhaps the best explanation of why this particular encounter became a 32 Battalion commemorative day can be found in a recent email sent by Colonel Jan Breytenbach to former members of 32 Battalion:

British paratroopers still remember Arnhem as a costly failure, but also as a magnificent example of paratrooper courage in the face of terrible odds when pitched against several German divisions, one of which was [an] SS 'Panzer' division.

The French Foreign Legion remembers the heroic and stubborn stand of a small force of legionnaires when attacked and totally wiped out by an overwhelming force of Mexicans.

The Paratroopers of the SADF remember a tough contest that almost ended in disaster when they fought and won a battle against tremendous odds at Cassinga.

Similarly, 32 Battalion had adopted the Battle of Savate as the 'leitmotif' to forever afterwards remember 32 Battalion comrades who fell during Savate, mainly because it was the highest casualty rate they ever had after Bravo Group had become part of the South African Army.

The first account of Operation Tiro-Tiro was written by Colonel Breytenbach and published as *They Lived by the Sword* in 1989. My book, *32 Battalion: The Inside Story of South Africa's Elite Fighting Unit*, followed in 2003 and included some additional information. Dr Louis Bothma's *Die Buffel Struikel* (*The Buffalo Battalion*), published in 2005, added even more. The account of the battle was still, however, incomplete.

I continued to intensively research and collect information in order to write a more definitive book about the battle, and in 2012 published *The Terrible Ones: A Complete History of 32 Battalion*, which I believe contains the most complete and accurate coverage of Operation Tiro-Tiro written to date.

Since then, however, a few things have happened.

After a long and costly struggle, I finally managed to obtain the declassification of top-secret Operation Tiro-Tiro documents stored in the military archives (permission to declassify these documents had been previously refused).

Then, in 2012, men from the 32 Battalion Veterans' Association visited the Savate battlefield as part of the 32nd commemoration of the battle. Unbeknown to the chairman of the association, he would meet the man who had been the FAPLA brigade's acting commander on the day of the attack. Before this unsolicited meeting, I had been trying, through every possible channel, to determine the identity of, and make contact with, the FAPLA commander on that day. But either the Angolan military did not know who he was or, more likely, they were reluctant to give me the information.

And so it was from the chairman of the veterans' association that I learnt the identity of the commander and acting commander at Savate: respectively, the then governor of the Cuando Cubango Province and the then administrator of Cuangar, a town and municipality in Cuando Cubango and with jurisdiction over Savate. Both were retired FAPLA generals and now politicians. I also learnt that a few Savate battle veterans lived in Cuangar.

After the 2012 Angolan elections, both the governor and the administrator were replaced and it took me a while to trace their whereabouts. I used friends and acquaintances – mostly former SADF and 32 Battalion members now working in Angola – to try to make contact with the men, but this prompted late-night visits to their houses by the Angolan security and intelligence agency. I therefore advised them to drop the issue, as I did not want to see anyone get arrested on my account.

In the meantime, I managed to make email contact, first via a middleman but then personally, with the administrator who had left Cuangar and was now administrator of Rivungo, a small town on the Angola–Zambia border. What started off as a healthy exchange of useful information deteriorated into his denial of documented facts, claiming they were false propaganda of the South African apartheid regime (maybe because I had questioned some of his original remarks). He told a different version of events, which painted FAPLA in a good light but contradicted what happened on the ground. After a while he became vague and eventually disappeared into thin air. I then learnt that he had been transferred to Jamba, the old UNITA hometown, after a riot against his style of governing broke out in Rivungo.

Interestingly, at around this time, many aspects regarding the Battle of Savate, which for more than three decades had gone unquestioned, were now being queried in publications and on other platforms. When the first books were written about the battle, no documentary proof or evidence was available and the authors had to rely on individuals to obtain information. Ironically, it was some of these individuals who were now questioning their own recollections. And others who had originally accepted their accounts were also now expressing doubt. It was time for me to use my new insights to tell the full story.

While it is unfair to analyse Operation Tiro-Tiro because the SADF commander on the day has passed away and cannot defend the decisions he made, I can nevertheless explain how the operation was planned and executed, what went wrong and what went right, and the results of the attack. I can outline the SADF strategy of the early 1980s and delve into why 32 Battalion attacked Savate on behalf of UNITA in the first place. I can attempt to explain why the events and figures that are now being questioned are in fact correct.

When soldiers speak about battles or about contact with the enemy, one often hears expressions like 'no, that's not correct, it did not happen like that. Ask me. I was there. I know.' It is true that what one person experiences and sees during an event is not necessarily the same as what another experiences and sees. During enemy contact, a soldier on the left flank of the attack line, for example, does not have the same experiences, fears or challenges as a soldier on the right flank, even though they may be only a few metres apart. While the personal recollections of soldiers who have lived through conflict are valuable, eventually memories fade, especially those concerning names, places, dates and times.

Not many official documents concerning the Battle of Savate are available, so, like many other operations in which 32 Battalion took part over the years, this battle also has its myths and unanswered questions. During my research for my first book, *32 Battalion*, Major General Deon Ferreira gave me his handwritten orders. These, however, were the deployment and attack plans, and it is known that the operation did not go according to plan.

This account is therefore based on a number of sources: the official war diary, situation reports, the original operation order, which includes a sketch of the Savate base defence, the aforementioned recently declassified documents and the personal recollections of 35 former 32 Battalion members who took part in the battle. My only regret is that there are not more recollections and personal experiences of the Portuguese-speaking men involved. I tried hard to get these, but gave up after I offered a middleman (the son of a 32 Battalion soldier) a substantial sum of money to interview Savate veterans on my behalf. All I got was a word-for-word copy of the battle as published in *They Lived by the Sword* masquerading as six interviews with Savate veterans. Only one of those men, whom he called Savate veterans and had supposedly interviewed, had a name that appeared on the Savate battle nominal roll.

The official Operation Tiro-Tiro war diary was updated in the Omauni operations room as the battle progressed. I include pages from the diary in this book to confirm facts and to put to bed some of the arguments that still rage around the attack, such as that regarding the strength and composition of the teams that did the initial reconnaissance. The war diary is, after all, the only official document available to confirm dates and times of events that took place during the Battle of Savate.

A note on nomenclature: the South African Border War was fought in South West Africa, at the time under the control of its southern neighbour. The territory received independence in 1990, when its name was changed to Namibia. Because the war was fought in what was then South West Africa, I will refer to it as such throughout this book.

I have followed the standard writing procedure of identifying a person in the first instance by their rank, initial (and in some cases their full Christian name or nickname) and surname. Thereafter, only the surname is used. This is not a sign of disrespect towards a particular person's rank, but a convention.

PIET NORTJE
DUBAI, UNITED ARAB EMIRATES
2015

Battle of Savate

Fear,
Subdued by the magnitude
Of aggressive events,
Developing into a level-headed mechanism
To survive.

Despair,
Sinking into a chasm
Borne of friends suddenly no more,
Becoming an animal's indifference to killing.

Caught in a void,
Walls of unleashed destruction
Cemented by the roar of vices,
Death ... the opening of a window.

Mindless helplessness,
A nothing ...
Enveloped in winds of fear,
Values and morals of shifting dunes.

Relief,
Pathetic in its intensity
Familiar faces –
Bastian's of trailing lifelines ... shreds of hope.

Drained,
In vacuums of the aftermath,
New lights of oppressive realities
... shadows.

– Second Lieutenant Justin Taylor
32 Battalion Signals Officer 1980
Written 28 January 1981

32BN

OORLOGSDAGBOEK VIR OPS TIRO-TIRO
17 MEI 1980 tot 24 MEI 1980

The cover page of the 29-page official war diary

1

War on the Border

By 1975, the writing was on the wall: the Rooi Gevaar (Red Peril) – the South African popular term for communism – was knocking on newly independent Angola's door. It was an unwelcome visitor for South Africa, which controlled neighbouring South West Africa. The 1974 coup d'état in Lisbon, Portugal, which saw the leftist Movimento das Forças Armadas (Movement of the Armed Forces) overthrow the Portuguese regime of Marcelo Caetano, had resulted in independence for Portugal's former colonies abroad.

In Angola, a war for independence had been raging since 1961. As a Western ally, South Africa had clandestinely supported the Portuguese military in the conflict against the resistance movements fighting for independence. The main resistance, the Movimento Popular de Libertação de Angola (Popular Movement for the Liberation of Angola, MPLA), had sided with Russia, the Eastern bloc leader in the Cold War, and was therefore branded as communist. The other resistance movements – Frente Nacional para a Libertação de Angola (National Front for the Liberation of Angola, FNLA) and União Nacional para a Independência Total de Angola (National Union for the Total Independence of Angola, UNITA) – had originally also sided with the Eastern bloc.

Even before Portugal had fully withdrawn from the territory, however, friction between the three resistance movements had resulted in a split that saw them fighting one another for control of independent Angola. The three resistance leaders met several times with Portuguese authorities towards the end of 1974, and eventually agreed to end their armed conflict. On 15 January 1975, in Alvor, Portugal, they signed what became known as the Alvor Agreement, granting Angola independence on 11 November 1975 and establishing a transitional government.

This cooperative agreement was short-lived. Fighting between the military arms of the three, now political, movements – the MPLA's Forças Armadas Populares de Libertação de Angola (People's Armed Forces for the Liberation of Angola, FAPLA), the FNLA's Exército de Libertação Nacional de Angola (National Liberation Army of Angola, ELNA) and UNITA's Forças Armadas de Libertação de Angola (Armed Forces for the Liberation of Angola, FALA) – escalated quickly, and the FNLA and UNITA requested support from the West.

At America's request, South Africa this time sided with the FNLA and UNITA to put a non-communist government in power in Angola when colonial rule officially came to an end in November. In the latter part of 1975, the South African Defence Force (SADF) therefore helped ELNA and FALA try to defeat FAPLA militarily, but the MPLA managed to seize Luanda and formed a new government with Agostinho Neto as the nation's first president. Neto established a one-party state and his government developed further ties with the Soviet Union and other nations in the Eastern bloc, as well as other communist states, especially Cuba.

The civil war, however, continued to rage. In early 1976 the SADF left Angola due to mounting political pressure from overseas. After the withdrawal, the FNLA disintegrated, leaving the pro-Western UNITA to continue the struggle against the Marxist MPLA government on its own. For a while, with no declared war between South Africa and Angola, FAPLA was forgotten by the South Africans, even though the SADF continued to clandestinely support UNITA operations logistically in Angola as part of the South African government's Cold War strategy.

In 1975, Colonel Jan Dirk Breytenbach of the SADF had gathered the remnants of ELNA at Mpupa in south-east Angola, where he trained them and formed them into what became known as Bravo Group. In March 1976, the South African Army authorised Colonel Breytenbach to move Bravo Group to South West Africa. Bravo Group, which would become integrated into the SADF, was tasked with fighting the South West Africa People's Organisation (SWAPO) and its military arm, the People's Liberation Army of Namibia (PLAN), which had been waging an insurgency war in South West Africa since 1961, infiltrating the territory from bases in Angola. In October 1976, Bravo Group became 32 Battalion.

What is commonly known as the South African Border War officially started in 1966, when the first shots between PLAN insurgents and the SADF were fired. Now, 10 years on, enough was enough. 32 Battalion would fight PLAN not only inside South West Africa, but also clandestinely in southern Angola.

The SADF had divided the northern border zone in South West Africa into military sectors, with each sector commander responsible for countering the PLAN insurgency in his operational area. Sector 10, with its headquarters at Oshakati, was responsible for Kaokoland and Ovamboland; Sector 20 (originally called 1 Military Area), with headquarters at Rundu, was responsible for the Kavango; and Sector 70, with headquarters at Katima Mulilo, for the Caprivi. Almost all the infiltration and fighting between SADF and PLAN forces took place in central Ovamboland, because 25 per cent of the population lived in that area and it bordered Angola, from where the PLAN insurgency was being launched.

In Angola, FAPLA had divided the provinces into military regions. The Cunene Province (5th Military Region) and the Cuando Cubango Province (6th Military Region) bordered the South West African operational area.

UNITA's FALA, for their own military command-and-control purposes, had also divided Angola into 17 military regions with each region subdivided into zones.

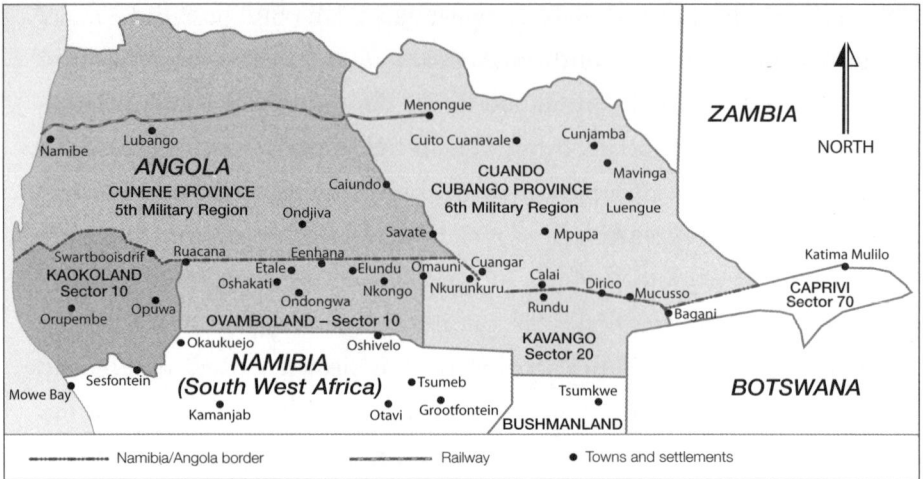

SADF and FAPLA military areas. Map shows the SADF sector areas of responsibility and the FAPLA military regions (not to scale)

FAPLA's reorganisation and strategy

Beginning in 1977 and under the guidance of Russian and Cuban advisors, and as part of a reorganisation and training programme, FAPLA withdrew most of its forces from the areas bordering South West Africa in the 6th Military Region. This left most of its bases along the Okavango River, which it had occupied since mid-1976, either manned by a skeleton force or totally abandoned. They had little to worry about though, as FALA deployments in this specific area were nothing more than poorly trained and ill-equipped compact guerrilla companies, lacking both the capability to hold ground or defend bases should they occupy them.

By the middle of 1978, most of FAPLA's reorganisation and training was complete. Organised in line with Soviet military doctrine, it now had motorised infantry brigades (*brigadas de infantaria motorizada*; BRIM) equipped with heavy weaponry, such as artillery, tanks and anti-aircraft systems, to deploy in conventional warfare, and light infantry brigades (*brigadas de infantaria ligeira*; BRIL) to deploy in counter-guerrilla operations.

FAPLA established its 6th Military Region headquarters in the Cuando

Cubango provincial capital of Menongue, which later also hosted the main recruit training centre for southern Angola.

The FAPLA regional commander at Menongue deployed 16 Brigade (BRIM) to Cuito Cuanavale, from where it was responsible for the defence of Mavinga and the occupation of towns up to the Zambian border. Mavinga was seen as a strategic position because of its airstrip. If FALA succeeded in occupying Mavinga, it could allow clandestine logistical support to be flown in from South Africa.

At the same time, 67 Brigade (BRIL) established its headquarters at Caiundo. The brigade was tasked with conducting anti-FALA operations in the area between the Cubango (the name given to the Okavango in Angola) and Cuito rivers, and up to the border with South West Africa. It was a vast area for just one brigade to cover, but, again, FALA's military capacity in this area was limited to guerrilla hit-and-run tactics, ambushes, sabotage and general disruption.

During their August/September 1978 offensive, 67 Brigade took the town of Savate – which lies 135 kilometres south of Caiundo and 75 kilometres

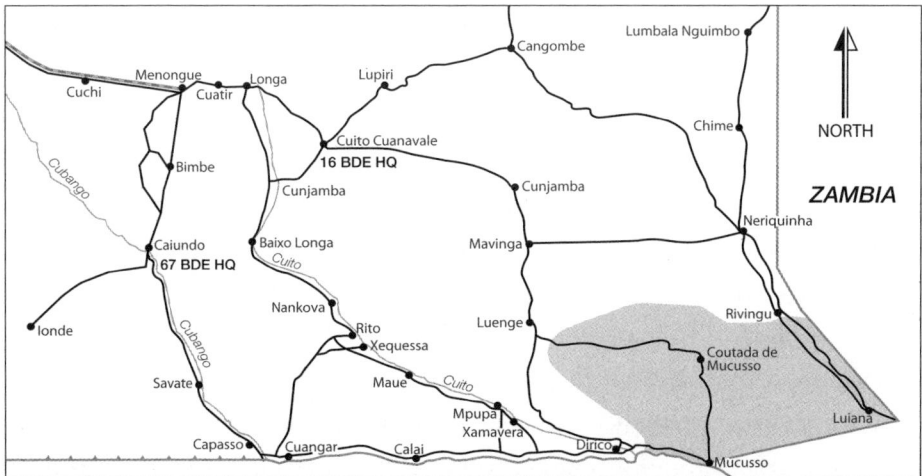

The southern Cuando Cubango Province in 1978, showing the positions of the FAPLA brigade headquarters and the area dominated by FALA (grey). All towns outside the FALA area were occupied by FAPLA

north of Cuangar on the border with South West Africa – from UNITA's FALA guerrillas, and established a battalion-sized base there. The brigade also occupied all their former bases along the Okavango and Cuito rivers as far as Mpupa. The reoccupation not only gave back the initiative to FAPLA, but also effectively cut off all resupply by road from the FALA guerrillas operating in the area.

A new South African strategy

An important strategic objective of the South African military in the Border War was to eliminate any insurgency from Angola into Kaokoland, Kavango and Caprivi. By doing this, the main effort – to clear Ovamboland – could be achieved more cost-effectively.

When the minister of defence, P.W. Botha, became South Africa's prime minister in 1978, the country's until-then low-level military aid to UNITA in the form of food, weapons and ammunition, and codenamed Operation Silver, escalated. In light of FAPLA's recent reorganisation, the South African generals were of the opinion that there was no point in supplying weapons to an untrained resistance movement and that FALA soldiers should, therefore, be trained. UNITA leader and FALA supreme commander, General Jonas Savimbi, met with Botha on 10 December 1978.

A decision was made to accelerate and expand the training of the FALA guerrillas, who until then had been organised into three fighting groups. The dispersed guerrilla group numbered around 8 000 men, operated in groups of about 10 and carried only their personal weapons and occasionally explosives. They wore a combination of military uniforms and civilian clothing. The 3 000 or so men of the militia group each carried a personal weapon – typically a vintage World War II rifle, with the odd AK-47 between them – and had only a few rounds of ammunition. The compact guerrilla group, with around 4 000 men wearing various military uniforms and operating in companies of about 180 strong, was more organised and locally trained. The men carried AK-47s as personal weapons and each company had two 81-millimetre mortars and one 75-millimetre recoilless gun.

SADF Chief Staff Intelligence (CSI) Colonel Flip du Preez had been coordinating the support to UNITA from an office in Rundu since 1976. He was now given the task of converting the Dodge City military base on the Caprivi into a FALA training base. (Until early 1977, Dodge City had belonged to 32 Battalion.) Before he could complete the task, however, Du Preez was transferred to Military Intelligence Division (MID) headquarters in Pretoria, with special responsibility for Operation Silver.

On 26 December 1978, fresh from a year-long South African Army command and staff course, Commandant Marius 'Mo' Oelschig was posted to the Rundu office as the officer commanding (OC) the Special Tasks field office. Oelschig, a paratrooper, had served as military attaché in Luanda in the early 1970s and had experience with Angola and UNITA. He spoke fluent Portuguese, which Du Preez did not, and this gave him an advantage in communicating with the FALA commanders. Oelschig's main responsibility was as primary liaison and executive officer for Operation Silver in the Cuando Cubango Province. He reported to Major General Jannie Geldenhuys, the General Officer Commanding (GOC) of South West Africa Command, headquartered in Windhoek. Geldenhuys, in turn, was under the command of the chief of the South African Army, Lieutenant General Constand Viljoen.

The strategy regarding the nature and scope of support to UNITA was significantly influenced by Geldenhuys's strategy for the region as a whole. At their first meeting, Oelschig received his first strategic guidelines:

In one of my first meetings with General Geldenhuys, he told me, in no uncertain terms, that he expected me, meaning UNITA, to 'keep Sector 20's doorstep clean'. The ensuing operational concept was to harass and interdict the lines of communication to such an extent that continued occupation by FAPLA of isolated bases like Calai, Dirico, Cuangar, Savate and Mpupa would be unsustainable.

By 1979, the South African military had changed its strategy to such an extent that the Reconnaissance Commando (the 'recces'), 32 Battalion and, on a smaller scale, 31 Battalion (later renamed 201 Battalion) were now allowed to provide clandestine combat support to UNITA. Five years after fleeing before FAPLA and its Cuban allies, former ELNA cadres, now in the guise of a fully fledged, well-disciplined SADF military battalion (32 Battalion) led by white South Africans, would once again get the opportunity to engage their former enemy.

In line with Botha's directives, Oelschig had set up training programmes. On 5 December 1978, 180 of FALA's best guerrilla fighters reported to Camp Delta, a small clandestine training base on the Caprivi, to receive training in basic intelligence from South African Recce Commando instructors. Savimbi's presidential guard would be derived from this group. At the same time, two experienced 32 Battalion officers, Captain Piet Botes and Lieutenant Des Burman, were transferred to MID. On 22 January 1979, together with six national servicemen, they began training the first 350 FALA compact guerrillas. These would form the basis of what would become FALA's fourth group, the semi-regulars, which, by the end of June 1980, numbered around 5 000. The semi-regulars were organised into battalions based on the South African Army's model and armed as such.

In the meantime, FALA guerrilla activities continued throughout the Cunene and Cuando Cubango provinces. The headquarters of FALA's Colonel Samuel 'Mwanangola' Chiwale was at Cafima, about 100 kilometres south-east of Cassinga in the Cunene Province, which itself was controlled from a CSI field office in Oshakati. By the end of June 1980, Chiwale would be the FALA commander, with 800 compact guerrilla fighters in the area north-east of Ionde alone.

Since FAPLA's reoccupation during its August/September offensive of

```
FALA Supreme commander
Gen Jonas Malheiro Savimbi
        |
Chief of General Staff
Col Demosthenes Chilingutila
        |
    FLA Commander
    Col Samuel Chiwale

Commander Urban Warfare ——— Chief of Staff    Intelligence – Capt Huambo Kassito
    Maj Altino Sapalo                          Operations  – Col Renato Mateus
                                               Finanace    – Lt Col Samakuva Lissumbisa
                                               Logistics   – Lt Col Eugenio Ngola

  Dispersed          Militia (3 000)    Compact Guerrillas (4 000)    Semi-Reular Force (5 000)
Guerrillas (8 000)   Personal weapons
                                              Coy  Coy  Coy  Coy        Bn  Bn  Bn  Bn  Bn
10 Guerrillas in group
Personal weapons                          Operates in company Weapons  Weapons
                                          180 x AK-47                   652 x AK-47
                                          2 x 81mm Mort                 6 x 81mm Mort
                                          1 x 75mm RG                   9 x RPG7
                                                                        9 x 40mm GL
                                                                        27 x LMG
                                                                        9 x 60mm Mort
                                                                        1 x 75mm RG
```

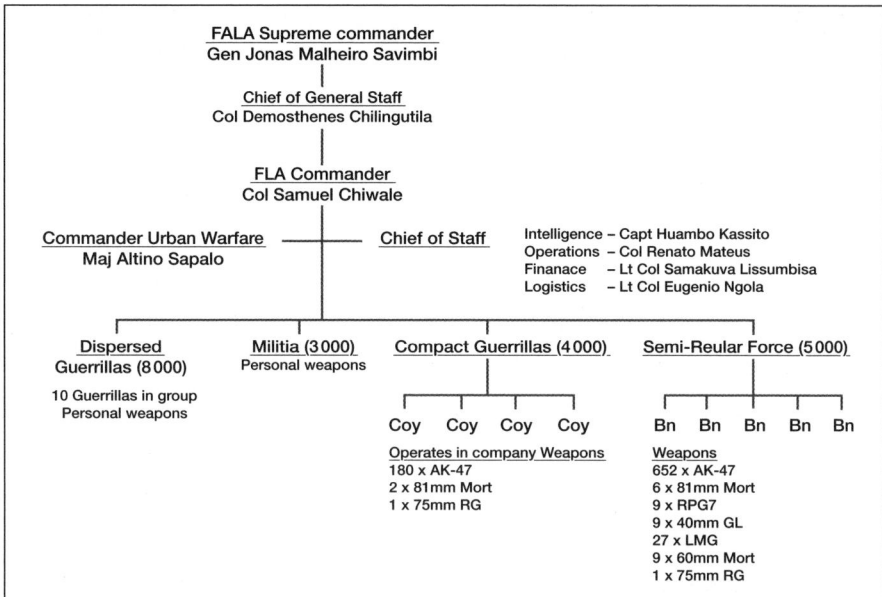

FALA organisation by end of June 1980

the previous year, UNITA had not made any effort to upset the stalemate. It was now time for the South Africans to act. On 23 February 1979, Savimbi and Brigadier Miguel N'Zau Puna (UNITA's secretary general) met with Du Preez and Oelschig, as well as Colonel P. Moller, Commandant J. Swart and Major H. Venter from 1 Recce Commando, at Camp Delta. The decision was made to deploy four recce commando teams of eight men each, starting in March, with the aim of assisting UNITA in operational planning, intelligence gathering, performing reconnaissance tasks, and establishing communications between the SADF and FALA. The deployment, codenamed Operation Broadcast, would entail sending two teams to Chiwale in the Cunene Province and two to support Savimbi in the Cuando Cubango Province.

Four days later, on 27 February, an operational planning meeting was held, again at Camp Delta, between Savimbi, N'Zau Puna, Geldenhuys and his second in command, Brigadier P.E.K. Bosman. At this meeting,

9

two approvals were given: one for joint operations between the SADF and FALA (although with separate tasks), and the other for the provision of SADF fire support (in the form of 81-millimetre mortars) for FALA attacks. The change in SADF strategy was being clearly marked and the ball was now rolling.

On 8 March in Pretoria, Savimbi met with General Magnus Malan (chief of the SADF), Constand Viljoen and representatives from MID. At this meeting, the overall UNITA strategy and objectives for 1979 were finalised:

> The Cuando Cubango border area, which was occupied by FAPLA in their offensive, should be re-taken by UNITA as a matter of priority within six weeks, with the assistance of 32 Battalion troops, if necessary, so as to provide UNITA with a safe base area in which to form the nucleus of an alternative government, as well as to restore the logistical lines and communication between south-east Angola and South West Africa. [Department of Defence Documentaion Centre, File DI/311/1/3 Silver Vol. 8, Enc. 106, 113–15.]

A decision was also made to establish an operational headquarters for UNITA at the Rundu field office, from which FALA operations could be controlled. FALA's chief of staff, Lieutenant Colonel Demosthenes Amos Chilingutila, would fill this post.

Until this point, UNITA was in control of southern Angola, as the operational planning thus far had been guided by politics. Now, however, the first signs of SWAPO's PLAN insurgents infiltrating the Kavango region of South West Africa began to surface. Intelligence reports suggested that PLAN was looking to activate the Kavango and create a foothold for further infiltration of the Mangeti – the traditional white farming area – and beyond. The area west of the Cubango River in southern Angola was uninhabited and had no water resources, making it virtually impossible for

PLAN to establish bases or successfully infiltrate the Kavango from there. The insurgents would have to follow the longer route south via Beacon 34 into the military-patrolled area east of Nkongo base, along the 17°30' cut line and, when south of the Chandelier Road, turn east to the Kavango. Not only was this a lengthy journey, but the insurgents would also risk making contact with security forces.

FAPLA's occupation of all the towns along the Okavango River meant that PLAN had readily available bases to supply logistical support and protection. Those bases located some distance from the border, like Savate and Mpupa, were conveniently situated to serve as staging areas for PLAN operations against the SADF's 1 Military Area (called Sector 20 from late 1979). Such insurgencies would be a major problem for the SADF, potentially leading to extended call-ups of Citizen Force units and additional budgetary allocations, things that the South African Army wanted to avoid at all costs. Therefore, while there were no indications that it was going to happen as yet, FALA, with South African support, nevertheless went on a six-week offensive.

The first action occurred on 21 March, when 600 compact guerrillas under the command of Lieutenant Colonel Kanjimi, along with Savimbi's two recce commando teams, attacked the town of Xamavera, on the bank of the Cuito River. Recces Lieutenant A.J. Verwey and Lance Corporal J.G. Olivier were in the attack group, while the rest of their recce commando delivered fire support. Within an hour, the town was taken, but Olivier was killed and Verwey wounded. The latter concluded that the FALA guerrillas were not ready for conventional attacks and advised a long-distance mortar bombardment on the FAPLA base at Mpupa, which would hopefully result in the enemy fleeing the town as well.

In the Cunene Province, Chiwale received instructions to prepare for an attack on Savate using the 1 200 men he had grouped at Ionde. This attack, however, never materialised.

The first fully trained and equipped semi-regular FALA battalion was

deployed from Dodge City to the Cuangar area between 1 and 3 April.
Not long after, the 32 Battalion Reconnaissance Wing was ordered to help
the FALA battalion attack the Cuangar base, to provide mortar fire support and to destroy a Soviet-manufactured Coke-type transport aircraft,
which had broken down on the airfield.

After a week of rehearsals, 40 men of the 32 Battalion Recce Wing
were instructed to move to the Rundu headquarters. They were to take
with them civilian clothing to wear during the attack, as they would be part
of the FALA battalion and South African involvement was not to be
revealed. They arrived at Rundu and awaited deployment. After four days,
it was decided that using so many South African soldiers in a direct attack
in support of UNITA at this early stage was too sensitive, so Recce Wing's
participation was called off. On 17 April, the FALA battalion, with no
South African support, successfully attacked Cuangar in a confrontation
that lasted just 15 minutes. FAPLA fled, leaving behind eight vehicles and
the aircraft, which was later destroyed.

Following this success, 32 Battalion's Corporal Etienne 'Ore' Venter
and his mortar group, assisted by recces, bombarded the Mpupa base on
19 April. As predicted, the enemy vacated the base.

Savimbi was eager to follow up with further successes. At a meeting in
Rundu on 24 April – chaired by Major General F. Loods (commanding the
recces) and attended by representatives from South West Africa Command,
1 Military Area, the South African Air Force (SAAF) and the Rundu field
office – Savimbi said he wanted to open the logistical routes to central
Angola from the south. It was decided at the meeting that the recces would
become more involved in direct attacks, with the first targets being Caire
and Calai.

Although a planned attack with 32 Battalion mortar support on Caire
did not materialise when a final reconnaissance proved that the base was
empty, Calai was successfully attacked on 19 May. Four recce commando
teams, consisting of a total of 30 men and under the command of Major

H. Venter, penetrated the town, killing 29 enemy soldiers. At the same time, a FALA battalion attacked an enemy base four kilometres north of Calai, killing one enemy and allowing 150 to escape. This attack signalled the last of UNITA's activities for a while, as preparation for its national congress at Coutada do Mucusso, starting on 27 May, was already under way. Savimbi seemed to think it was more important for his commanders to attend the congress than conduct operations. In the meantime, however, training continued at Dodge City and Camp Delta.

The seasons determined and influenced the fighting in the Cuando Cubango and it was not long before a clear pattern for control of the province developed. FAPLA would launch its offensives during the dry season (June to October), which allowed for the large-scale transport of forces by road. FALA would then infiltrate and retake the towns during the rainy season (March to June), when the roads were impassable for vehicles and the thick foliage gave cover for guerrilla attacks. When the dry season came round again, and it was clear that FALA was not sufficiently trained and equipped to hold the towns it had captured, FAPLA would launch another offensive. In a meeting between Savimbi and Oelschig on 15 July 1979, it was decided that FALA's tactics for the dry season would remain the same and that FAPLA would be allowed to reoccupy the towns.

FAPLA's 16th and 67th brigades launched their next offensive, code-named Operation Kilo-Kilo, in July 1979. FALA compact guerrillas concentrated on delaying the pace of the FAPLA advance by deploying ambushes, planting mines on approach routes and trying to isolate the besieged towns until such time when a full-scale attack could be launched. By the middle of July, 67 Brigade had captured Cuangar, but it quickly became evident that FAPLA had lost momentum due to the logistical difficulty of supplying their units all the way from Caiundo.

Following FAPLA's reoccupation of the towns, FALA continued with what it was good at: using hit-and-run tactics to cut FAPLA's logistical supplies, resulting in the brigades' gradual starvation.

At the beginning of August, SADF staff in Pretoria identified certain strategic targets, such as bridges, in southern Angola that were to be destroyed. On 10 August, Malan was informed and gave his approval. On 18 September, Geldenhuys met with Savimbi and other high-ranking FALA officers with the objective of integrating South West Africa Command's operational plan for southern Angola with the overall planning and strategy of Operation Silver. In line with the earlier decision taken in Pretoria, Geldenhuys asked Savimbi to attack and destroy specific targets in southern Angola.

On 24 September, two months after capturing Cuangar, FAPLA's 67 Brigade managed to capture Calai. Three days later they also occupied Dirico, which until then had no or few military activities.

By 15 October, FALA had 1 993 trained and equipped fighters organised in almost three semi-regular battalions, which included a mortar group of 32 men fresh from training at Camp Delta. The number to be trained put tremendous pressure on Dodge City, with the result that instructions were issued to open another training base at Bwabwata, on the Caprivi. Called Tiger, this base became operational in February 1980.

FALA forces attacked Rito and Mavinga in October, but saw little success in November and December. By year end, FALA had lost the initiative and FAPLA had reoccupied all captured towns.

Strategic success

In 1980, FALA expanded its compact guerrilla operations west of the Cubango River and north of the border with South West Africa by sending a mixture of untrained compact guerrillas and militia to set up base north of Beacon 40 in the Anhara Capembe area. The guerrillas were logistically supported from the CSI base in Rundu. Under the cover of darkness, South African Army trucks belonging to CSI would transport supplies from the Rundu base by driving west on the Chandelier Road and then north along the 18-degree cut line into Angola.

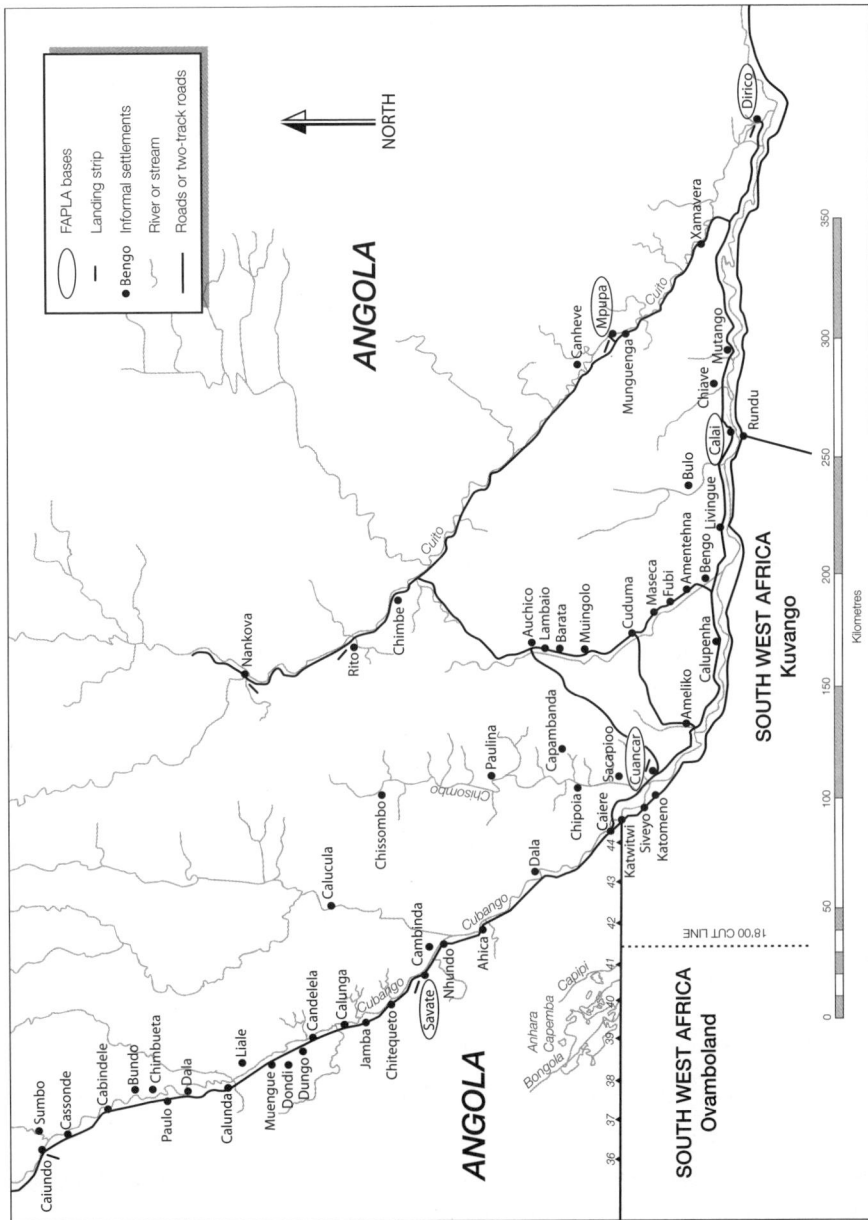

Towns occupied by FAPLA at the beginning of 1980

From its new base, FALA slowly expanded its guerrilla activities northwards. Before long, it had established a small guerrilla presence at Tandaue, north-west of Savate, with the aim of joining up with Chiwale's guerrilla force operating in the vicinity of Ionde. The harsh and dry landscape, as well as restricted logistical support from their southern base, made conditions almost unbearable for the guerrillas at Tandaue.

Operationally, FALA kept a low profile in the first months of the year. In January, Operation Silver's headquarters was compelled to ask Geldenhuys to use 32 Battalion to reoccupy Dirico, because in enemy hands it was a threat to the FALA logistical route being used to supply forces east of the Cuito River from their stronghold in Mucusso. A final reconnaissance on 10 January, however, found that the FAPLA occupiers had already left Dirico, leaving only individual enemies in the base, who departed soon after. The 32 Battalion Recce Wing nevertheless completely destroyed the bridge spanning the Cuito River, cutting off the only means of crossing the river from Dirico.

On 21 January, a new FALA semi-regular battalion of 567 men started training at Dodge City. At Camp Delta, starting 30 January, French instructors presented an intelligence course to 15 students. One of the graduates was Captain Huambo 'Wambo' Kassito.

During a meeting in Rundu on 31 January – attended by Dr G. Viljoen (the administrator general of South West Africa), Geldenhuys, Major General D.J. Earp (the director general of operations), Bosman, Brigadier R. Badenhorst (the OC of Sector 10), Colonel G. Nel (the OC of Sector 20), someone named Du Plessis and Oelschig – the Forward Angolan Joint Management Centre (F-AJMC) was established to coordinate the strategy that had been developed for Operation Silver.

The F-AJMC was to take into consideration the strategic objectives and operational planning of both the South West Africa Command, whose name, in the meantime, had changed to the South West African Territorial Force (SWATF), and the civil administration of the administrator general's department. It was reasoned that Operation Silver operated from South West African soil and that it was necessary to coordinate with the general security activities of the defence and civil administration in South West Africa, particularly when it came to planning and conducting operations in southern Angola.

Before the F-AJMC had a chance to meet, in mid-February FAPLA led an unexpected offensive in the Cuando Cubango Province. This was unusual because FAPLA did not normally operate during the rainy season. The Rundu field office also received intelligence from UNITA that three FAPLA battalions, supported by MiG-17 fighter jets and three Mi-8 helicopters, were operating in the area at the confluence of the Cautir and Luatuta-Capango rivers (north-east of Caiundo) with the intention of moving south along the Chissombo River to reinforce Cuangar. It was deduced that FAPLA wanted to catch off-guard FALA guerrillas in the Cuando Cubango and destroy them to achieve their 1979 objectives in the province. South African intelligence sources, however, thought it might be a reaction to a sudden upsurge in FALA attacks and ambushes between 11 and 13 February. On 11 February, a FALA battalion had attacked Baixa Longa, but failed to capture it. On 12 February, they killed eight of the enemy in an ambush on the road near Caire and, on 13 February, they bombarded Dirico after a small force from Mpupa moved down and occupied the town.

But both the South African and UNITA intelligence communities were wrong regarding the FAPLA offensive. FAPLA high command had realised the tactical impossibility of effectively occupying and supporting bases along the Okavango and Cuito rivers, and of conducting anti-FALA operations with only one brigade from a brigade headquarters at Caiundo, 210 kilometres from the border with South West Africa. The reported activity was FAPLA's 60 Brigade (BRIL), commanded by Captain Eusébio de Brito Teixeira. Until two weeks before, 60 Brigade had been busy training in Huambo, but was now conducting operations with the objective of taking over the Savate base from 67 Brigade, which was earmarked to conduct operations from Caiundo north towards Menongue, east to Baixa Longa and west to Ionde. Teixeira's brigade took over the bases along the Okavango River.

It was clear that better cooperation and coordination were necessary between the SADF and UNITA. For this reason, the first F-AJMC meeting, headed by the administrator general, was held on 16 March to coordinate UNITA's plan of action with the SADF's own concept for operations in Angola until July 1980. The first order of business pertaining to the Cuando Cubango Province and Sector 20 was that, between UNITA and the SADF, they had to secure FALA's logistical routes into the interior of Angola. Secondly, and more importantly for the SADF's strategy, they had to control the illegal border crossing of civilians and the PLAN infiltration into the Kavango.

A plan formed around the intended capture of Cuangar, Calai, Mpupa and Rivungo before 31 May, and the towns of Rito and Savate before 30 June. While FALA would be responsible for these attacks, recce commandos and 31, 32 and 35 battalions would provide clandestine support in the name of UNITA. To facilitate operational planning and control, a joint SADF/UNITA command-and-control committee was established in Rundu under the chairmanship of Nel, who would be assisted by Major D.W.K. 'Des' Lynch (OC of 301 Air Component) and Oelschig. Representing UNITA were N'Zau Puna, Lieutenant Colonel Manovakolo (operations), Major Samukuva (logistics) and Captain Kassito (intelligence).

The joint plan to regain control over the Cuando Cubango Province began to be implemented at the beginning of April. Cuangar was the strongest and best defended of the bases along the Okavango River, and so the committee decided that the attack on Cuangar should start without delay. A Dodge City–trained battalion, supported by a 32 Battalion mortar platoon, was used for the attack. From 3 to 5 April, Captain Daan de la Rey, the commanding officer of Dodge City, reconnoitred Cuangar. This was followed by an air reconnaissance on 7 April.

The attack started at first light on 14 April, and by 10:00 the town and base had been captured and secured. FALA lost 12 men. The enemy fled, leaving behind some vehicles. FALA occupied and reinforced the town, and pursued FAPLA to the Chissombo River.

The focus now shifted to Mpupa and Rivungo. On 6 April, a four-man 31 Battalion recce team had started a reconnaissance of Mpupa. When they returned on 12 April, they had only covered 50 per cent of the area. To gain more information on Mpupa, CSI approached the 32 Battalion commander, Commandant Deon Ferreira (nicknamed 'Falcon'), and asked him to send 32 Battalion recce teams on 'snatch' operations to Calai and Dirico, hoping to get information from captured enemy. On the night of 26 April, the Dirico snatch went terribly wrong but the Calai one was a success and enough information was received to plan attacks.

The attack on Mpupa was nevertheless delayed, because in the first week of May it was reported – but not confirmed – that FAPLA forces were regrouping at Caire with the intention of launching a counter-attack on Cuangar. After the snatch operation, the FAPLA forces in Calai and Dirico either realised that a possible attack was forthcoming or that they were cut off from supplies at Savate after the capture of Cuangar, and they vacated their bases.

In the meantime, FAPLA's 60 Brigade commander, Teixeira, was transferred from Savate to Cuito Cuanavale and a 23-year-old *alferes* (Portuguese for ensign or second lieutenant) named Daniel Rufino took his place. Rufino was not an experienced commander; he had been the brigade's political commissar. As a teenager in 1974, he had enrolled in FAPLA and received recruit and weapons training at Comandante Kwenha's base in the Namibe Province; thereafter, he had joined a unit in Menongue, then still Serpa Pinto. On 1 August 1975, the 18-year-old had experienced his first combat in clashes with ELNA near Menongue.

'Inexperience dictated in combat; you see for yourself but never forget,' says Rufino, recalling his first engagement. 'We left in disarray. Some fled to the woods and others were captured. I also ran away.'

Rufino went to Cuito Cuanavale, where he found refuge with his family. Months later, 'the sense of patriotism led me to return to military life,' he said. By 1976, he was back in FAPLA.

Starting on 21 June 1976, Rufino attended a six-month political-commissar course at Comandante Gika's military school in Luanda. On 12 January 1977, he was promoted to sub-lieutenant and placed in the 4th Military Region, Huambo Province. On 28 January 1980, he was appointed political commissar of 60 Brigade.

On 2 May, a second trained FALA semi-regular battalion was sent from Mucusso to reinforce Cuangar, which meant that only one semi-regular battalion was available for an attack on Mpupa, which was not enough. On 7 May, the joint planning committee decided instead to concentrate on Savate, because its capture would relieve the threat of a FAPLA counter-attack on Cuangar.

2

Planning Operation Tiro-Tiro

After considering the available FALA forces, the joint planning committee decided that it would be too risky to withdraw a FALA battalion from Cuangar for the attack on Savate. The attack, therefore, would be undertaken by 32 Battalion alone. FALA would merely occupy the town once it had been captured.

To give the impression that this was an attack on Savate by purely FALA forces, no South African artillery or close air support would be provided. A FALA guerrilla force would be used to prevent the FAPLA forces, which were reportedly regrouping in the Caire area, from intervening and another FALA guerrilla force would block any attempt at reinforcing Savate from Caiundo. (From the start, however, there were doubts whether FALA would deploy as required.) Once FAPLA had been driven from Savate, FALA would occupy the town and, together with the two other FALA guerrilla groups, would prevent FAPLA from returning and thus also cut off the FAPLA supply route to Cuangar.

On 24 April 1980, an SAAF Impala jet flew an air-reconnaissance mission over Savate from its base in Ondangwa. The aerial-photograph analysts at Ondangwa identified a trench system and detected indications of an understrength FAPLA battalion in Savate. They also found evidence of a small enemy deployment at the airfield, consisting of a group that protected what was interpreted from the aerial photographs to be the vehicle park. There was no indication of enemy advance posts on the roads north and south of Savate. UNITA intelligence confirmed these last two findings,

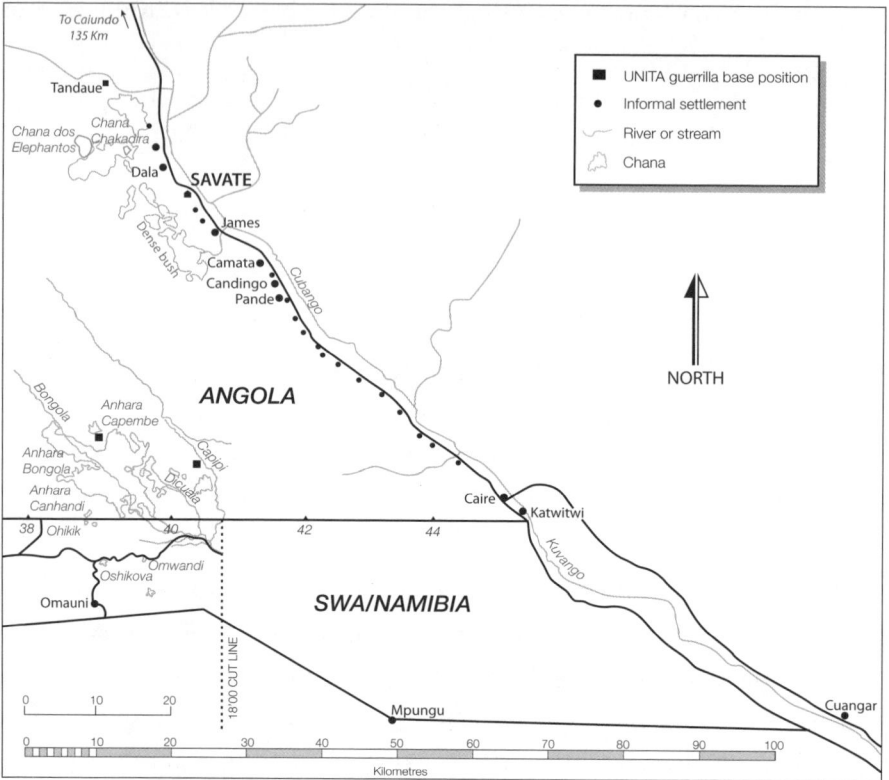

Savate and the position of FALA guerrilla bases in early 1980

but contradicted the aerial-photograph analysts by reporting the presence of a company-strength enemy element at the base.

At an Operation Tiro-Tiro planning meeting in Rundu, Oelschig presented an intelligence intercept stating: 'The enemy positions at Savate complain that the general shortage of food, ammunition and weapons makes it impossible for them to defend the position against an attack.' This report seemingly confirmed the air-reconnaissance results that the Savate defences were weak. It was estimated that, because of the relief process, a FAPLA force of about a company (approximately 150 men) would occupy the town at the time of the attack. The joint planning committee therefore focused their plans for the attack on the trench system surrounding the kraals and town of Savate, as well as the military base between the airstrip and the town.

To be safe, a decision was taken to send reconnaissance teams to Savate to determine, firstly, if the base was occupied at all and, secondly, if so, the exact enemy strength. A signal was sent to SWATF explaining the plan – a reconnaissance followed by an attack – and requesting authority to execute. The reply received by the joint planning committee was in Afrikaans: '*Gaan voort met die werk*' (Proceed with the work). Both the 32 Battalion commander, Deon Ferreira, and the committee understood the message to indicate that he was to continue with the attack.

Ordered to plan an attack based on unconfirmed intelligence that an understrength battalion held Savate and occupied the base complex, Ferreira prematurely left the tactical headquarters of Operation Ferreira (an operation in Sector 10).

Using the aerial-photograph interpretations of the base's layout, as well as UNITA's intelligence, Ferreira planned to attack Savate with three rifle companies, relying on two mortar sections (four weapons) for indirect support fire and the Recce Wing for stopper groups. He also planned to use two rifle platoons for protection and reserve purposes, an assault pioneer section, and individual elements from one company for echelon protection and to assist with base clearance. The only other authorised support for the operation was provided by the SAAF Tactical Air Unit (later renamed 320 Air Force Command Post) in Rundu. The air support approved was one Alouette gunship and one Puma helicopter for the evacuation of casualties only. A Cessna 185 was also available for command-and-control purposes. The helicopters were not permitted to overnight in Angolan territory. Instructions were clear: to limit the use of the helicopters to the absolute minimum and to avoid making their presence known to the enemy.

Not knowing what their mission was, the tasked companies started preparations at Buffalo, the battalion's base in the Caprivi. The companies put on standby for the operation were Alpha Company (strength 74), commanded by Lieutenant Charl Muller (the adjutant) in the absence of company commander Lieutenant Tony Nienaber, who was recovering from injuries sustained in a motor-car accident while on a course in South Africa; Charlie Company (strength 62), commanded by Lieutenant Sam Heap; and Foxtrot Company (strength 75), commanded by Echo Company commander Lieutenant Jim Ross. Ross was put in command of Foxtrot because two of his Echo Company platoons (strength 47) were to be deployed on protection tasks. The two mortar sections (strength 26) were commanded by Second Lieutenant Chris 'C.B.' Brown.

All the companies were understrength to begin with, but, luckily, the January 1980 recruit intake finished training in time to make up the numbers. Most of the companies' white leaders were either on leave or on courses in South Africa, and therefore had to be replaced with leaders from other companies. Fortunately, they were able to supplement the leader group with former Rhodesian servicemen, who had arrived in the unit two weeks before and were busy with orientation training.

Corporal Leon Grobler, Alpha Company Platoon 1 (Alpha 1), remembers the preparations:

> We had a slow start to the year and were looking forward to a real operation, one with many bangs and kills. I remember Falcon's briefing: it was long and thorough. Any Infantry School instructor would get goose pimples and an erection listening to such a presentation. Everything was covered, very accurate and thorough. We received a group of recruits (just finished with training) before the operation. Caliango, a tall, thin chap, and some others joined Alpha 1. They had heard about the operation and were not very enthusiastic about the whole affair. We, however, had a very good leader element.
>
> We prepared for the clandestine operation. All the South African marks had to be removed. We were supposed to be UNITA. We removed all marks on the mortars, grenades and boots. (We had to cut

the boot soles in order not to leave South African tracks.) We also received unmarked ammunition. All South African ammunition was marked R1M1. Also, our rations. No tins, papers, or anything that could be recognised. We listened to 'House of the Rising Sun' many times. We practised the attack at Buffalo. Long extended lines, fire and movement. Then we trooped.

Corporal Johan Anderson was the second in command of the mortar sections, which would do the preliminary bombardment to destroy the infrastructure and soften up the target to such an extent that it would be easy for the assault force to enter the extended trench system and bunkers. Anderson remembers:

We trooped from Buffalo to Omauni, knowing that a big operation was coming. This was the first big operation for our intake and we were looking forward to it. The troops sang all the way. It was nice. We, however, did not know that big things were going to happen.

Not everyone was so excited. Coincidentally, the battalion paymaster arrived for a routine 'bush pay' payout. His arrival caused some of the Portuguese-speaking men to believe that there was something sinister to the operation. Corporal Antonio Mendes of Charlie Company, however, saw this as motivation to go into battle. Recce Wing member Sergeant T.T. de Abreu (who would later be commissioned to officer) remembers the payout:

While we were busy with our preparation, somebody came to us and told us that it would be a big operation, even the paymaster was paying out a lot of money to all infantry. After that, they called us and for sure we got the bush pay, back pay. For the first time in our lives, we get R900 in cash before we go on operation. Why?

25

Ferreira decided to send two recce teams to Savate before the attack. On 15 May, he briefed Lieutenant Willem Ratte in detail at the headquarters in Rundu. Ratte and Second Lieutenant Justin Taylor, the battalion signals officer responsible for confirming radio communication, returned to Omauni that same day to prepare two recce teams for the task. Ratte explains:

> Now, the intelligence that came down to us when I was first briefed by Commandant Ferreira was that before we attack Savate we must make sure that, firstly, it's occupied, because UNITA wasn't sure whether it was occupied at all. The strength of the garrison was assumed not to be too strong; they normally don't have a lot of people there, and one battalion should be enough to take them out … and their big problem was to launch a big operation in turn to find that there is nobody there … so I was tasked, the Reconnaissance Wing was tasked, to first establish whether there was any enemy at Savate and where they were in relation to the airstrip and the river. Secondly, another team of ours was to recce the route in for the battalion, because they obviously had to come afterwards and move into position to attack. Thirdly, our blokes were to form a stopper line, so that if FAPLA withdrew from Savate we could basically stop them. Now, the composition of a stopper line gives you an indication of what was expected, what strength was expected, because we had 10 stopper groups of three men each – 30 men [This is contradicted by other men who confirmed that some teams had five men] – so you don't put up that sort of stopper line if there is a whole brigade, which is basically three battalions, 3 000 men. So, our intelligence, whether it was a deliberate attempt to mislead by UNITA or not, I don't know, but we were under the impression that it was at most a small garrison of 100, 200, or maybe 300 who were holding the town. Our main mission was to establish whether it was occupied at all, whether there was anybody there.

Unlike routine reconnaissance missions, the recce teams were heavily armed. De Abreu remembers how, for Savate, their team composition and weaponry were changed:

> Before W.R. [Willem Ratte] departed, he briefed all the team leaders. My surprise was when my team leader was changed, of which I was not happy. I normally worked with Lieutenant Opperman (Oppies) or Botes (Cara de Kambwa, Dog Face). This time I had Swanepoel (Swannie), a new lieutenant from Delta Company.
>
> My new stick leader told me that all of us will wear enemy dress (SWAPO uniform), including weapons [this is incorrect; everybody was dressed in the standard 32 Battalion camouflage uniform]. I told him I did not want to take an AK-47, but my R1 rifle and my 60-millimetre mortar. Lieutenant Swannie said no; he then gave me an RPD machine gun. I stole from our store an M72 anti-tank rocket launcher and hid it in my mochila [backpack]. I went to the shooting range; the RPD was okay. When Lieutenant Swannie saw the M72 he laughed. This guy did not know about the 81-millimetre mortar he was going to carry.

At 07:00 on 16 May, Ratte and Second Lieutenant Stephanus 'Oppies' Opperman's recce teams were airlifted by Pumas and dropped on the Angolan border. There they would be met by CSI guides, who would take them by vehicle to drop-off points from where they would leave to do a detailed reconnaissance of the FAPLA base, to find positions to deploy the mortars south of Savate, and also to confirm the detail on the aerial photographs and the intelligence provided by UNITA. Opperman had to confirm the route to the dispersal point and lead the assault group to it.

With the reconnaissance operation under way, the tasked companies continued to prepare at Omauni. By now everybody believed they were to launch an assault on a SWAPO base somewhere in Angola. Anderson recalls:

At Omauni, ammunition was distributed. Order groups were held and it sounded like we were just going to walk in and take the base without much resistance. We all slept outside the base, but the leader group could eat inside the base. There we heard that Piet van Eeden and Willem Ratte were already busy with a reconnaissance.

Early on 17 May, Alpha Company commander Muller, Regimental Sergeant Major (RSM) 'Ikes' Ueckermann, Second Lieutenant Tim Patrick (intelligence officer) and Lance Corporal Laubsher (operation clerk) arrived by helicopter at the Omauni base to start preparations for Ferreira's briefing and orders. They built a sand model of the Savate base, which Ferreira would use to explain his plan. At roughly 08:00, Ratte and Opperman's recce teams left Omauni to begin their reconnaissance.

At 09:00, Private Louis du Plessis, a national serviceman who would complete his two years' service at the end of June and the driver of one of the first two of the 10 Kwêvoël trucks transporting the assault force, left the Buffalo base for Omauni. The balance of the vehicles left in groups of two at 30-minute intervals. By late afternoon, the assault and support groups had arrived at Omauni to prepare and rehearse for the attack.

The Omauni base war diary showing the strength of the recce teams to be five men each. Team 1: Lieutenant Ratte, Second Lieutenant Baumeister, Sergeant van Eeden, Corporal Paulo and Lance Corporal Casoma. Team 2: Second Lieutenant Opperman, Second Lieutenant Botes, Sergeant Maree, Rifleman Kaliva and Rifleman Kassubu

TOP SECRET/UITERS GEHEIM

OPERATIONS WAR DIARY/OORLOGSDAGBOEK OPERASIES

OF/VAN 32 BN Tak HK

DD1991

BAND/VOLUME................
MAAND/MONTH.. May 89.....

PLEK
PLACE..... O.mauni.................. TYDPERK VAN
PERIOD FROM.. 17/0800/h ....TOT ... 18/0800/h..................

Reeks no. Serial no.	Datum en tyd Date and time	Opsomming van voorvalle en informasie Summary of events and information	Verwysing Reference
On Saturday (17 May) Lt Muller, WO2 Buchmann (RSM), 2 Lt Patrick (Int off) + Lt Ldubxdw (Ops Med) left for Omauni by Chopper. Later that same day A, C, & F coy arrive at Omauni from Buffalo by vehicle, accompanied by two (2) mor. plt and (mil) assault pioneer section. Earlier that morning (at approx. 0800) two (2) recce stick under command of Lt Ratte left Omauni to go recce target			
			DEFENCE INTELLIGENCE DECLASSIFIED 2 3 NOV 2009
			F SMIT 6898405 PE WO1

OPS/1/32 BN   TOP SECRET/UITERS GEHEIM

The Operation Tiro-Tiro diary

At 06:00 on 18 May, the SAAF component, Ferreira, Major Eddie Viljoen ('Big Daddy', the battalion second in command), Captain Andre Erasmus (intelligence officer) and Captain Johan Louw (logistics officer) arrived at the Omauni base. The Puma was put on standby, not only for evacuation of the two recce teams if it became necessary, but also for the duration of the operation. At 09:30, Ferreira gave his briefing and orders to the assault force.

The Sector 20 operations room would be used to relay radio messages to SWATF in Windhoek. The attack would be led by Ferreira. Major Viljoen would man the tactical headquarters at the Omauni base, from where all the deployments would take place. The plan was that the mortar sections, protected by two understrength Echo Company platoons commanded by Lieutenant Dave Thompson and Sergeants Russell Organ and Billy Faul, would use four 81-millimetre mortars with high explosive (HE) and white phosphorus (WP) bombs. They were to take up positions approximately

TOP SECRET/UITERS GEHEIM		DD1991

OPERATIONS WAR DIARY/OORLOGSDAGBOEK OPERASIES

OF/VAN 32BN Jct HQ

BAND/VOLUME.............

MAAND/MONTH...May 80...

PLEK PLACE......Omauni..............

TYDPERK VAN PERIOD FROM...18./0800/b......TOT ....19./0800/b.........

Reeks no. Serial no.	Datum en tyd Date and time	Opsomming van voorvalle en informasie Summary of events and information	Verwysing Reference
		On Sunday (18 May) Cmdt Ferreira (OC), Major Viljoen (2IC), Capt Erasmus (SO3 Int), Major Lynch and air crew arrived at Omauni from Rundu. At ± 0930 all middles participating in Ops 7i10-7i10 were briefed by Cmdt Ferreira personally..	Rundu
		DEFENCE INTELLIGENCE DECLASSIFIED	
		2 3 NOV 2009	
		6848496 PE WO1	

OPS/1/32 BN   TOP SECRET/UITERS GEHEIM

two and a half to three kilometres south of the base along the north–south road, from where they would mount a pre-bombardment. Faul would also mine the road south of Savate, preventing any interference from forces in that direction, as well as cutting off any enemy trying to flee the base.

Alpha Company would attack the main base complex situated to the north and around the Savate town complex, advancing from west to east, with the aim of pushing the enemy towards the Cubango River, leaving them little choice but to flee north towards Caiundo, about 135 kilometres away, the obvious escape route for the Savate defenders. Charlie Company would use two platoons to attack what was interpreted from the aerial photographs to be the vehicle park, on the eastern tip of the airstrip, about 500 metres north of the town. The airstrip would form the border between Alpha and Charlie Companies. Foxtrot Company would attack the southern part of the town and base complex. The third Charlie Company platoon, commanded by Second Lieutenant Andre 'Trompie' Theron, was the reserve for the main assault force and, together with some men from

Echo Company's third platoon and Second Lieutenant Rolf Heiser's nine men from Bravo 6, they would walk in a spread-out line behind the assault line to attend to any wounded and take them to the medical point.

The assault pioneer section (12 soldiers), commanded by Second Lieutenant Coenie Nolte and Warrant Officer Class 2 José D. Lourenco, would protect the echelon where Louw was in command. They would also help clear the base after the attack. The Recce Wing was divided into 10 three-to-five-man groups and would deploy north of Savate to stop individuals of the enemy forces trying to escape towards Caiundo. The SAAF component, under the control of Major Lynch of the Mobile Air Operations Team (MAOT), would be stationed at the Omauni base on standby to evacuate casualties only.

A medical evacuation post would be set up by Lieutenant (Dr) Richard van Zyl, the Buffalo base doctor, who would accompany the assault force from Buffalo. This medical post would be near Ferreira's headquarters, on the road forming the border between the Alpha and Foxtrot Companies' attack force. Van Zyl would be assisted by Lieutenant (Dr) Stefaan Bouwer, the Omauni base doctor. Bouwer had Corporal Grand Larkan, a trained South African Medical Service (SAMS) operational medic stationed at Omauni, to help him. Lieutenant (Dr) Breedt from Rundu and Lieutenant (Dr) Dunlop from Ondangwa would man the Omauni sickbay in the absence of Bouwer and would be responsible for treating casualties, who would be evacuated by helicopter. Company medical orderlies would support the medical teams.

Second Lieutenant Dave Hodgson, Alpha 1 platoon commander, remembers that there were many questions after Ferreira's orders and briefing:

The result of the order group was that each company commander planned his part of the operation and this was then passed by his order to his platoon commanders. Disturbingly, many questions that were raised as to the enemy's strength and weaponry remained unanswered.

We were convinced by the intelligence section that it would be a walk in the park. The enemy was possibly a maximum of 300 persons and their heaviest weapon would be at most PKMs, RPDs, and 82-millimetre mortars. At no stage did we doubt that we would be attacking a target for UNITA, and therefore it must be FAPLA. This deduction was clearly apparent when we heard that there would be no air support – only, if absolutely necessary, a casevac chopper, should there be the small possibility that we would have casualties.

In the meantime, the recce teams had arrived on the border. Staff Sergeant Lopez Francisco, known by 32 Battalion men as 'Senhor Lobbs', was a

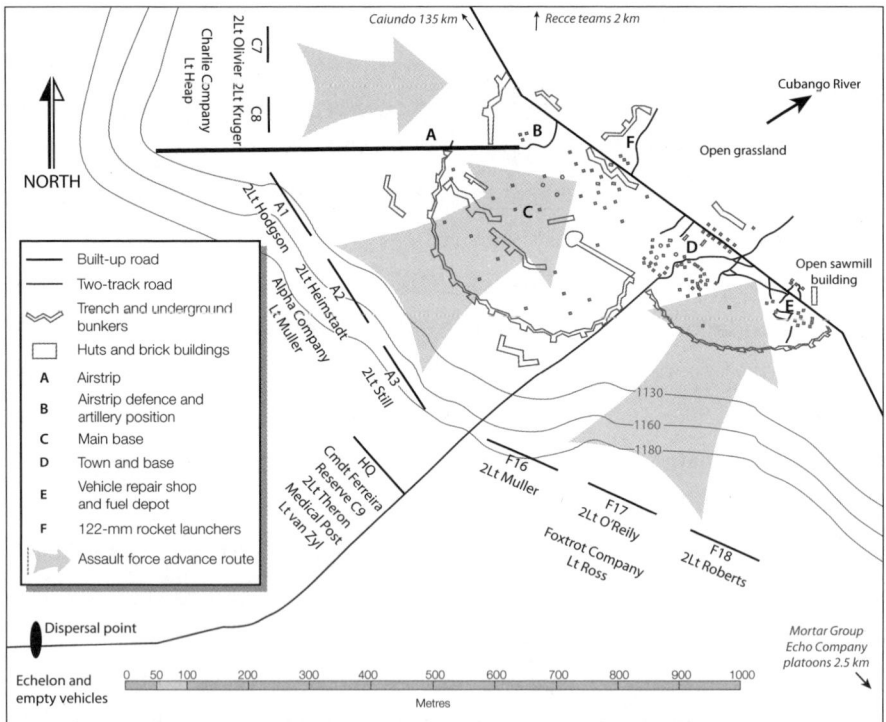

The attack plan. A computer-generated copy of the base layout, as provided by the photograph-interpretation analysts in Ondangwa. Except for A, C and D, other positions or installations were identified after the attack

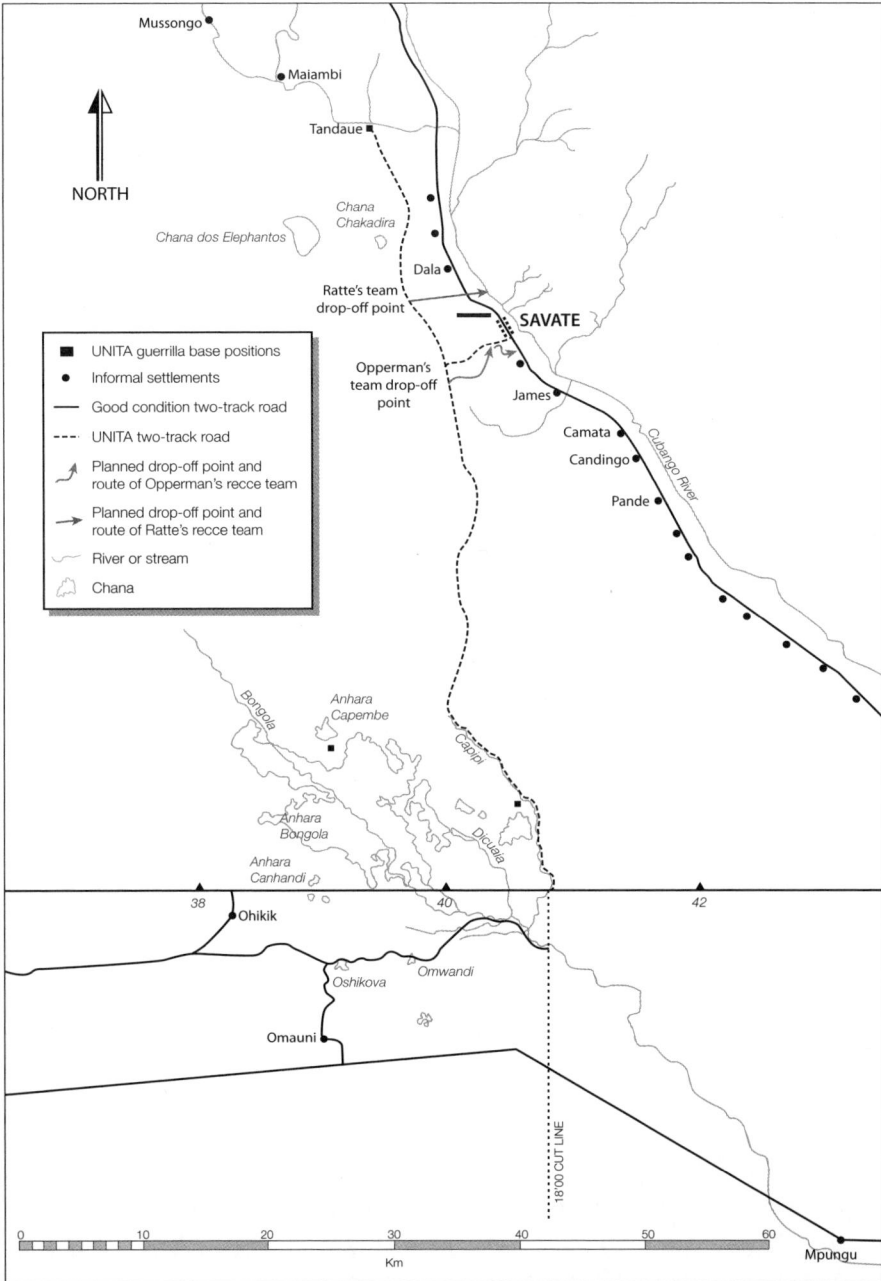

NORTH

Legend:
- ■ UNITA guerrilla base positions
- ● Informal settlements
- ── Good condition two-track road
- --- UNITA two-track road
- ↗ Planned drop-off point and route of Opperman's recce team
- → Planned drop-off point and route of Ratte's recce team
- ∿ River or stream
- ⌂ Chana

Places and features labelled on the map: Mussongo, Maiambi, Tandaue, Chana Chakadira, Chana dos Elephantos, Dala, Ratte's team drop-off point, SAVATE, Opperman's team drop-off point, James, Camata, Candingo, Pande, Cubango River, Bongola, Anhara Capembe, Capipi, Anhara Bongola, Anhara Canhandi, Dicuala, Ohikik, Oshikova, Omwandi, Omauni, Mpungu, 18'00 CUT LINE, 38, 40, 42

Scale: 0 10 20 30 40 50 60 Km

The reconnaissance plan showing the road positions, as reported by FALA guerrillas, the recce teams' drop-off points and the planned routes to the base white Portuguese man, previously a resident of Angola, who had been employed in road construction and as a professional hunter in the southern Angolan hunting concessions, and was now employed by CSI. He and another UNITA guide met the two recce teams at the border – along the route used by CSI convoys to resupply the FALA guerrillas at their base at Anhara Capembe – and from there transported them to their drop-off points. They first dropped Opperman's five-man team at a point, according to Francisco, south-west of Savate, from where they would walk east for a certain distance and then turn north, walking until they found the road coming from Savate, and from there walk along the road to the proposed dispersal point.

Francisco dropped Ratte's six-man team (five Recce Wing men and the UNITA guide) at a point, according to him, north-west of Savate, allowing them to walk east until they reached the Cubango River north of Savate, where they would assemble their Klepper Aerius kayaks and paddle downstream to the target area.

Unbeknown to Opperman at the time, he would never find the route or do a reconnaissance of the dispersal point, which would later influence the movement of the assault force. By the morning of 19 May, Opperman had still not found the road. He explains:

> I was to take in a group to do the reconnaissance of the access route to the dispersal point, where the whole fighting force would disperse from. Willem went in with another group, he went in to check up on the base itself ... I chose Tabo, Botes, Kaliva (the machine gunner) and Kassubu (the medic). So, the five of us, we went in to do the route in. Senhor Lobbs, he took us in, both teams in one of their vehicles.
>
> We checked the aerial photographs and we also took the maps and they would have taken us up, dropped us off at a specific point, where then we would walk north. It would have been a night walking in and out, checking out the dispersal point ... we were supposed to lead in the

main fighting force. They dropped us off that afternoon, three or four o'clock, somewhere there, it could have been one o'clock, but middle of the day, we travelled most of that day, until they dropped us off. We had one water bottle each because it should have been in and out.

We were dressed lightly, and they took Willem further on. We started walking and walking and walking. Eventually came daybreak; we were out of water at that stage and we still couldn't find the road. We started doing a 360, meaning you go one kilometre, two kilometres, making a square, to find this road.

By one o'clock that afternoon, we hadn't found anything, but then we were basically stuffed because the water was finished and we were thirsty: it was a hot day. By then, it was 40- or 50-odd kilometres that we had walked without finding anything, so we started talking back to Omauni, where the main fighting force was at that stage, and said, 'We've got a problem,' so they sent Big Daddy. He came in with a spotter, he started looking for us and, for some reason or another, I told him, 'Listen, you're still south of us.' I could hear that aeroplane, but to me it sounded like they were still south of us.

Early morning on 19 May, Lieutenant Graham Chisholm, the Cessna 185 pilot, and Major Viljoen (Big Daddy), who was not supposed to take part in the operation because he had just returned from a kidney operation, searched for Opperman and his team. They flew much farther north than expected, but could not find the men. Eventually, at 10:20, they established radio communication with Opperman and determined his position as seven kilometres south-west of Savate. Opperman explains:

Eventually, they were like 30-odd kilometres north of Savate, there's another establishment there and they said they are going to get into trouble now by going that way; they were much too far north. So they came back, and suddenly the plane passed overhead and I said, 'Wait,

TOP SECRET/UITERS GEHEIM — DD1991

OPERATIONS WAR DIARY/OORLOGSDAGBOEK OPERASIES

OF/VAN 32 BN Tact. HQ

BAND/VOLUME..........
MAAND/MONTH May 8..

PLEK/PLACE...... Omaun...... TYDPERK VAN/PERIOD FROM... 19/0800/b ... TOT/TO ... 20/0800/b .

Reeks no. Serial no.	Datum en tyd Date and time	Opsomming van voorvalle en informasie Summary of events and information	Verwysing Reference
1	19/1020/b	Comms made with c/s Romeo 2 Lt Oppmann (Recce) at grid reference Iz Y6...	Informal
2	19/1200/b	2 Lt Oppman ready at location to be picked up by tiger (that is Puma). They also require white to be taken for them when picked up 2 Lt Oppman picked up at 19/1240b May by Puma..	Informal
3	19/1135/b	Lt Botti (Recce leader) at grid reference Y2 S8	Informal
		Conway (4 cap; recce; coy assault pioneer section, 2 mortar groups, Int team, maintenance element + med element) leave this c/s at 19/1418/b May	

OPS/1/32 BN   TOP SECRET/UITERS GEHEIM

TOP SECRET/UITERS GEHEIM — DD1991

OPERATIONS WAR DIARY/OORLOGSDAGBOEK OPERASIES

OF/VAN

BAND/VOLUME.............
MAAND/MONTH.............

PLEK/PLACE.................. TYDPERK VAN/PERIOD FROM.......... TOT/TO ....

Reeks no. Serial no.	Datum en tyd Date and time	Opsomming van voorvalle en informasie Summary of events and information	Verwysing Reference
4	19/1840/b	309/1/A5 Ops Trio – Trio (Siku) Situp no1, Period 18/1700/b – 19/1700/b May 80	OPS/184/May80

OPS/1/32 BN   TOP SECRET/UITERS GEHEIM

36

wait, you just passed over us!' So then they realised what had happened. The road we were supposed to take was going in a northerly direction, but they took a completely different route which went basically north-west, so the time scales as we had it, where we were supposed to be dropped, got messed up by this other road. We went through a UNITA establishment, the first time in my life I had actually seen UNITA in the veld.

We went through one of their towns, or bases, and from there it went north, meaning they dropped us off about five to 10 kilometres too far to the west, and about five kilometres south from where we were supposed to have been dropped off. We were in no-man's-land.

By then, they said we must just walk back to the river and they'll pick us up when they come in, the main fighting force, and we said, no way, we're stuffed. We slept there that night, and the next morning we started drinking drips because we didn't have any water – saline drips, it tasted so shit that I put condensed milk in it, and the condensed milk actually made it worse. But by then we were dehydrated ... I said, 'I'm not walking any more. If you want me, come and fetch me,' and they said from the base, 'No, just start walking.' And I said, 'No ways, if you want us come and fetch us.'

The next day, at 09:00, Captain Theuns Meyer flew his Puma to pick up Opperman's team and return to the Omauni base, just in time for them to join the main force, which was to move shortly.

Ratte's team – comprising Second Lieutenant Erwin 'Smoothy' Baumeister, Sergeant Pieter van Eeden, Corporal Chivale Paulo, Lance Corporal Pedro Casoma and the UNITA guide – were dropped at the prearranged point at 18:10 on 17 May and started their journey eastwards towards the river, according to them about a six-hour walk. They did not reach the river that first night and so decided to find a lay-up place for the following day. Ratte became concerned when they heard vehicle movement. He explains:

And then we laid up by day, and we didn't reach the river, we didn't even come close to it in the first night, so we knew that something was wrong, but we didn't know what, and we still assumed that we were north of Savate. Then, during the day, we heard vehicles [due] east, in other words in the direction where we were going, so we assumed – well, it can't be Savate, because Savate must be south, so it could be a convoy that is passing up there north of Savate – so we decided that we didn't want to walk into that convoy so we went off slightly to the right, to miss them, and to then launch our boats.

At last light on 18 May, Ratte's team continued on their route towards the Cubango River. When they reached it, they assembled their kayaks and started their more-or-less seven-kilometre downstream paddle towards the target area, still in time, according to Ratte, to do the reconnaissance the same night.

From the beginning, the UNITA guide was not very comfortable because he was not familiar with the terrain. The team continued rowing south, however, hoping that he would find the terrain more familiar the closer they got to Savate. Eventually, they reached a small former Portuguese settlement on the western bank of the river, which they assumed was Savate. They went into a lay-up place on the eastern side of the river for the day of 19 May, but did not detect any movement the entire day. The UNITA guide went silent when Ratte told him they would enter the town that night to confirm the FAPLA presence and deployments. When darkness fell, the team rowed across to the western side of the river and sneaked into the settlement, which they found to be deserted. Suddenly the UNITA guide recognised where they were. Ratte explains:

But what actually happened was that he [Lobbs] had dropped us off far to the south – not north of Savate, but west of Savate, actually opposite Savate. In other words, where he had dropped us off, if you draw a line

Mussongo

Maiambi

Tandaue

Chana Chakadira

Chana dos Elephantos

Dala

NORTH

SAVATE

Ratte's team
drop-off point

James

Camata

Candingo

Cubango River

Pande

Opperman's
team drop-off
point

	UNITA guerrilla base
●	Informal settlements
—	Good condition two-track road
---	UNITA two-track road
	Actual drop-off point and route taken by Opperman's recce team
	Actual drop-off point and route taken by Ratte's recce team
	River or stream
	Chana

Bongola

Anhara Capembe

Capily

Anhara Bongola

Dicuaia

Anhara Canhandi

38

Ohikik

40

Oshikova

Omwandi

42

Omauni

18°00 CUTLINE

0   10   20   30   40   50   60

Mpungu

Km

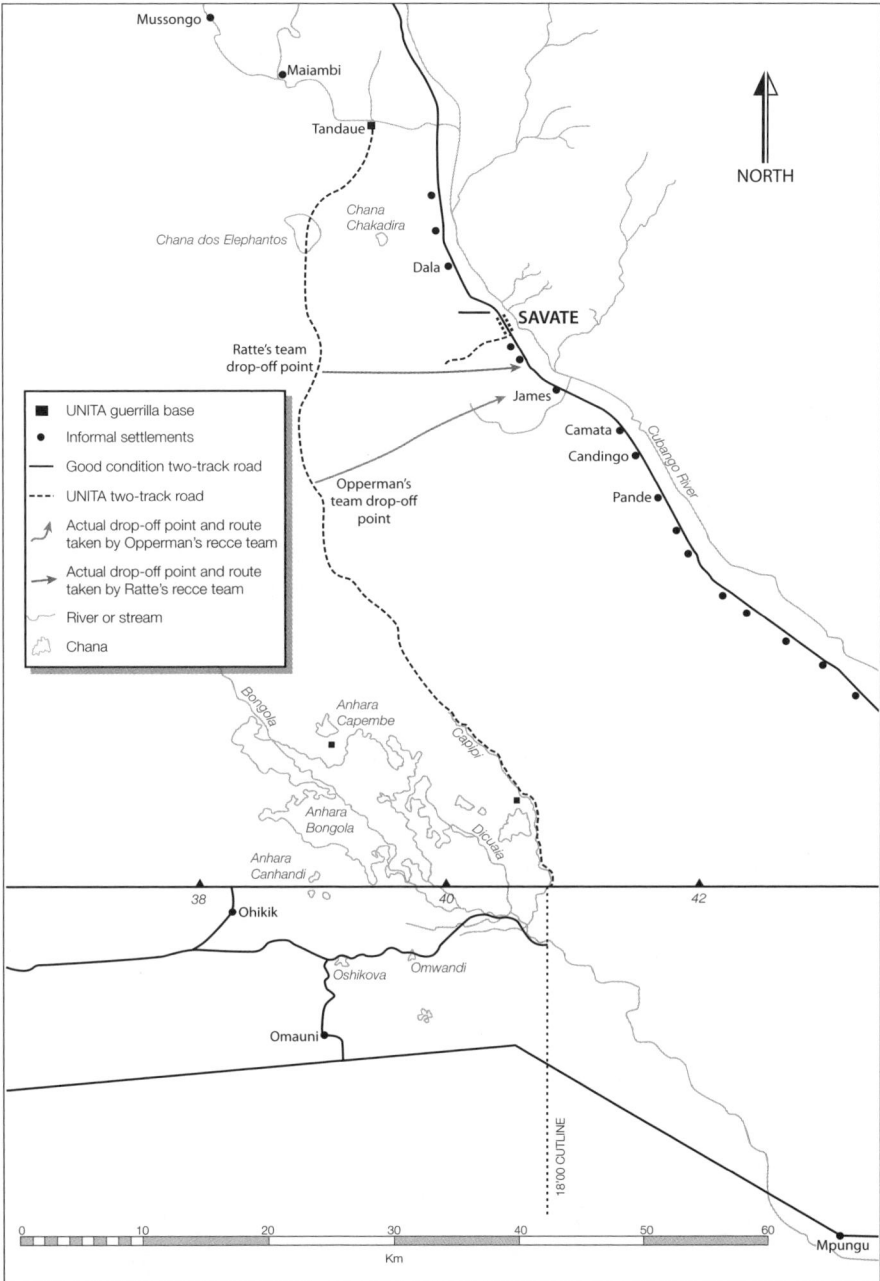

The actual reconnaissance. Map showing the actual position of the road, the drop-off points and the recces' routes

39

to the east, we would have walked right into Savate itself. The vehicles that we heard were actually vehicles in Savate itself, so when we veered off to the right the next night we continued walking, and then in the middle of the night, we got to the river and we launched our boats. We saw tracks and a little road and I think we even heard vehicles that evening again, but at that time, from where we launched, it would be north, but we just assumed that it was just a vehicle convoy and that Savate was to the south, so we rowed downstream through rapids as well; at one stage there were rapids there and we made good progress, but all the time, the guide was puzzled.

They had paddled south for approximately nine kilometres before reaching the small deserted settlement of Pande, about 17 kilometres south of Savate. At 11:35 on 20 May, Ratte reported his predicament by radio to Ferreira.

Ferreira had set the attack date for first light on 21 May and was awaiting final authority to move out. No reconnaissance on the entrance route or dispersal point had been done because of Opperman's wrong position and Ratte's team were 17 kilometres from their target. H-hour was 24 hours away and he still had no final reconnaissance!

3

Advances

Ferreira could wait no longer. At 14:15 on 19 May, the 370 company men, the mortar sections, the assault pioneer section and the support elements left for Savate on Kwêvoël trucks. Ferreira's small command element – which included his intelligence officer, Erasmus, RSM Ueckermann, signals officer Taylor, signaller Lance Corporal Bruce Anders, operations clerk Laubsher, Doctors Van Zyl and Bouwer, and Charl Muller, who was responsible for navigation and some of the Recce Wing men – travelled in four Buffels. Each Buffel was armed with a 7.62-millimetre mounted Browning machine gun and manned by a Recce Wing man. The other Recce Wing men travelled on one of the Kwêvoël trucks. Louw controlled the seven Kwêvoël trucks on which the companies travelled. I was sergeant at the time, and I was tasked with ammunition resupply during the battle and had one 10-ton Kwêvoël, loaded with ammunition and supplies.

The planned route was the same as for the recce teams, except that when the road (which was barely visible on the aerial photographs and was supposed to have been reconnoitred by Opperman) that ran towards Savate was reached, the force would debus and advance on foot towards the base. All the planning was based on the assumption that the assault force would reach the debus point long before last light on 20 May.

The navigation of the main assault force to the assembly point was once again left to 'Senhor Lobbs' Francisco, who confirmed that he knew the route and insisted that he had dropped Opperman and Ratte at the correct locations. The driving was time-consuming and difficult. The two-track road they were on had been bundu-bashed by FALA with GAZ or IFA

G.P.-S.

MESSAGE FORM—BERIGVORM

DD 978
(DD 977A)

File reference
Lêerverwysing 32BN/309/1/A5

Number
Nommer

For signals use
Vir gebruik van seindiens

Precedence action Voorrang uitvoering	Precedence info Voorrang info Routine—Roetine	Date time group Datumtydgroep	Handling instructions Hanteringsinstruksies
P		19/140	

From/Van ØA

To/Aan ØC

DEFENCE INTELLIGEN- DECLASSIFIED 23 NOV 68...

Prefix
Prefiks GR

Security classification
Sekerheidsklas U/C

Info

Originator's Number
Opstellersnommer OPS/184/MAY 8Ø

1 (.) 3Ø9/1/A5 OPS TIRO-TIRO (SILVER) SITREP NO 1 (.)

PERIOD 18/17ØØ/b — 19/17ØØ/b May 8Ø (.)

2 (.) ENEMY

A (.) — HU NTR

3 (.) OWN FORCES

A (.) LN LEFT OMAUNI AT 19/1615/b MAY 8Ø (.)

B (.) CROSSED CUTLINE AT 19/1615/b MAY 8Ø

C (.) WILL PROCEED ALONG ROAD UNTIL 19/19ØØ/b MAY 8Ø

AND WILL THEN LAY UP FOR THE NIGHT (.)

LOC (.) UNKNOWN (.)

Page Bladsy	1 of 2 pages van bladsye	Refers to a classified message Verwys na 'n geklassifiseerde berig Yes/Ja No/Nee	Drafter's name Berigskrywer se naam	Appointment Aanstelling	Phone No. Foonno.

For signals use Vir gebruik van seindiens	Q R	Date Datum	Time Tyd	System Stelsel	Op Bdnr	V D	Date Datum	Time Tyd	System Stelsel	Op Bdnr	Releasing officer's signature Goedkeuringsoffisier se handtekening Rank Rang Designation Ampstitel

G.P.-S.

MESSAGE FORM—BERIGVORM

DD 978
(DD 977A)

File reference
Lêerverwysing

Number
Nommer

For signals use
Vir gebruik van seindiens

Precedence action Voorrang uitvoering	Precedence info Voorrang info Routine—Roetine	Date time group Datumtydgroep		Handling instructions Hanteringsinstruksies
From/Van			Prefix Prefiks	GR
To/Aan			Security classification Sekerheidsklas	
Info			Originator's Number Opstellersnommer	

D(.) WILL PROCEED FURTHER ON 2ø/ø63ø/B MAY 8ø
TO ADMIN AREA (.)
E (.) C/S R (LT RATTE) AT GRID Y2 S8(.)

F (.) NOTHING ELSE TO REPORT (.)

Page 2 of 2 pages Bladsy van bladsye	Refers to a classified message Verwys na 'n geklassifiseerde berig		Drafter's name Berigskrywer se naam	Appointment Aanstelling	Phone No. Foonno.
	Yes/Ja	No/Nee ✓	7 Heyman		

For signals use Vir gebruik van seindiens	Q	Date Datum	Time Tyd	System Stelsel	Op Bdnr	V	Date Datum	Time Tyd	System Stelsel	Op Bdnr	Releasing officer's signature Goedkeuringsoffisier se handtekening
	R					D					Rank Rang Designation Ampstitel

trucks. While the Buffels had a similar wheelbase, the 6×6-wheel-drive, 10-ton Kwêvoël trucks were much bigger, with a much wider wheelbase. Private Nico Groenewaldt, who was driving behind the lead Buffel, remembers the difficulty of navigating the sandy road, and the later bundu-bashing he was required to do with his vehicle when transporting reserve mortar bombs to the mortar position:

> In front of me was a Buffel, with Charl Muller standing up, holding onto the roll bar most of the time. Dressed in camo, with a scarf around his head and face, he looked every bit the great soldier that he was. I felt very proud to be part of this operation. The driving was hard work. The sand was thick and we were bundu-bashing all the way. The wheelbase and turning circle of my Kwê were much wider than those of the Buffels, so I had to make a new road all the way.
>
> Much further, I was met by a dark figure and recognised one of our guys. He jumped onto the ladder next to my open door and guided me deep into the bush. The bundu-bashing damaged some of the brake air pipes on the truck. To drive without brakes in the bush is not a problem. The problem is that if all the air leaks out of the system, the back brakes lock up automatically and then you go nowhere. You become a sitting duck with a target as big as a house. I spent some time under the truck clamping shut the broken pipes and disconnecting the back brake boosters. This was done by the light of a borrowed cigarette lighter. I was mobile again.

At one stage, the assault force was delayed when a doctor had to stitch up Corporal Andy Falcus's forehead. Bouwer recalls:

> During the bundu-bashing, we stopped on one occasion because one of the troops stood up and hit his head against a tree. He gashed open his whole forehead and Dr Richard van Zyl had to put in sutures while

we all waited. This [Falcus] was an ex-Rhodesian chappie that had just joined 32 Battalion.

With Ferreira on the move, Ratte's team had no choice but to turn around and start paddling back upstream to Savate. Stealing some daylight, at 17:00 on 19 May, they began their return journey. Ratte and Casoma, who was also the team medic, were in one kayak, and Van Eeden, Paulo, Baumeister and the UNITA guide in the other two. About 12 kilometres from Savate, they narrowly escaped being spotted by an enemy control point, which had been set up on the road near the riverbank. Nobody was aware of this control point, as it was not visible on the aerial photographs. They made it to within eight kilometres of Savate and stopped at a daytime lay-up place just before the first rapid in the river. Paddling upstream took time, and instead of having two nights for the reconnaissance, there was now only one.

By 22:00 on 19 May the assault force had still not reached their assembly point. Finding themselves instead at a chana, Ferreira realised that Francisco had taken them past Savate and that they were actually at Chana dos Elephantos, 16 kilometres north-west of Savate. The road from Savate, barely visible on the aerial photographs, which joined the UNITA supply road on which they were travelling, was nowhere to be found. Again, Francisco had taken the wrong road. Ross (Foxtrot Company) expresses the men's feelings about their guide's navigational ability:

The guide, Lobbs, was a curious choice, as we were eventually convinced he had never been into southern Angola, let alone near Savate. Ratte had an uncanny ability to get himself to the target regardless of who had dropped him 'you know where'. We were, at the time, oblivious to all these facts and were delayed by a day. We eventually got 'plotted' and found the correct road to Savate. The most curious thing was that we passed many a sizeable tree and not in any of them did I see Lobbs strung up.

Ferreira had no choice but to laager south of Chana dos Elephantos that night. Early the next day, he tasked Viljoen and Chisholm with an aerial reconnaissance of the route, so he could decide where they should go next. Flying out of earshot and sight of Savate, or so they thought, Chisholm and Viljoen scouted the route they would later direct the convoy to, as Chisholm explains:

> My mission was to fly Viljoen and recce the route the convoy was to take to get within striking distance of the target. This took a couple of hours before Viljoen was happy with the intended route ... we flew within five miles of Savate at that time. Once the convoy got under way, I again got airborne to give directions to the rendezvous until last light.

Knowing that he was falling behind schedule, Ferreira decided to travel in daylight and left Chana dos Elephantos at 14:00 on 20 May, moving south. When they were west-south-west of Savate, Chisholm, who was still airborne, guided the convoy towards the correct road. Fifteen kilometres from Savate they found it. Half overgrown and running from Savate, it stopped in the bush with no junction with any existing road except for two-track roads disappearing north and south into yet more bush.

Meanwhile, the CSI liaison team commanded by Oelschig arrived by light aircraft at Omauni at 17:30. Oelschig was accompanied by Major Johan 'Redheart' Schutte, his logistics officer, who was to determine the nature and scope of logistics requirements so that UNITA/FALA would be able to remain operationally functional in the area once FAPLA had been driven out of Savate. Another team member, Major D.D. 'José' de Oliveira, was interested in finding or identifying elements from Savate who would be willing to provide information regarding FAPLA military activities in the area.

The plan was for the CSI team to fly with the Puma to Savate after the attack. However, when it became apparent that he would need to liaise with the FALA forces, which would deploy north and south of Savate, to coordinate times, Ferreira ordered Oelschig and his team to be flown by helicopter to his position. Oelschig would then accompany Ferreira's force, travelling on Francisco's two-ton Fiat truck.

The assault-force convoy followed the road to the assembly point nine kilometres from Savate, reaching it at around 19:00 on 20 May. The plan was for the echelon vehicles, empty Kwêvoël trucks and Buffels to stay at the assembly point under my and Louw's command.

Just after last light, Ratte and his men resumed paddling. They predicted that they would reach Savate with enough time for a reconnaissance. Ratte and Paulo would confirm the enemy deployments in the town, and their defences and strength. Van Eeden and Casoma would do a reconnaissance of the mortar positions, so that they could lead the mortar platoon to them the next morning. Baumeister would be the rear link manning the radio and guarding the boats. Ratte explains:

So, we decided to go in that next night and we had basically two tasks: the one was to establish the mortar position where our mortars were to be set up ... so they could plot themselves and from there they could plot the enemy. The other was to establish the perimeter of the garrison ... so when it became dark we pushed the boats into the water again and rowed upstream and we arrived opposite Savate and got out ... the houses started a bit further back. I think we got going just after midnight. So Piet van Eeden, who was a mortarman, he went off to one side to establish a mortar position and I took another guy, Paulo, and we went all around the trenches. In other words, the perimeter trenches that the Angolans had dug all around Savate ... we went all the way around until we got to the airstrip and then walked down the airstrip back to the river. In the process, we established the extent of the base, which was far bigger than we expected and also that they must have some heavy weaponry there ... it was not just a normal little garrison.

We walked outside the perimeter, all the time staying close to the perimeter; in other words, the trenches and the fires and the guards and so on, but trying to keep out of earshot so that they didn't realise that we were there. We just watched and saw there is a trench, there is presence there, there is a fire there. Coming down the runway it was coming on to early morning; normally that's the time when nobody moves, and we just openly walked down the runway and just checked on the side, there is presence there and there is presence there, and we just carried on because we didn't have any time any more; we just had to leg it back to the river. Then, before first light, we withdrew across the river.

Van Eeden and Casoma did not have a complicated task and reached the projected mortar positions long before Ratte was done with his reconnaissance. Van Eeden marked the mortar positions and waited there to receive the mortar sections before first light on 21 May. He remembers:

We prepared the Kleppers, and without taking any breaks, started to row north; time was against us. At about 01:00, we arrived at Savate. I was the first to get out of the Klepper and climbed up against the riverbank. I told W.R. that it looked like a big town because of the activities still going on at that time of the morning. W.R. left in the direction of the base. He gave me and Casoma instructions to go to the position where the mortars would deploy. I waited at the place where the mortars had to deploy.

When Ratte had completed his circuit of the base, he confirmed the deployment of FAPLA forces in and around the town. Their strength was much more than a battalion. He also noted extensive conventional trench and underground bunker systems, and confirmed a strong deployment of 14.5-millimetre anti-aircraft guns at an airfield that the aerial-photograph analysts had supposed was a vehicle park.

Paddling through the rapids had been difficult, and Ratte's high frequency (HF) B22 radio was no longer working, as it had been submerged underwater twice. As Ferreira's force was now well out of reach of his small very high frequency (VHF) A52 radio, Ratte had no means of communicating his information. Ferreira, for his part, kept to the time schedules, trusting that Ratte would at some point come on the air and speak to him.

While the recce team were conducting their reconnaissance, Ferreira's headquarters group, Van Zyl's medical team, the assault force, the mortars with two platoons of Echo Company and the remaining recce teams were preparing to move on foot to the dispersal point two kilometres west of Savate. From here the mortar and protection platoons would move to their set-up place south of the town. The moment the bombardment on Savate started, the empty vehicles, the assault pioneer section – divided among the four Buffels under the command of Sergeant Ron Gregory – and the echelon were to move to the outskirts of the enemy base, where a second medical evacuation post under Bouwer and an echelon area under Louw would be established. Casualty evacuation and ammunition resupply to the companies

49

G.P.-5.

MESSAGE FORM—BERIGVORM

DD 978
(DD 977A)

File reference
Lêerverwysing 32 BN / 309 / 1

Number
Nommer

For signals use
Vir gebruik van seindiens

Precedence action Voorrang uitvoering	Precedence info Voorrang info	Date time group Datumtydgroep	Handling instructions Hanteringsinstruksies
P	Routine—Roetine	20/1930/B	SLICODE.

From/Van ØA

To/Aan ØC

Prefix
Prefiks   GR

Security classification
Sekerheidsklas   U/C.

Info

Originator's Number
Opstellersnommer   OPS / 195 / M80

REFERENCE INTELLIGENCE
DECLASSIFIED
29 NOV 2009

1.) SITREP NO 2., PERIOD 19/1700/B - 20/1700 B

MAY 80.,
2C.,
2C., ENEMY.,
2C., UB₁   PX₄   RS₃ /
A.) ENEMY ACTIVITY IN SAVATI., VEHICLE
MOVEMENT IN SAVATI AND VICINITY.,
UT₃ CO₂ PA, VM2 QD₄ / YE (FUT₅) AA₂
SMALL ARMS FIRE HEARD IN VICINITY
UO₂ DR₂ LD₄ NR₂ / SM₂   UO₂ DR₂ LD₄ NR₂
OF TOWN., K OBSERVED IN TOWN.,
XC₃
3.) OWN FORCES.,
PP₄   B F₂
A.) REACHED ADMIN AREA AT GRID
REFRENCE. (K7 L7   )

Page 1 of 2 pages
Blady van bladsye

Refers to a classified message
Verwys na 'n geklassifiseerde berig
Yes/Ja   No/Nee

Drafter's name
Berigskrywer se naam

Appointment Phone No.
Aanstelling Foonno.

For signals use Vir gebruik van seindiens		Date Datum	Time Tyd	System Stelsel	Op Bdnr		Date Datum	Time Tyd	System Stelsel	Op Bdnr	Releasing officer's signature Goedkeuringsoffisier se handtekening
	Q					V					
	A					D					Rank Rang Designation Amptitel

G.P.-S.

MESSAGE FORM—BERIGVORM

DD 978
(DD 977A)

File reference
Lêerverwysing_____

Number
Nommer_____

For signals use
Vir gebruik van seindiens_____

Precedence action Voorrang uitvoering	Precedence info Voorrang info	Date time group Datumtydgroep	Handling instructions Hanteringsinstruksies
	Routine—Roetine		

From/Van

Prefix
Prefiks   GR

To/Aan

Security classification
Sekerheidsklas

Info

Originator's Number
Opstellersnommer

B(.) BUSY DEPLOYING TO BN DISPERSAL
POINT(.)

US, US₂ (+

23 NOV 2009

DEFENCE INTELLIGENCE DECLASSIFIED

4(.) M.T.R(.)

5(.) N.T., R(.)

6(.) GENERAL(.)

A. EVERYTHING PROCEEDING ACCORDING TO
RA₃
PLAN(.) UNLESS SERIOUS PROBLEMS
MF₁ SD₄ QP₃ WH₄
ATTACK TO GO IN ON 21ˢᵗ MAY 89(.)

Page Bladsy 2 of 2 pages van bladsye	Refers to a classified message Verwys na 'n geklassifiseerde berig		Drafter's name Berigskrywer se naam	Appointment Aanstelling	Phone No. Foonno.
	Yes/Ja	No/Nee X	MAJ. E.G. VILJOEN	2IC	

For signals use Vir gebruik van seindiens	Q	Date Datum	Time Tyd	System Stelsel	Op Bdnr	V	Date Datum	Time Tyd	System Stelsel	Op Bdnr	Releasing officer's signature Goedkeuringsoffisier se handtekening
	R					D					Rank Rang / Designation Amptstel

51

would be done from this point. Casualties would first be treated by Van Zyl at a medical point near Ferreira's headquarters before being moved to Bouwer's post for further attention. Bouwer explains the medical plan:

> I came at the rear with the logistics guys and had most of the medical equipment with me. Richard van Zyl decided on what he needed for the little casevac station in front, following our briefing that there was not expected to be heavy opposition. He therefore only took a few drip needles, a few injections and a few drip sets that he could carry in a little bag. The rest of the stuff I had in a few trommels [steel trunks], which we would use once we met up.

Preparations were done at the debussing point. The assault-force men, dressed in combat kit, were given one 81-millimetre mortar bomb each to carry, to help the mortar platoon move the 300-odd mortar bombs to the dispersal point. From there, the mortar crews and Echo Company platoons would have to carry their four mortar tubes as well as at least three mortar bombs per man. The balance of the mortar bombs would be transported by vehicle to the mortar position once the bombardment began.

The backpacks belonging to the company men were stacked on the Kwêvoël trucks to be redistributed in the echelon area after the attack. As the recce teams would have to stay in the vicinity of their stopper-group positions after the attack as an early warning element, they took their heavy backpacks with them.

Before moving out, Ferreira once again confirmed that everything was ready. Oelschig recalls:

> Commandant Deon Ferreira came over to my position to confirm that everything was in order for the operation to proceed. He confirmed that the enemy were in their defensive positions and that this fact had been communicated to the operations room at Bastion in Windhoek.

He told me that he had been given the go-ahead for the operation. For my part, I confirmed that all UNITA forces were in position and that there had been no reports of movement towards Savate, either from Caiundo in the north or from Cuangar in the south. It was agreed that my headquarters would remain approximately one kilometre to the rear of 32 Battalion's headquarters until called forward.

At 21:00 on 20 May, on time to reach the target before first light, the assault force started their march towards Savate. Walking in a prearranged order would allow for quick separation once they reached the dispersal point. Charlie Company led in single file, walking on the left (north) of the road,

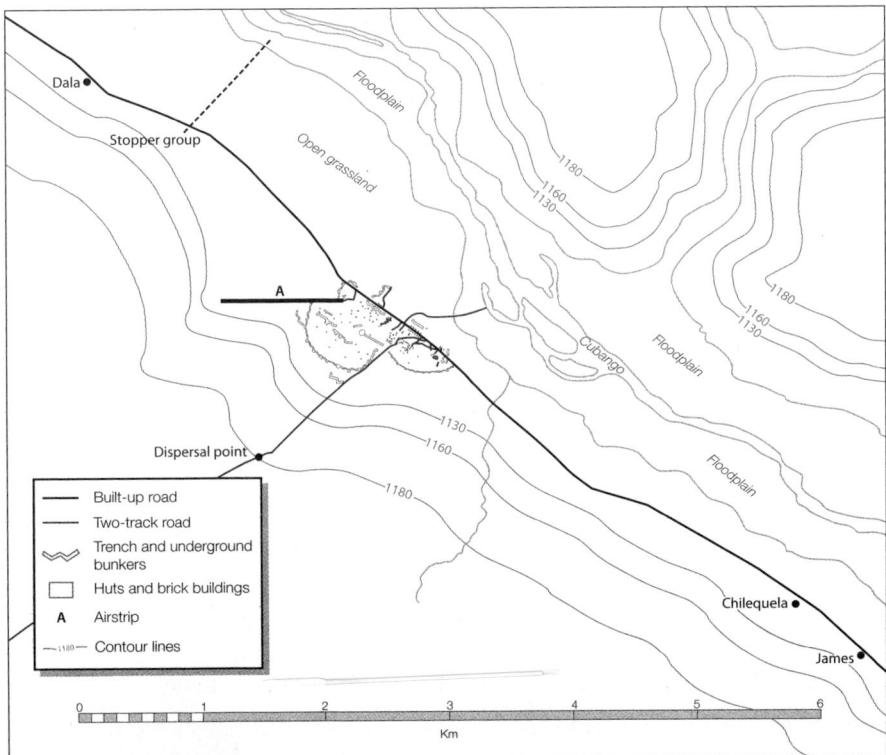

Map showing the topography, dispersal point, and stopper-group and mortar positions. The men had to advance down a slope to the base area

followed by battalion headquarters, the recce teams and the mortar sections. Alpha Company led on the right (south) of the road, followed by Foxtrot Company. When they fell behind schedule, Ferreira pressed the force to move on. With no reconnaissance of the route, nobody knew what to expect in the vicinity of Savate. The advance to the dispersal point did not go as planned. At 22:30, an enemy vehicle approached from the front. Grobler of Alpha 1 remembers:

> I will never forget the night before the attack. We prepared, covering up with 'black is beautiful'. I helped Tim Patrick with his. This was his first bush trip. We even helped him with his equipment, what to pack where. Then we started to walk.
>
> We walked in single file. Alpha 1 in front. Dave Hodgson was the platoon commander, therefore he was leading in front behind the blokes that led us in. I walked near the back of the platoon. Charl Muller (company commander) was behind me, then Alpha 2 with Horst Heimstadt leading. Foxtrot was behind Alpha. We all carried extra 81-millimetre mortar bombs. Late that night, we heard a vehicle. When the lorry (a GAZ truck) arrived, the shots were fired (small arms and MAGs). Afterwards, Charl called me to go with him.
>
> We had to sweep the area to ensure that there were no other surprises waiting for us. That was not necessary. The driver was dead. I took the driver's AKM rifle to use the butt. The bloke was really shot up. Some of the passengers had got away. However, if one looked at the damage, it was not possible for them to get far. Then we walked again. Late at night, we laagered. In a long single file we just lay there and slept; we did not have sleeping bags and because of the adrenalin could hardly sleep. I remember how Charl and Jim Ross joked about FAPLA now cleaning the barrels of the 14.5s in anticipation. They shared a space blanket. Early the next morning, we started to walk again. At 09:00 we were in position and the mortars started to fire.

TOP SECRET/UITERS GEHEIM

DD1991

OPERATIONS WAR DIARY/OORLOGSDAGBOEK OPERASIES

OF/VAN

BAND/VOLUME..............

MAAND/MONTH..............

PLEK
PLACE.................................. PERIOD FROM.................. TYDPERK VAN TOT ....

Reeks no. Serial no.	Datum en tyd Date and time	Opsomming van voorvalle en informasie Summary of events and information	Verwysing Reference
4	26/1945/6	Setup no 2. Period 19/1700/6 — 26/1700/6 May 86.	Ops/195/May 86
5	26/2236/6	From ФВ (maintinanu element) to ФА(tactical HQ, Omuni): Heard icy short small amo fire to thu southeast. On further investigation it was found that a car had to be stopped on the road, and the occup taken out. No casualties. Happened ± 5 km south east of c/s ФВ. Everything will proceed as nomal.	Informal
	PACE INTELLIGEN DECLASSIFIED 2/3 NOV 2009 SMIT		

OPS/1/32 BN   TOP SECRET/UITERS GEHEIM

Heap, the commander of Charlie Company, which was to attack the so-called vehicle park, also recalls the drama during the advance:

> It was a relief to eventually arrive at the point where we all had to debus from the vehicles. Everybody took the minimum of equipment because we all had to carry at least one 81-millimetre mortar bomb together with our own more than normal first-line ammunition and ample water for one day. The expectation was that the attack and rounding up of the base should be finished by midday the same day. The logistics vehicles would then bring our equipment to the front.
>
> I remember it was very dark that night. We could not even see the vehicle track, which we had to follow in an easterly direction. The assault force, together with the mortars, advanced in two single files walking on the dirt track. I walked about an arm's length behind Attie [Sergeant Attie Roestof from Alpha 2] – it was so dark that we had to hold each other from the back. Falcon and the command group were behind us.

I do not know where the recces and mortar group walked in the formation, most probably with Falcon in the middle.

It was cold, but everybody sweated because of the heavy load of ammunition and [the] mortar bombs. I think we walked at a pace of about two kilometres an hour. At one stage we heard a vehicle to the east, but the sound soon faded away. Not long after that, we again heard a vehicle, the sound coming closer and closer. I informed Falcon by radio that a vehicle was approaching in our direction.

He ordered us to take cover on the left side of the track and let the vehicle pass. They would jump the ambush from the middle of the formation where he was. We went down on the left side, about 10 metres from the track, lying on our stomachs. The vehicle headlights were switched on and I could clearly see the dust caused by our walking through the glare of the lights. I was afraid that the driver would realise that there was dust hanging in the air. However, the vehicle passed our position without any problems. It was too dark to see how many people were in the vehicle but we could hear their voices. Suddenly, there was heavy small-arms fire and just as quickly silence again. I wondered how many of the enemy were killed.

By now everybody's nerves were at breaking point. Everybody at Savate must have taken notice of this incident and thus would be on alert: no more surprise first-light attack. We again started to walk east. At one stage, we walked into a very thick bush. Attie suddenly stopped walking and I bumped into him; in front of us, we could make out a big dark object. I thought maybe it was an elephant. Falcon inquired why the advance had stopped. I informed him that there was something big blocking our advance. He instructed us to investigate.

Carefully, with tensed body, I moved forward – it was a vehicle. Many thoughts went through my mind: is the truck booby-trapped? Where are the driver and passengers – are they in an ambush position waiting for us? I used my knowledge, which I had learnt from a demolition course which I did in 1976 in Kroonstad, and opened the door carefully, feeling for any wires – there was nothing. This vehicle most probably had run out of fuel or had just been left there, not able to turn around because of the thick bush, when the other vehicle drove into our ambush. We continued to walk.

I had to walk on a compass bearing and I navigated for the Charlie Company platoons. We battled, it was pitch dark, and the haak-en-steek was thick. Everybody was extremely tired from the heavy weight we had to carry. Everybody was nervous because of the surprise element being given away.

After battling for about 30 minutes through the haak-en-steek, everybody's arms and faces were covered in bloody scratches. I asked Falcon if we could wait until daybreak so that we could see where we were going through the haak-en-steek. He agreed. Everybody went down in his tracks, lying or just sitting, waiting for first light. As mentioned already, we had the bare minimum of equipment. By now it was very cold and we were soaking wet because of the sweat.

Attie had a groundsheet. He, myself and another person lay down and covered ourselves with the groundsheet. Luckily, I was in the middle and could feel how the others struggled to cover themselves. The groundsheet did not make much of a difference, as we were still very cold. It was actually a blessing to start walking again. Very carefully, in the first light of the morning, we navigated to the dispersal point and took up position. I informed Falcon when we were in position. I cannot remember the time; all I know is that we had to wait for the mortar bombardment to start, which would be the sign to cross the advance line.

We reached the dispersal point, where the mortar group turned southeast. Myself and Charlie 7 and 8 walked in a north-easterly direction. Charlie 9, commanded by Second Lieutenant Andre 'Trompie' Theron, was the reserve element and moved with the battalion command group. It was a massive relief to get rid of the 81-millimetre mortar bombs

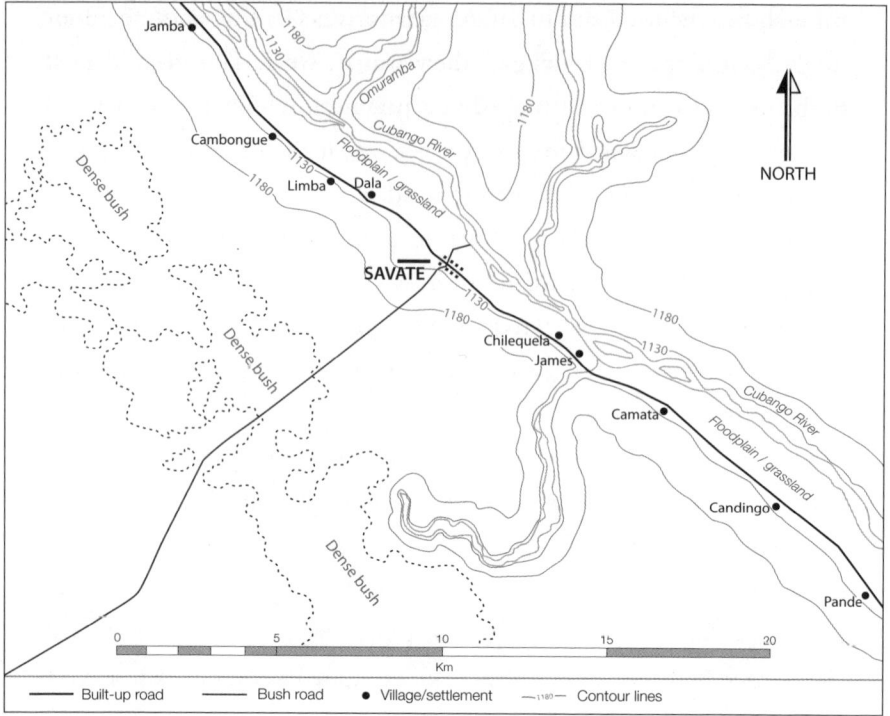

The terrain west of Savate showing the position of the dense bush that brought the advance to a halt

when we handed them to the mortar group to carry. I felt sorry for the mortar group, as they had to carry about 300 bombs on their own.

Ross had been walking with his company in the middle of the file when the vehicle approached:

Advancing down the road that night, Sam [Heap] called on the radio from the head of the column that vehicles were approaching. It was decided that should he encounter any, he was to get off the road and let them through. I was in the middle of the column and tasked to stop whatever came up the road.

We were raising a fair cloud of dust so we could not let them go through and then get back to Savate. Inevitably, a GAZ truck came trund-ling down the road and Sam gave the warning. We all took off to the left of the road and lay down. After about five minutes, the vehicle appeared and two of us rolled out into the road and gave it a solid spray of machine-gun rounds. I do not recall how it was decided how many soldiers had escaped and reported back to Savate. They need not have bothered going back, as the base would have heard the gunfire and been able to position us. That was, after all, the reason the vehicle came out. To look for us.

I remember it being cold that night and Sam had reported that going forward in the dark was impossible because of the bush. Falcon ordered us to stop and try to get some sleep. Sleep was not possible, as it was freezing. I had a space blanket and shared it with Charl while the troops sought comfort in a bit of happy weed. No doubt the occupants of Savate were having as bad a night, but surprise there was to be none.

Taylor, who was walking with Ferreira, was opposite the vehicle when it was shot out:

> In the silence following the brief burst of rifle fire, we heard the left cab door open and someone fall into the grass alongside the track. He crawled off into the undergrowth and was left to his own devices, most likely to die of his wounds. As we passed the GAZ truck, I could see a dark shape on the right-hand side of the cab and smell the strong, sickly sweet smell of blood. It was a left-hand-drive vehicle and the passenger, not the driver, had been shot to pieces.

During this time Ratte had been trying to reach Ferreira on the A52 VHF radio, but to no avail. While he waited on the western side of the river, Van Eeden was at the mortar position. Just before first light, Ratte decided to cross the river to evade FAPLA's early-morning patrols. Van Eeden remembers:

It started to become daylight and there was vehicle movement in the base. A vehicle loaded with troops drove past my position and I became concerned that the enemy would see the marks I had made in the road. I contacted W.R. by A52 radio to ask what was going on. At that stage, he was finished with his recce and at the Kleppers. He told me to also return to the Kleppers. We could not get radio communication with the headquarters because the B22 radio had been underwater twice because of the rapids.

Casoma was waiting with Van Eeden:

We were finished before first light and waited at the road for the mortars to arrive. We sat in the bush when we heard cars coming; it was already becoming light and we hid in the long grass. There were four trucks full of enemy forces driving towards the town. Not far from us the trucks stopped, but luckily nobody saw us. We waited there until the trucks left and we quickly went back to the river. When we arrived at the river, we could not find our boat. We had left it behind when it was dark and found it difficult to locate again because in daylight the place looked different. Sergeant Pict [van Eeden] called the lieutenant, who we had left at the boat, on the radio and after a while we found it. We quickly crossed the river and went with Lieutenant Ratte to the observation post.

Hoping to establish communication with Ferreira when he was nearer to Savate, the recce men took up an observation post from where they could direct the mortar fire. Van Eeden remembers Ratte's assessment of enemy strength in the base:

W.R. put us in position opposite the base (on the other side of the river). W.R. took his A52 radio and climbed a tree. He said to me that Charlie Company was going to walk into the 14.5 [anti-aircraft guns] when they start the attack. There were many movements in the base and W.R. said there was not only a company but maybe a battalion in the base.

From the dispersal point the burden of carrying the mortar bombs fell to the mortar sections and the two Echo Company platoons. The assault force would wait for the mortars to start the pre-bombardment, which was scheduled to last about an hour. The night march was particularly difficult for the mortar troops, some of whom had not fully recovered from wounds sustained during a previous deployment and were finding walking difficult. Anderson describes the hellish night:

We debussed from the vehicles about 10 kilometres from the town, and while we were walking, there were some recce teams, our recce teams from Omauni. The recces walked in front, and while we were moving towards the attack point, we heard a vehicle approaching and we were told, 'Everyone move to the left-hand side of the road,' thinking that if you shoot from the left to the right you'll kill the driver. We didn't take into consideration that all the Russian vehicles were left-hand drive … they shot the vehicle out, but the driver managed to get away and I think he got to the town and managed to warn them of a possible attack.

I remember walking past the vehicle that night with four or five guys sitting there, all having been shot, and getting that weird smell of blood mixed with diesel and gunpowder, and I knew we were in for something big.

We walked to the point where the mortar group and two platoons of Echo Company, who were to act as protection, met up. The mortar group walked at the back of the column. When there is such a long column, it is natural that it would 'concertina'. We only heard that the blokes went down for a break; we continued walking. We were still

walking when we heard on the A52 radio that the columns were starting to walk again after their rest break – we were still walking without
having had a break. The troops battled with the walking. The night was
so dark that we lost contact with each other. Every now and then we
had to call to each other; this made it very difficult to walk.

What made it even more difficult was that many of the mortar
troops were wounded blokes who had not fully recovered from their
wounds. The mortar pipes and the number of bombs we had to carry
also took their toll on the men. At one stage I helped a troop to carry
a mortar pipe. I was glad when we arrived at the mortar positions. At
that stage I was still young and full of fight. I hit a troop with the rifle
butt in his face when he again lost the route. He was angry and wanted
to shoot me. Everything was forgotten when we arrived at the position
and started with the bombardment.

Bouwer also recalls passing the enemy truck and getting into position for
the attack:

On the way I remember we drove past the GAZ truck that had been
shot up by the advance guard as they walked towards the base. I remember that we were still quite worried that they would have heard the
gunshots and alerted the base, but it looked like it had not happened.
The main attacking group set off and I was then diverted with some of
the echelon guys to an opening just behind the front line. We waited in
this opening while the attack started. We had our radios on and followed
the progress of the attack to hear when we had to move forward.

The 10 recce teams were ordered to take up ambush positions north of
the base to cover the most probable escape routes. Second Lieutenant
E. Swanepoel's team was tasked with leading the men from the dispersal
point. They were to walk with Heap's Charlie Company until they reached

the end of the runway at the airfield, where they would split up. Their advance to the ambush positions was not without problems. De Abreu recalls:

We walked in two single files throughout the night of 20 May to the place where we were to hand over the 81-millimetre bombs to Echo Company and the mortar people. Not wasting time, Lieutenant Swannie took my compass, put the bearing on plus/minus north and told me that after no more than two kilometres we would reach the end of the airfield, then we would have to turn north-east towards the river where we would find the Caiundo road. Our stick would be the first to stop at the road and put up our stopper group. For sure, most of us were already tired before we started moving to the position.

We arrived at the airfield, but not at the end. Instead, we arrived at a new enemy open bunker with two enemy soldiers sleeping and snoring in it. That time my hearing was 90 per cent good. I stopped and gave the enemy signal to the man behind me. It was night and for sure nobody saw my signal anyway. I talked very low, saying, 'Inimigo.' We changed direction for approximately 50 metres, then moved north again until we reached the end of the airfield. We turned north-east and luckily about 800 metres further we were on the Caiundo road.

We laid our ambush facing Savate and the rest went in the direction of the river, according to plan, leaving 200 metres between stopper groups. The sun had not yet risen, but you could see. As usual, we started the round-the-clock guard system. Lieutenant Swannie started with one-hour each and I was supposed to be the last. I took a chocolate from my ration pack and drank half a bottle of water lying down behind my RPD machine gun, ready for action. I fell asleep immediately due to fatigue. I believe all of us slept like rocks. I even dreamt that our dead man, R. Alberto [Rifleman Rodriques 'Space Monkey' Alberto was killed later], and I were together enjoying drinking somewhere in South West

Africa, he with long hair like a pop musician. No one woke me when the battle started in Savate.

Opperman also recalls that night:

At that point, Zack [Second Lieutenant Paul Q. Garret] would have taken over the recce group operation. As we entered the bush that one vehicle came and we all jumped into the bush, that's my recollection, and that driver, as we entered the bush area, I think he saw the tracks on the road and the dust still hanging in the air and tried to make a U-turn. He stopped, turned around, and ran slap-bang into the main fighting force.

They shot him up; they shot that whole vehicle up, but never hit the driver. He got away, and I think that what happened eventually at Savate might have been one of the results; he might have made his way back to base, I don't know. So eventually, we got to the dispersal point, the main group went down, we prepared from there, and that's where Zack took over with the recce group. He would have then led us into our stopper-group position, to the north of Savate. I still remember talking to Rassie [Alberto]: he was the intelligence office and he was killed there. I remember putting 'black is beautiful' on his nearly bald head, and said, 'Remember you've got a wife and kids, so look after yourself.' Those were my last words to him. Eventually we dispersed.

We were not in position yet when they started bombing. We were at the road at that stage and started dispersing from there. That's when I fell asleep that night, because we were in single file, going towards our place, and I just fell asleep, because for the last three, four days we'd been at it, and when I opened my eyes again, I couldn't see the guys in front of me: they were gone.

Eventually, Botes [Second Lieutenant Antonie 'Billy' Botes] was behind me. He said, 'No, they went that way,' so we caught up again.

He was walking with his hands in his pockets, and at one stage he stood on a branch and his foot slipped off and he fell down. We had kind of fun that night, but we were stuffed. Come sunrise, we were at the road. We stayed behind, we were supposed to be three in the stopper groups all the way down, but the terrain did not allow that, so two or three of our sticks stayed there at the road, and the bushes allowed enough cover. We thought the most obvious escape route might be on the road, which is why we actually took three groups, with enough firepower to stop vehicles. Eventually, when we reached the road that morning, the first mortars had already started falling at nine o'clock.

While the recce teams were taking up their positions, Ferreira's headquarters group waited by the side of the road. It was early morning and, as was customary, the locals were making their way from the town. Taylor remembers one particularly heart-stopping moment:

We watched Sam Heap's company file silently past us off to the left to get into position to the north of the base. They were behind schedule and still had a way to go. The mortar guys were also seriously behind schedule, having been hampered by thick bush while trying to get into position. The sun rose while we waited. A message came to us that there were three young boys walking up the road towards us. Ferreira's orders were to bayonet them should they try to run back, but leave them should they continue walking away from the FAPLA base. I sat there with my heart in my mouth, quietly willing them not to turn around. As they drew level to where we were sitting, one of them looked to his right and saw me sitting quietly a few metres away in the tall grass. He visibly caught his breath and his eyes flew wide. I must have looked like the devil incarnate dressed in my dirty camouflage uniform with the 'black is beautiful' camouflage cream streaked from the sweat on my face ... and they kept on walking away from the base. Once past us

65

they could contain themselves no longer and broke into a wild sprint down the sandy road, elbows pumping wildly and the pink under-soles of their bare feet flashing up nearly as high as their shoulder blades!

The mortar bombardment was supposed to start at 06:00 on 21 May, but the first bombs were not fired until 09:00. Sergeant John P. Botha, who was on his last operation (he had resigned from the South African Army and would leave at the end of May) and had deployed with Sergeant Kevin Sydow's Recce Wing team, explains how the recce teams were deployed when they eventually reached their positions:

At 09:00, the mortar bombardment commenced while we were walking into our stopper-group positions. We started dropping off stopper groups, one at a time, generally consisting of three to five men each. Our team took up position just west of the main supply route. The stopper-group area consisted of open grassland with very few trees in between. It was totally opposite to what we were accustomed to in the savannah bush of southern Angola. The teams were deployed in three- or five-man teams 200 metres or so apart, with the ability to move closer to support the next team in case of emergency. The team closest to the river consisted of Sergeant Kevin FitzGerald, the team leader, Lance Corporal Peter Lipman and a machine gunner with the nickname Space Monkey [Alberto].

We took up our position, Kevin Sydow to my right and the machine gun to my left. Remember, Kevin was the team leader. In front of me was an anthill next to a small tree. I crawled to it and used the anthill and small tree as cover not to break any silhouette. The reason for this action was that the grass was dry and very long, up to knee height, and if you did not have any other form of cover you would expose yourself. From there, I had a view over the grassland up to the perimeter of trees where Savate base was situated.

The attack force lay in position waiting for the mortar bombardment to stop and for the signal to attack. Soon after the first bombs exploded in Savate, FAPLA delivered a counter-bombardment with 122-millimetre mono-Katyusha rocket launchers and 82-millimetre mortars in the direction of the attack force. Nobody expected there to be those types of weapons at the base.

Corporal Jim 'Pip' Freeman had reported to 32 Battalion with other junior leaders in November 1979. After orientation he was assigned to the recruit-training team as an instructor. The recruit training came to an end two weeks before Operation Tiro-Tiro and Freeman was allocated to Alpha Company Platoon 2 (Alpha 2). While he lay waiting for the signal to attack, Freeman shared his fear of going into battle and possibly dying alongside an unexpected companion. He remembers:

As far as I can recall, the attack on Savate was supposed to commence with a mortar bombardment at first light, but, when the sun rose, I found myself with my back to a tree and only the sound of birds in the surrounding bush disturbing the silence. It had been a truly horrible night – I was cold and very nervous – so I was anything but peaceful. I wasn't particularly worried, though: after all, there were 250 of us; we were 32 Battalion; and there were only 350 of them, very lightly armed (remember, this was what we'd been told in Omauni).

I was grateful for the tree at my back. I was heavily weighted with about 11 magazines for my AK in my chest webbing and the zip-up pockets of my jumpsuit. Other pockets and pouches were loaded with M26 offensive hand grenades. I had a penchant for these, having been a fast-bowler at school, and could hurl them pretty far and accurately. They'd come in handy later.

In front of me, as the morning got warmer, was an anthill with bushes growing thickly around its base. I think I dozed off. Chris Brown launched the first mortar rounds at 09:04 by my watch. Being an insignificant little cog in the whole machine, I had no idea why the bombardment started so late.

The bombardment intensified and continued for several minutes – how long, precisely, I have no idea – before the day's first shock. Away in front of me was a detonation, followed by the whistling shriek of a rocket directed back towards where the enemy believed the 32 Battalion mortar position was located. It was the first time I'd heard the sound, but I'd listened to the Angolan old-timers talk about them often enough to know immediately that the counter-fire was being led by 122-millimetre Katyusha rockets. If there was one thing the 32 Battalion soldiers hated, it was the Katyushas.

More Katyushas were launched and a mortar counter-barrage commenced. Southern Angola was beginning to rock 'n' roll. The earth started shaking heavily and, from the depths of the scrub surrounding the anthill at my side, an adult caracal (a rooikat) emerged. Clearly deeply disturbed by the bombardment, its tufted ears were erect and it was panting. I can truly say I was more terrified at that moment than I would be for the rest of the day (pound for pound, the caracal, or lynx as it is commonly known, is as vicious a predatory cat as the leopard). I sat very, very still.

The animal was disoriented and – believe me, I know this sounds wildly improbable – began to rub itself against my pulled-up knees like a domestic cat. A very big, very solid and very wild domestic cat.

After a while it began to twine itself between my legs, in and out, round and about, again and again. Very slowly, I took my right hand off my rifle (C00453, I remember its number as well as I remember my service number) and let my fingers trail in the air above its body until I was at first lightly stroking its back and later softly scratching its head. I had completely forgotten the impending battle. I swore to the Lord right then that somehow, sometime I would honour this cat. In 1994, I registered a company called Linx Communications. I also have RedCat Photography and Caracal Productions.

TOP SECRET/UITERS GEHEIM

OPERATIONS WAR DIARY/OORLOGSDAGBOEK OPERASIES

OF/VAN 32 BN TACT. HQ

DD1991

BAND/VOLUME..............

MAAND/MONTH May 82......

PLEK
PLACE.......... Omauni..........TYDPERK VAN
PERIOD FROM.....21/Ø8ØØ/B...TO ....22/Ø8ØØ/B.

Reeks no. Serial no.	Datum en tyd Date and time	Opsomming van voorvalle en informasie Summary of events and information	Verwysing Reference
1	21/1ØØØ/B	± 21/1ØØØ/B May 82 Own force attack Savate	Informal
2	21/1139/B	3Ø (C coy) report that there are more than one (1) enemy companies in the trenches.	Informal
3	21/	Following ammo urgently required direct runno at C/S Ø (ENHQ): 1) 12 boxes of R762 rounds 2) 5 cases of AK rounds 3) 10 x boxes of 60 mm mortar 4) 50-100 kg of P4 explosive Send to them by Puma (tiger)	Informal

DECLASSIFIED 2 3 NOV 2009

OPS/1/32 BN

TOP SECRET/UITERS GEHEIM

The 122-millimetres fell silent – we heard subsequently that C.B. [Chris Brown] had dropped a WP-loaded 81-millimetre bomb right into the middle of the Katyusha battery so that it exploded on top of a launcher tube and took out everyone around it – and the orders came for us to stand up and start the advance on Savate.

The caracal disappeared into the bush.

4

The assault

When the assault started, there was still no communication from Ratte, so Ferreira decided to send Viljoen with the Cessna 185 to try to reach him. For the second time, Chisholm would fly unplanned and continue for most of the day:

> On the day of the attack, E.V. [Eddie Viljoen] ran the war from the air, being in contact with all the stopper groups and observation posts. We flew slightly to the west of the target due to the heavy ground fire from the enemy and also while they were firing their 122-millimetre rockets, which were landing about six or seven kilometres on the other side of the river beyond W.R. [Willem Ratte].

Via the Cessna, Ratte managed to make contact with Ferreira on the A52 radio and informed him that Savate was much bigger and stronger than expected. But it was too late to stop: the bombardment was in progress and the attack force was advancing towards the base. Van Eeden remembers:

> A plane arrived, E.V. was in it, and W.R. made contact with him. W.R. informed him what was going on, but the next moment we heard the 14.5 at the airstrip and knew Charlie Company had arrived there. Then the heavy weapons in the base opened up on 32 Battalion. From the tree, W.R. gave fire control orders to the mortar group, which was a huge success because we could clearly see what was happening in the base.

The FALA guerrillas deployed between Cuangar and Savate either did not deploy or did not do their work when the bombardment started to prevent FAPLA interference from Cuangar or, more likely, from the forward post that Ratte had come across. Anderson recalls vehicles carrying FAPLA soldiers approaching Savate from south of their mortar position:

> Everything did not go according to plan. Billy Faul mined the road to the south of Savate. We deployed about 500 metres from the road in the tree line. While busy with the bombardment, two or three GAZ trucks approached on the road from the south.
>
> We ceased fire and waited for the vehicles to detonate the first mine. What we did not know was that FAPLA had debussed from their vehicles. I wanted to bombard them with the 81s firing 'out of the hand', only with the pipe mounted on the ground plate, but C.B. [Chris Brown] prevented me. I wanted to prevent at all cost the FAPLA convoy reaching the base. Because C.B. was the mortar group commander, I listened to him. He said it was more important for the mortars to protect the advancing battalion than to tackle a couple of vehicles. I did not agree and we had a hefty argument. My Calvinistic upbringing won and I just left it.

When the advance began, it was clear that the mortar bombardment had not had the desired effect of keeping the enemy's heads down and giving the assault force time to reach their positions. FAPLA were waiting for them before letting loose with their arsenal of weapons. Grobler was waiting for Muller to give the signal to advance and when it came the action soon turned out not to be the usual fight. Grobler remembers the Alpha Company attack:

> At 09:00 we were in position and the mortars started to fire. I opened a tin of meat and started to eat. According to plan, the bombardment

should be for one hour – more than enough time to eat. Some of the troops just shook their heads, they had other things on their minds, like kicking FAPLA's backside. All of a sudden, all hell broke loose. I heard strange whistling sounds coming from Savate. I asked the troops what it was; they replied, 'Mono-Katyusha.' It continued. If you think that the bombardment took one hour, and you look at the fight ahead, it would tell you that our bombardment was of no use. We would possibly have been better off without the bombardment, which gave FAPLA time to consolidate. When the bombardment started, they were busy preparing food.

After an hour we heard Charl Muller's voice: 'All stations forward', such a relaxed command. Charl sounded very gatvol [he'd had enough]. The effect of his voice, however, was wonderful. He was calm, not bothered with this massive firefight that we were about to walk into. It boosted our self-confidence. Just think for yourself what the effect would have been if he had given a panicked 'Forward!' We would have stayed just there. That just shows what calibre Charl was.

The leader element got up, shouting 'Avançar!' The troops followed and the shit started. It was rough. It was the heaviest firefight I had had up to then and since. It was intensive. Every now and then we had to take cover to regain control. Then again, Charl with his 'All stations forward' ... retreat was not part of his vocabulary, we would have walked through a wall with him.

We reached the trenches. Rod Howden's experience took over. He was the one who during all the adrenalin and excitement still remembered to do trench clearing. Some of the blokes forgot about it. We gave all the bodies another shot, just to make sure they were dead, making sure they could not shoot us in the back when we passed them. Some blokes forget to do it – this would cost Charl his life. According to Dave Hodgson, while the fire was very heavy and we had to lie down, Corporal Dave [Cline] had run forward, stood to attention and asked him for a hand grenade. Hodgson screamed at him, asking if he was mad and that he had to lie down, but gave him a grenade.

Charl gave his last command: 'All stations forward.' I remember it was so calm, so full of self-confidence. He was in control of the situation.

An explosion close to our line wounded Rifleman Pedro Vika so seriously that he could not move forward. Corporal Dave, the Rhodesian, was also wounded. He was basically out of action for the rest of the year in 1 Military Hospital in Pretoria.

What happened (according to Pedro) was that Charl [had] moved past a bunker. As company commander, he was behind the line to control it during the attack. Those in front of him had not cleared the bunker and when Charl jumped over the trench (apparently he was already wounded, I cannot confirm it because I did not see his body), a FAPLA grabbed him. He hit the FAPLA and jumped again. In that movement the FAPLA shot him. Pedro was also seriously wounded and could not help Charl. We started to run out of ammunition. The troops had AK rifles. They threw me full magazines to ensure continuous fire. Some of them used FAPLA weapons to continue the firefight.

Charlie and Foxtrot were pinned down (Sam by the 14.5s and Foxtrot in the firefight). We, however, continued; nobody was keeping us waiting. We were without Charl and did not know it. We reached the buildings and started with house clearing. I still remember, when I entered a building, I opened the door and started to shoot: it was a pantry. The tins were full of sausages, and when the bullets hit them, they burst open and the sausages looked like fingers coming out, wanting to grab me.

No one had ever imagined that so many people would be killed or wounded. The troops carrying the wounded followed behind the assault line and were in danger of being shot by the enemy running between the assault line and the echelon. Rifleman Alberto Fonseça was carrying

a wounded comrade to the medical point when he nearly fell prey to
FAPLA:

> We attacked and started to advance. What happened was, after the fight
> was already in motion … the enemy passed behind us. Once the enemy
> had flanked us, I was busy carrying a brother who had taken a bullet
> in his arm. Then, from there I was holding that brother of mine, the
> others just kept on advancing forward, and so when I lifted my brother,
> we could advance and go forward.
>
> When I got a fright behind me, I heard people calling behind me,
> 'Stop, stop! Don't move any more or we will shoot you!' So I stopped
> and when I looked back, there was that confusion of gunfire and bombs
> and stuff, so I was thinking that it was our brothers. And so I started
> calling them: 'Come, come! Look, our brother here has been hit!' When
> they reached me I saw what they were wearing and realised they were
> enemy soldiers. They were wearing black berets and I knew they were
> not on our side. 'Ay caramba! I'm caught.' I put my hands up. They
> came up to me and said, 'Don't you move! If you do, we'll shoot you.'
> And so I stayed like that with hands up and my brother was on the
> ground because he had already been wounded.
>
> And so one of them started saying to the others, 'Hey, comrades,
> this guy, we're not going to kill him. We going to take him because our
> boss said that if we capture anyone from 32 Battalion, we must not kill
> him!' There was a lieutenant with two stars on his shoulder, one of
> the enemy. He said, 'What about this guy that is injured?' and another
> person responded, 'That guy that is injured, we don't need him, we'll
> just take this guy that isn't hurt.' They said to me, 'Okay, let's start
> walking.' We started walking away; there was gunfire. We had walked
> about 200 metres when we heard a gunshot from behind. Bang! They
> had just killed my friend who was injured. I was also scared. I said to
> myself, 'Fine, they've already killed the other guy, today I'm going to
> die.' We continued walking.

As we were walking, the bombs that the enemy were firing from the cannons were landing in the area towards where we were walking. So as soon as the bombs started landing, we all fell to the ground, hiding so that we were not hit by shrapnel. Myself and the enemy all fell to the ground, so as these bombs were landing, the air became full of dust, and we were in the middle of the dust. I started crawling with my arms and legs, and I felt that I was not hit, so I got up and started running. As soon as I started running one of them that was on my left started shouting, 'Hey, comrade, that man is running away!' And so they all started running after me, screaming, 'Hey! Comrade! Stop or we will shoot! We are going to kill you! Stop! Stop!' I just kept on running and they started shooting at me, and I kept on running until I came out on this road, the road we came into Savate on.

As soon as I hit the road I carried on running and then our car came. Lieutenant Muller came in the car to make a blockade. So as soon as he came they started shooting, so I took off my cap and held it up to show them. I shouted, 'Don't kill me! Don't kill me! It's me!' and so when the car arrived they stopped, ordered me to get in the car, and as I was climbing up they asked, 'Hey, what's the problem?' and I said, 'I was captured by the enemy!'

'So you were captured?'

'Yes, I was, I was helping a friend that was shot and because of that I was moving slowly and trying to catch up, and the enemy came up behind me, and they wanted to take me alive, but they couldn't because of the bombs going off, and so from there I ran!'

Possibly because of the topography of the area, VHF radio communication between the platoons began to intermittently break down and for long periods it was impossible to speak to one another. Alpha Company were fighting to break into the trenches. Hodgson remembers they got fierce resistance:

Poorly trained and armed FALA militia

Better armed and equipped FALA compact guerrilla

Semi-regular FALA troops. They were trained by South African instructors, properly armed and generally issued with green fatigues

UNITA leader and FALA supreme commander General Jonas Malheiro Savimbi (left) and secretary general Brigadier N'Zau Puna in 1982. Savimbi's bodyguards are in the background

Colonel Samuel Chiwale (right), who in 1980 became the FALA commander

UNITA/SADF cooperation. Savimbi and chief of the South African Army, Lieutenant General Constand Viljoen, at a UNITA base camp in Angola

Well-equipped semi-regular FALA troops train with 75-millimetre recoilless guns

CSI's Staff Sergeant Lopez Francisco or 'Senhor Lobbs', seen here in Savate base after the attack. Behind him is a 32 Battalion soldier and on his left a FALA guerrilla dressed in a SADF nutria coverall

On route to Savate, the men from the companies are still in a cheerful mood on the back of a Kwêvoël

Final briefing: Lieutenant Sam Heap (seated with book in hand) gives orders to Charlie Company platoon commanders while Commandant Deon Ferreira (seated right) and RSM Ikes Ueckermann (standing) listen in

Troops rest before the long night march towards Savate

Savate Base

Left: Well-concealed, waist-deep trenches

Below: A 32 Battalion soldier stands at the entrance to an underground sleeping bunker. These were located at intervals behind the trenches and could accommodate about 10 men

Small grass shelters had been built all over the base to accommodate the temporary influx of soldiers

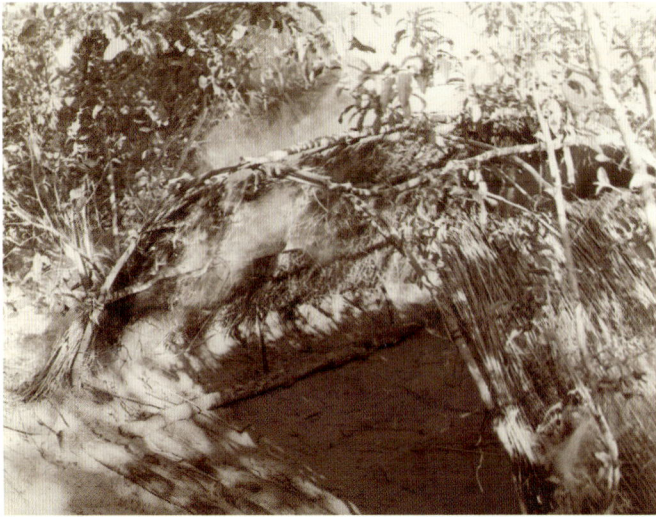

These temporary shelters were used as sleeping places

In the middle of the base were better constructed huts and tents

Abandoned and shot-out enemy vehicles at the recce group stopper position. Ferreira's command Buffel is in the background. To the left, recce group men load captured equipment and weapons into a Kwê

In Savate after returning from the recce group ambush site and the enemy convoy chase. Left to right: Ferreira, Major Johan Schutte (CSI), Ueckermann, Heap (with a bandage on his cheek after he was hit by shrapnel when Charlie 7's platoon sergeant accidentally fired a shot that ricocheted against the Buffel), Commandant Maruis Oelschig (CSI) and Lieutenant Jim Ross

Echo Company and the mortar sections arrive back at Savate. Lieutenant Dave Thompson is on the left of the vehicle

Recce group men offload supplies from an abandoned vehicle on the Cubango floodplain. Sergeant Kevin Fitzgerald (facing the camera) is in conversation with Sergeant Mike Kiley

One of the many dead enemy defenders lying near a trench

A BRDM armoured scout car near the headquarters complex

An enemy truck that did not make it across the Cubango River

CSI's Major José de Oliveira in front of the command Buffel

Oelschig and a tired-looking Ferreira, sill wearing 'black is beautiful' on his face, at the vehicle repair area. A brand-new STAR mobile workshop is being recovered behind them

opez Francisco (left) with the recovery truck drivers

Left to right: Major Eddie Viljoen, Ferreira, Corporal Rick Lobb, unidentified soldier and 2nd Lieutenant Justin Taylor with bandaged hand up on the spare wheel

Captured FAPLA soldiers

Above left is the youngster captured by Sergeant T.T. de Abreu

The other two were found in the base and sent to Rundu

At the airfield, Oelschig dismantles one of the 14.5-millimetre anti-aircraft guns

Loading captured equipment. Two 122-millimetre mono-Katyusha rocket launchers lie in the road, while men in the background drag a 14.5-millimetre anti-aircraft gun

One of the two amphibious pontoons that were later destroyed

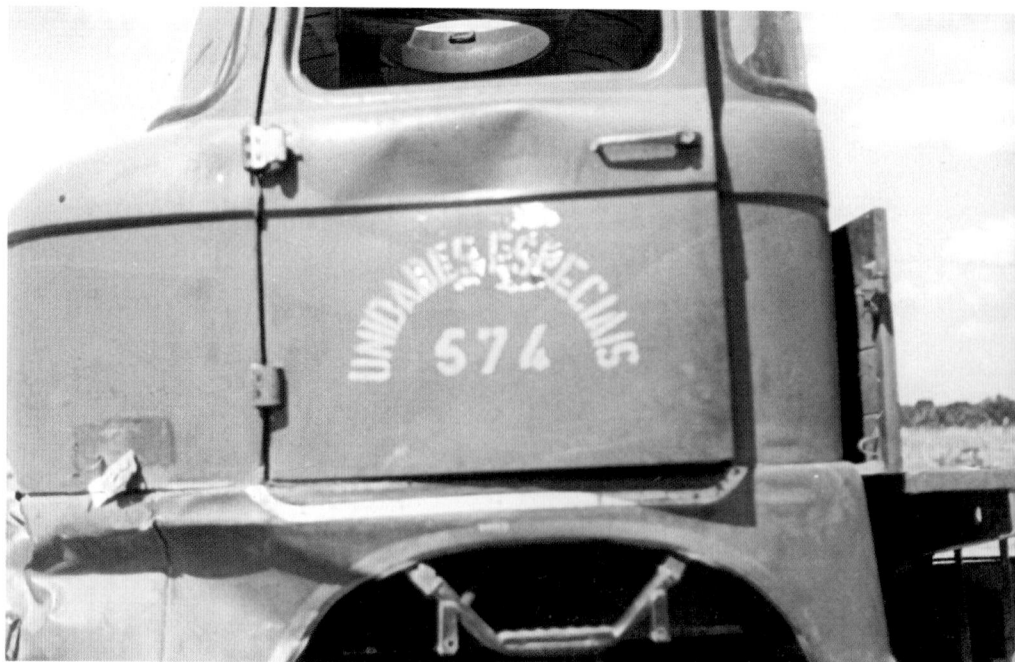

Captured vehicle with Reconnaissance Company markings

At the workshop, where at least 15 trucks were destroyed. The new STAR mobile workshop is in the background

An enemy truck left behind in the floodplain. Civilian clothes hang from the back

A convoy of captured vehicles lined up and ready to return to Omauni base

Captured weapons and ammunition are loaded from an enemy truck. A B10 recoilless-gun barrel is visible on the back of the enemy truck

The main road through Savate town with buildings on left and right. During the day of 22 May the civilian population started to return

Civilians helped themselves to food from the FAPLA stores. A young boy carries a bag of food

A 2013 satellite image shows the Savate base trench system. Blocks 2 to 6 show the trench positions (marked with white arrows) in more detail

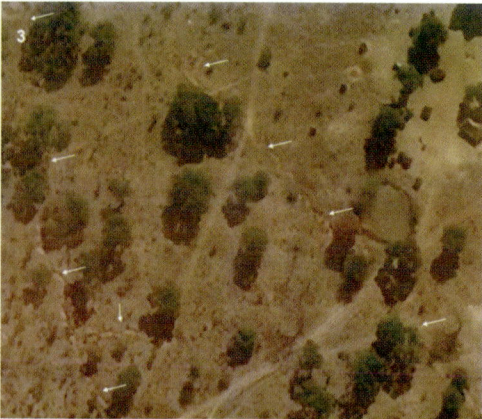

Three 122-millimetre rocket nose fuses are stacked against a metal trunk, with two B10 recoilless-gun ammunition containers in the background and a wooden crate for storage of the same calibre of ammunition in the foreground

Freshly dug extensions to the trench system near the 122-millimetre Grad-P rocket launcher positions. During the night of 20 May, the Savate defenders extended and dug new trenches

Buffalo base cemetery, 2013

Buffalo base cemetery, 1980. The final resting place for the Portuguese-speaking men

Rifleman Joaquim Matamba

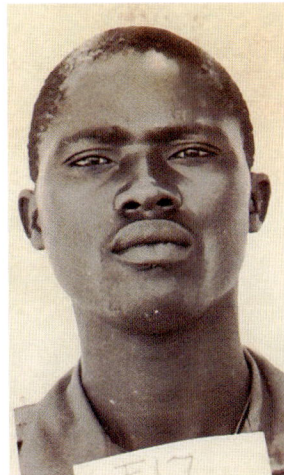

Rifleman Manuel Augusto

Erasmus's grave in the Voortrekker Hoogte cemetery

Captain Andre Erasmus

Page 2   THE CITIZEN   Saturday May 24 1980

Anguish of slain Captain's wife

By RIKA VAN GRAAN

MRS Linda-Marie Erasmus, wife of Acting Captain André Erasmus (28) lived through the anguish yesterday of having to tell their three toddlers what had happened to their father.

Capt Erasmus was one of five members of the South African and South West African Defence Forces killed in an ambush in which 81 terrorists were slain in the operational areas.

Also killed in the ambush were Lieutenant Charl de Jongh Muller (23), 2nd Lt Johannes Matthews Heyns Muller (19), 2nd Lt Timothy Simmons Patrick (18) and Corporal Eduard Coetzee Engelbrecht (19).

"I think they will understand better now that I have told them their father has gone to Jesus who will look after him. To have told them he was killed by terrorists would not have explained anything and could have puzzled them," a calm Mrs Erasmus (26) said from Rundu in Okavango last night.

Mrs Erasmus's three children are Tanja (4), Desireé (3) and Mark Andrew (8 months).

She said the family had moved to Rundu four months ago from Pretoria. I am satisfied that he died what he had lived for. . .for his country.

"I will fly to Pretoria on Monday for the funeral but the children will stay with a friend here until my return," Mrs Erasmus said.

Capt Erasmus was the youngest of three sons of Sergeant-Major Johnny Erasmus of Valhalla, Pretoria.

Lt De Jong Muller leaves his wife Zelma (23). They have been married two years and just after their honeymoon the couple settled in the Kavango town.

Charl matriculated in Windhoek where he was born.

He will be buried with full military honours in his home city on tomorrow afternoon.

Cpl Engelbrecht, also of SWA, was one of 12 children of Mr Pieter Engelbrecht and his wife Neeltjie of Otjiwarongo.

A bereaved Mr Engelbrecht told The Citizen from his home last night Edward started his compulsory national training in January 1979 and after an officer's course at Oudtshoorn he was based at Rundu.

"My son was a very lively person and he enjoyed life on the border," Mr Engelbrecht said.

Lt Heyns Muller of the farm Dagnreek in the Villiers district intended to become a farmer after his two years service his mother Mrs Ivonne Muller said last night.

Lt Muller, who matriculated at Villiers Hoërskool in 1978, started his national training in Potchefstroom and then trained for his commission at the Oudtshoorn Infantry School. Since November last year he was based at Rundu, his mother said.

"We had him here in March for two weeks and I can tell you he did not really want to go back. I think he was just tired of being in the battle field all day," Mrs Muller said.

The newspaper report on Erasmus's death

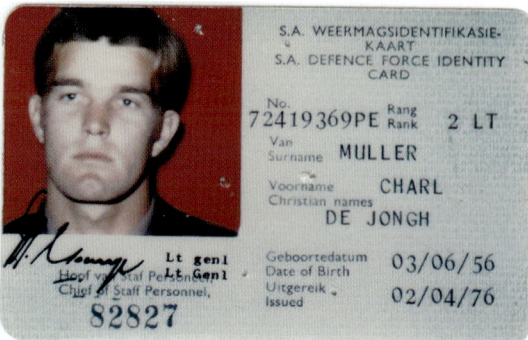

Lieutenant Charl de Jongh Muller

De Jongh's grave in the Windhoek cemetery

81 TERRORISTS KILLED IN SWA

FIVE members of the South African and South West Africa Defence Forces and 81 terrorists had been killed in an action in the operational area in northern SWA Defence headquarters in Pretoria and Windhoek said last night.

The soldiers were: Temporary Captain Andre Erasmus (29), Lieutenant Charl de Jongh Muller (23) Second Lt Johannes Mathews Heyns Muller (19) 2nd Lt Timothy Simmons Patrick (18), and Cpl Eduard Coetzee Engelbrecht (19).

Ambush

"The soldiers died after they had walked into a huge enemy ambush on the border. A hectic firefight started and the security forces went over to the offensive immediately.

"Although the Security Forces suffered losses, the terrorists were driven back and fled," the statement said.

The Security Forces followed them and in the ensuing contact, 81 terrorists were shot dead.

The Security Forces also confiscated and destroyed huge amounts of light and heavy weapons, ammunition, webbing and canvas equipment, including rucksacks.

"This large number of terrorists confirms the tendency that they are trying in desperation to improve their low morale by fighting in large groups in order to recover lost prestige," the Defence spokesman said. — Sapa.

A 24 May 1980 newspaper report on the Battle of Savate

Rundu headquarters, Christmas 1979. Left to right: Justin Taylor, Candidate Officer (later promoted to 2nd Lieutenant) Timothy Simmons Patrick, who was killed at Savate, Corporal John van Dyk (seated) and Signalman 'Gonzales'

The grave of 2nd Lieutenant Johannes Mattheus Heyns Muller, in the Heroes' Acre of the Villiers cemetery

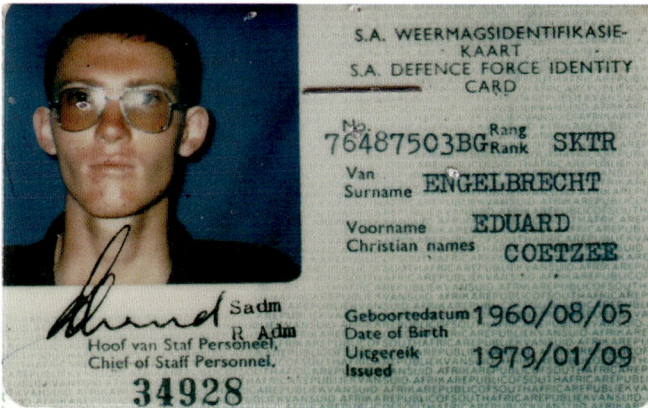

Corporal Eduard Coetzee Engelbrecht and his grave in the Otjiwarongo cemetery in Namibia

Lance Corporal Andrew Jeremy Falcus

Fulcus's grave in the St Lawrence Church cemetery in Surrey, UK

I still remember the muffled clicks of rifle safety catches being set from safe to fire. That was the last normal sound for the next few hours. As the mortars plopped down the pipes all hell broke loose. Charl shouted '*Avançar*, Alpha, *avançar!*' and we started moving forward. Then a whistling steam locomotive roared over our heads, leaves fell from the trees and progress halted for a second when the anguished shout came from one of our troops, mono-Katyusha 122-millimetre rockets whistled over our heads, and yet Alpha advanced. Our platoon mortars were firing so rapidly that by the time we reached the first bunkers we had no more shells. To add to this predicament, Johannes, my best LMG [light machine gun] gunner, let rip a long burst of fire at an enemy in FAPLA uniform who jumped from a bunker in front of us. She was almost cut in two. Johannes was so incensed that he poured automatic fire into the bunker's opening.

Then two things happened that almost stopped the whole Alpha Company advance. Firstly, Johannes's LMG seized up solid and, despite his attempts, would not fire a shot, and we drew deadly fire from the north, killing two of my guys: a troop and my radio man. The immediate reaction of the troops was to go down and the advance stopped. Screaming into the radio for clarity on whether it was friendly fire or not, we tried to get hold of Charl or Tim [Patrick]. There was no answer. Little did we know that neither was able to answer.

With no company commander to direct their attack and under heavy enemy defensive fire, Alpha came to a halt. Foxtrot Company continued advancing, which resulted not only in a gap opening between them and Alpha, through which some enemy broke to attack from the back, but also in a flank attack on Muller and Corporal A. Stolz of Foxtrot 17 platoon, in which Muller was shot and killed.

The platoon leaders had to get Alpha Company moving again. Freeman remembers how Sergeant Pedro 'Kioto' Gomes, a fearless former ELNA commander who, together with his battalion, joined 32 Battalion after the Angolan Civil War, got Alpha 2 to advance:

> I was utterly, completely, totally clueless in the ways of battle. I simply followed the example of those around me that day, and none more so than Kioto, who was now, realistically rather than nominally, in command of Alpha 2.
>
> The madman Kioto got up in a hail of fire, slung his rifle and started capering from foot to foot like an organ-grinder's monkey, while singing old FNLA battle songs and exhorting his Alpha 2 troops to get up and 'Avançar!' I can clearly remember his broad, white-toothed grin as he put his boot into one guy who showed extreme reluctance.
>
> The result was that Alpha 2 got up and, so as not to be shamed, Alpha 1 and 3 did too. It wasn't long before we breached the base. There was an intense escalation in the defensive fire but, despite it, Kioto and I (we were a bit ahead of the rest of the platoon, by accident not design) heard the clanking of a tracked vehicle. We were crossing the perimeter road and looked down; our ears hadn't fooled us, there was the spoor of what we thought was a tank.
>
> Kioto ran across the road and started taking heavy fire from a group of FAPLA hiding behind a corrugated-iron structure. He told me to toss a couple of grenades. I did, but before anyone else could respond, a slight, 'black is beautiful'-smeared figure came sprinting through and emptied a Tokarev pistol into the shocked defenders. It was Rod Howden, one of the original 'when-we's' who'd had a right topsy-turvy career in the Rhodesian Army before joining 32 Battalion just a week before Savate.

Hodgson's Alpha 1 platoon, however, was reluctant to advance. He recalls:

> Our orders were to advance, and that is what we did. We could not let the enemy in front of us outflank Charlie or Foxtrot companies. One

of either Peet [Sergeant Peet Horn], Rod or Grobbies [Lance Grobler] threw a white phosphorus grenade into the bunker. I threw my AK to Johannes, picked up a stick, and between us, Peet, Grobbies and myself, we started clobbering any troop who dared to stay behind cover. [Hodgson did not mention in his recollections that his AK, before giving it to the machine gunner, probably saved his life. A B10 recoilless-gun rocket detonated a few metres in front of him, not only killing his signaller and another troop, but also driving four pieces of shrapnel into the wooden butt of his AK rifle, splintering it completely, as it shielded his stomach.] Our goal was to reach the buildings in town and take cover, reconsolidate and try to make communications with Charl. Bullets, mortars, grenades – nothing was going to stop us reaching our goal. As we advanced, Rod came up to me and asked if I was fucking mad, and he gave me his backup pistol, a small 7.65-millimetre if memory serves. I was mad. My guys were dying and taking a hell of a beating from the north.

I will never forget that impish smile on Grobbies's face as he rushed behind anyone who looked as if they would stop advancing. Peet, in his unflappable way, was helping with the wounded and redistributing ammunition. Poor Horst [Heimstadt] was reeling from the northern fire, as he was directly adjoining the airstrip. Our instruction was to leave the wounded, and Charlie and Echo platoons would look after them.

Then the ultimate confusion: we were drawing heavy fire from behind. Could it be the unknown Charlie or Echo platoon, or was it an enemy in between? Your mind will not allow you to process this. How can Charlie and Echo be shooting at us? Impossible! Then a glimpse of a FAPLA uniform and we now knew we had big shit. Somehow, these arseholes had managed to get between us and Echo. We had reached the first buildings of the town. The only place that we were not receiving fire was from where the enemy were supposed to be, the east, and from the south we heard spasmodic fire, but at least none in our direction.

What was to have been an easy run for Charlie Company turned out to be a nightmare. They were formed up north of the runway, which marked the 'border' between Charlie and Alpha companies. At 11:39, Charlie Company's advance was cut short by a 14.5-millimetre anti-aircraft gun utilised in the ground role. What on the aerial photographs had been interpreted as a vehicle park was in fact the Savate air-defence position. During the initial planning phase of Operation Tiro-Tiro, no one had thought that the runway at Savate was functional and that FAPLA would defend it. Heap tried to advance, but soon realised it was suicide. He explains:

> Very carefully, in the morning's first light, we navigated to the advance line and took up position. I informed Falcon when we were in position, I cannot remember the time, all I know was that we had to wait for the mortar bombardment to start, which would be the signal to cross the advance line.
>
> Around 09:00 the mortar bombardment started, and we started our attack on the transport park north of the airfield. We advanced in an extended line. We heard the bombs exploding to our south. We advanced for about 100 to 150 metres when all hell broke loose on us! I first thought that we were in the killing ground of an ambush, as trees and plants around us were simply cut down by 14.5-millimetre bullets. I could not see any enemy yet and we attacked with battle talk, and fire and movement in the fashion we had done so many times at Lekkerhoekie [part of the training area in Buffalo] and during other enemy contacts.
>
> By now there was virtually no cover and everybody used what little cover they could find for protection. Still no enemy in sight, only the

sound of the 14.5 in everybody's ears. Over the radio my platoon commanders reported about troops that were already dead or seriously wounded and needed urgent medical treatment. We had not advanced even a hundred metres yet. It became clear to me that we would never win the firefight because the enemy weapons were much more numerous and dangerous than ours. I ordered a ceasefire and instructed everybody to move back to a safe area.

I tried to reach Falcon by radio, but did not succeed, as they were busy with a heavy firefight to the south of the airstrip. Big Daddy was in a Cessna. I communicated with him and explained the situation. I requested permission to stop the attack on the 'vehicle park'. He was furious and accused me of being a bang gat [afraid]. I felt humiliated, but explained to him that it was impossible to attack any further, as it would be suicide. He communicated with Falcon, after which we were tasked to join the echelon vehicles.

The enemy forces from the Charlie Company objective were now attacking Alpha Company from the north. Foxtrot Company's advance was steady and they did not encounter much resistance. They soon reached the town, leaving only one more objective to clear. Ross explains:

Details were not forthcoming, and the plan had Sam [Heap] attacking first, followed by Charl and then myself. We all went off at two-minute intervals. Falcon followed Charl at a short distance. The mortar barrage started proceedings, and the imbalance of firepower indicated that we were superior and that allowed us to advance to contact in reasonable spirits. Needless to say, what happened over the next five hours was going to change many people's perception about the glory of battle.

We advanced downhill and I remember thinking that it was not in our favour, as most people tend to shoot high when under fire. It has something to do with your anal sphincter pulling your head down and

81

pushing your rifle barrel upwards. This suited the enemy's situation, but not ours.

Virtually at the flick of a switch, the whole area around us was replaced by something that resembled a movie set and one would not be thought ridiculous were you to be seen looking around for John Wayne, or better, Private Ryan himself. The sound of ripping canvas magnified through Pink Floyd's sound system did not even come close. The trees were exploding and it started snowing leaves. The movie-makers were doing well – and then suddenly one was back in reality. There is a lot of verbal abuse that goes with shooting people. Noise wins battles, you would have been told at Infantry School, but I am sure not too many guys remember those lessons. What transpires in most individuals can never be the same in all of us, but to control lines of advance and keep the morale up, what can one do but shout and shoot? Foxtrot was doing so well though, and our advance was steady. We had three objectives to take and once I was in the town itself I knew we had only one to go. This was close to the river and I sent a platoon to go and clear it out.

Ferreira's headquarters and his reserve also became involved in the firefight, which explains why Heap could not get hold of him over the radio. Taylor remembers arriving at the base defence trenches:

The sound of the bullets had now changed to that deadly whip crack as they passed between us – and I knew that we were now close. Trompie's troops, a few metres ahead, started firing while moving steadily forward, but I couldn't see anything. Astonished, I realised that the trenches were but five metres ahead. They were an ingenious design, a metre wide, deep enough for a man to stand in with his head and shoulders sticking out, they zigzagged off to our left and right, not running straight for more than three metres. What made them almost invisible until you were on top of them was that they had no mound in front of them, but were flush with the ground. As we were soon to learn, they were difficult to clear unless you systematically worked down the trench line.

The companies ahead of us had advanced over them to get into the base, as we were about to do. I peered into the three-metre section in front of me and, seeing nothing there, backed up and took a running jump to clear the trench. We hadn't moved 30 metres into the base area than we started taking fire from behind us – the enemy were still in the trenches! Everyone around me dived to the ground.

With the weight of the backpack on my back I carefully knelt and put out my hand to lower myself to the ground when I was suddenly pitched face forward into the sand. Thinking at the time that it was the weight of the backpack, I later saw that a bullet had passed through the backpack, missing my neck by a few centimetres. Being the only one carrying a backpack (the HF radio was in the backpack) that stood nearly as high as the back of my head, I must have stuck out like a sore thumb, making an obvious target. Trompie's troops immediately engaged the enemy behind us. I rolled on my side and pulled my arms free of the backpack. I had had enough of carrying it and I shouted to my signaller to take over. He was clearly not happy at the prospect, but it was his turn, and rank certainly had its privileges.

At one point, Major Lynch made the decision to take the Puma and gunship closer to the battlefront in case they were needed for casualty evacuation, and landed at the echelon and medical post established at Oelschig's position. He also arrived with helicopters, so that he could better coordinate air support, if needed. The assault force was progressing slowly and taking heavy casualties, which had not been anticipated.

When Heap had to regroup, a gap opened in the line and soon some enemy appeared behind the assault force and between the echelon vehicles. The echelon protection element had to take part in the fight, shooting at

FAPLA soldiers as they ran from the bush across the access road between the assault force and the echelon. Louw, in the meantime, had sent some of the Kwêvoël trucks to the front to pick up the wounded and transport them to the first-aid post. The assault force was running out of ammunition, especially 60-millimetre mortar rounds and 7.62-millimetre R1 ammunition. Commandant Ferreira called me and my ammunition vehicle to the front.

The enemy were fighting from their trenches, supported by their own 82-millimetre mortars, B10 recoilless guns and 122-millimetre Grad-P (mono-Katyusha) rocket launchers. The FAPLA commander and his troops were probably under the impression that a FALA force was attacking them. They remained in position, returned disciplined fire, retained command and control, and stuck to their defensive fire plan. After about two hours, however, their fire started to slacken and their resistance showed less resolve. They stayed in the trenches and did not launch a frontal counter-attack, but instead used small groups to attack. Unbeknown to Ferreira, FAPLA forces were systematically withdrawing from the base and consolidating north of the runway at what was thought to be the vehicle park.

Alpha Company took the main hammering and things did not go well, as they had to leave behind many wounded. Hodgson remembers how Ross and Foxtrot Company rushed to their assistance:

> As we ducked under cover in the buildings and faced west and east, Horst and Attie joined us and said that they had wounded that were left behind, as per orders, and that the enemy would take them out. Horst, Peet and Grobbies gave us covering fire, and Attie, [Corporal C.] Augusto and myself rushed out to where they were hysterically screaming, more with fear than pain. The only reason that the three of us went to assist is that we were the biggest and would be able to carry a wounded person better than the others. I remember Attie slinging a wounded troop over his shoulder, taunting the motherfuckers to try to get us. We worked on a buddy-buddy system, Augusto covered and we carried.

Two trips were made and the nearest wounded were brought under cover. Horst came scrambling up as we returned and said that we had a huge problem: the enemy had regrouped and were forming up between the river and where we were situated. This meant that the only way out was south. I think that more prayers were said in that moment than at any other during Tiro-Tiro.

Following this, a silence descended and then we heard the most beautiful sound. Unbelievably, Jim Ross was organising his company in an extended line moving from the river over the flats towards us. A cheer went up from all of us. One minute, we were all heading for hell, and the next, a reprieve. Jim took over and we started sweeping the base. All were in a euphoric state of shock. We had seen our comrades blasted out of existence and, but for the grace of God, we could have been too.

To his left, Ross had noted that Alpha Company troops were exhausted from the battle and decided to go and help before the enemy could over-run them. He explains:

Observing troops from Alpha over on our left flank was worrying, as they looked severely depleted in numbers. The radios did not have a clear signal due to the undulation of the geography. Once I had been told that half of Alpha was still pinned down back up the hill, I decided to take Foxtrot back up our line of advance and go see if we could help. Advancing from the side on one's own troops can prove hazardous in any circumstance, but to do so just after they had had a monumental shootout would be scary. Nevertheless, it had to be done, and I eventually joined up with Falcon, and the rest of Alpha carried on down into the town.

From his observation post, Ratte reported a group of enemy moving on foot to the north along the road. Some of them were carrying 122-millimetre mono-Katyusha rocket launchers. This group would most probably walk north and mount the rocket launchers to bombard the assault force – the launchers were useless firing from their original positions in the base because of the short distance between them and the assault force.

From his position, Stolz could see Ferreira's headquarters group advancing along the road (the border between Alpha and Foxtrot companies). It was becoming increasingly difficult for Ferreira to control the assault, as the headquarters protection element regularly had to physically take part in the assault because of the numbers of enemy they encountered. Taylor and Erasmus were for a moment on their own firing at the enemy, but they made it back to the protection of Theron's platoon before Erasmus was killed in a firefight not far from Ferreira. Taylor remembers:

Trompie's headquarters defence platoon was strung out expectantly in a skirmish line running down the slope, facing towards the river. No sooner had we arrived than all hell broke out. Unencumbered by the dreaded backpack, I dived onto the sand. I fired half a magazine between the two-man MAG machine-gun crew a few metres to my left and Erasmus in a clump of grass on my right, before crawling forward into the firing line.

It was very comforting to hear the roar of the MAG to my left and to know that we were back with the platoon. Running the risk of losing the initiative if we stayed stationary, I shouted through the noise to advance. The MAG gunners began gathering their glistening ammunition belts, draping them over their shoulders and preparing to hoist up the machine gun. Changing to my second-to-last magazine as I got up, I realised there was no response from Erasmus. 'Captain, Captain, we have to advance, we have to advance' … no response again. My signaller shouted behind me, and I realised he was telling me that there appeared to be something wrong with Erasmus.

I went back from the firing line and crawled round alongside him in the grass. To my horror, I saw he had a hideous throat wound and blood was gushing out of his mouth as he struggled to breathe. Something snapped in me and, jumping up, I ran down the skirmish line screaming for the medic. Thirty metres down the slope I saw Sergeant Major Ueckermann on all fours crawling up towards me – an unusual posture for this big, burly RSM with his red handlebar moustache and bellowing voice that struck the fear of God into all around him! He reached up and pulled me down by my webbing as I was about to run past him, screaming for the medic.

'*Looty, wat's fout?*' [Lieutenant, what's wrong?]

Not making much sense at first, I took a deep breath and told him about Captain Erasmus and that he needed a medic, in fact, he needed a doctor, fast.

'The medics are all busy, Looty, and so are all the doctors … there's nothing we can do right now.'

'Fuck!' Numb, I began crawling back up to Erasmus. I looked over my shoulder and to my amazement I saw Commandant Ferreira strolling up the firing line with his AK-47 slung casually by its strap off his shoulder. With two VHF radios strapped to his web belt, he was listening intently, an earpiece pressed to each ear. He was completely oblivious to the firefight raging around him, and while the rest of us were slithering around like lizards, he looked every bit as if he was out on a Sunday-afternoon stroll.

The advance had faltered on my side of the line when I had gone apeshit looking for a medic. I lay helplessly next to Erasmus in the clump of grass as the fight continued. His left arm was thrust forward, twisted crookedly above the elbow. I watched helplessly as he slowly died, gulping for air as blood gushed from his mouth each time he tried to breathe. The firefight slowly died down and I got up when I saw Commandant Ferreira standing behind me, still talking intently on his radio command network. Hoisting the backpack up against a tree, I plugged a whip antenna into the big HF radio and switched it on in case Commandant Ferreira needed it. When I tried testing comms I got a strange 'bbbrrr' in the earpiece. Lifting the HF radio up, I saw a bullet hole through it. Inspecting the rucksack, I could see the neat entry hole at the back and the jagged exit. I realised with a chill that had I not leant forward to lie flat when the enemy opened fire from the trenches behind us, the bullet would have hit me in the top of my back.

Anders, the Omauni base operations clerk and now Taylor's signaller, was given the radio backpack to carry. He describes the gruesome reality of war in which there is no mercy:

I took the backpack from Justin as we came under fire for the first time. I continued walking. Erasmus was on our right a few metres away. We came to a clearing and there was heavy machine-gun fire to my front, about two o'clock to my right. I heard it, but could not see where exactly it was coming from. We moved forwards quite quickly. Erasmus opened fire and moved to a small bush. This seemed to attract fire in our direction. I dived down flat onto the ground. I could not move because the pack was very heavy. Erasmus stopped firing. There was heavy firing from both directions. Commandant Ferreira appeared and shouted that we must give the command to cease fire. Everything went quiet. I think we were firing on one another.

After Erasmus was killed, Ferreira, Justin, Lappies [Lance Corporal Laubsher] and I were standing together. Lappies was very upset, as we had just heard that Muller had been killed or captured. There was a captured, wounded Angolan soldier sitting against a tree. He was young and I remember the friendly look on his face. He looked at me. I thought that because he was captured he would have received medical treatment. Lappies wanted to shoot him. Ferreira said to Lappies that he must not get his hands dirty and turned around to another soldier who was standing over him and said, 'Floor-board him.' I turned away and heard the shots and did not look back. I was now numb to all the noise and what was happening, and just walked on.

Moments later, Ferreira's headquarters came under mortar bombardment. He contacted Lynch, requesting the Puma to evacuate the casualties and the Cessna to assist with radio communication.

Oelschig and his CSI team were waiting for instructions to move forward when Ferreira contacted him by radio:

Deon Ferreira spoke to me on the radio. He reported that his forces had encountered very stiff resistance and that they had sustained a number of casualties. He reported that one of his company commanders had been killed in action. About 15 minutes later, Deon again spoke to me by radio. He reported that his forces were progressing slowly, but that they had suffered very heavy casualties, especially in his own headquarters. He reported that the headquarters had been hit in an apparent mortar counter-bombardment, in which his intelligence officer had been killed. He reported that he had a number of serious casualties that required immediate evacuation. He had submitted his request for the casevac to Des Lynch, but asked that I reinforce this request. I spoke to Des Lynch and together we decided that there was nothing for it but to send in the helicopter to evacuate the most seriously wounded. We informed Deon Ferreira of our decision and told him to make smoke on the most suitable landing zone.

I arrived with the ammunition vehicle at Commandant Ferreira's headquarters, which by now had moved slowly forward behind the Alpha Company advance line and was situated near a Soviet amphibious pontoon standing behind the first trenches. At 14:50, before I could start distributing ammunition, the mortar bombardment on the headquarters began. I remember that Falcon had instructed people from the company to load the seriously wounded onto the ammunition vehicle and another vehicle that Louw had sent to the front to take them to Bouwer's medical post for treatment.

We loaded while the mortar rounds fell, and drew some rocket-propelled grenade (RPG) and small-arms fire too. Falcon shouted to get the ammunition vehicle out of danger. I managed to get it away from the bombardment and later returned to Falcon's position. Falcon then decided to bring the Puma forward to evacuate the casualties and instructed me to go with the vehicle to prepare a landing zone. The RSM took charge of the vehicle and instructed me to sit in the back with the dead and wounded. The doctor and some medics were still desperately working on the 15-odd wounded while we drove to the back. Their moaning was horrible. We could do nothing for them. The ammunition boxes were covered with blood dripping from the wounded and dead.

By now Gregory had joined us in a Buffel. I found an open area about a kilometre or so away from the base and asked some of the company people who were still in the back of the vehicle to secure the area. While waiting for the helicopter, the doctor was doing everything he could to attend to the wounded. Like so many others, the driver of the ammunition Kwêvoël, Private Du Plessis, was scared of being killed. He remembers picking up the wounded:

I remember how, throughout the operation, I constantly prayed, 'Lord, I do not want to die now. I only have six weeks left of my two-year national service.' Later, RSM Ueckermann told us to pick up the wounded. I remember we stopped at the body of Lieutenant Patrick, but do not remember the reason why we did not pick him up. The back of the vehicle was packed with wounded.

I was told to return by the same route we had entered the town in order to find a landing zone. Sergeant Ron [Gregory] accompanied us with a Buffel on which a Browning was mounted. On the way, I saw troops ahead who took cover on the side of the road. Sergeant Ron stopped alongside my vehicle and asked what was the matter. I said to him, 'I do not know if it is our troops or enemy.' He said to his driver, 'Let's go.' Luckily it was some of our troops, whose leader group had been shot, on their way back to Savate.

We found a landing zone, and the wounded, including a wounded black woman and her child, were loaded in the chopper. I will never forget the fear in the eyes of that mother and child, not knowing what was going to happen.

The FAPLA mortar bombardment had a devastating effect on the Alpha Company men, as Hodgson explains:

This was too much for Alpha Company. There was a mass rout. The same troops that had faced overwhelming odds had seen their comrades killed, maimed and wounded, and wanted no more. Low on ammunition, they ran, heading west to get as far away as they could from the hell they had survived. Our leader group followed them. They finally stopped when they reached a place where Sam [Heap] and the vehicles were waiting. When I got there, Sam gave us instructions to head back immediately. Shit, this was the last thing our minds wanted to process. Discipline kicked in, orders were orders. The only way we could achieve this was by walking ahead of them. Funny thing was that no one hesitated. They just followed. Most of them had little or no ammo. It was as if we had faced something so bad that nothing could be worse. As long as we were together, we would be fine.

Just before the Alpha men took flight, Ross jumped in a Buffel heading out of Savate. Grobler thought Alpha Company left Savate because of Ross's departure. However, Ross had been called to Ferreira's position and not to the echelon area, where Heap and his men were. Grobler explains:

Alpha had no leader and we looked to Jim Ross for direction (he was close to us). He got into a Buffel, showed the driver the direction out of Savate towards the echelon and drove off. As far as I know, he said nothing to anybody why he drove away. Needless to say, when the troops saw this they followed in a long line. Attie and I and some of the Alpha troops tried to keep them back. They probably thought Jim knew something we did not and followed him. Well, Attie and I followed too, as we did not feel like staying all by ourselves. On the way to the echelon the troops started to drop the loot – it became too heavy to carry, as the echelon was a long way.

It actually looked very funny. Everywhere were chairs, sewing machines, food, etc., lying where they dropped it. When we arrived at the echelon everybody was there except Falcon. I thought he was further back. We sat next to a Kwêvoël. At one side a couple of 'when-we's' were sitting as well. [Corporal] Trevor Edwards and another one whose name I cannot remember were crying. Falcon contacted us and said we must return to the base. He was still in the base at Savate (this says much about his guts). That was when the two, Edwards and another one, shouted, 'He has no respect for human lives.' We swore at them and chased them back to Savate. They got paid to be soldiers!

Falcon wanted a volunteer to go back to the big echelon to lead in the vehicles and mortar guys. It had to be one person who could move carefully, as the area was still full of FAPLA. Attie Roestof immediately volunteered and off he went. That must have taken lots of guts (the blokes in the Recce Wing were more used to such things; we in the platoons always had lots of firepower around us). When he returned we noted that he was shot through his hat.

Freeman also recalls Roestof's bravery. Ferreira needed the Echo Company men and Louw's echelon to move forward, but because radio communication had broken down, his only option was to send somebody on foot to fetch the reserves. Roestof, realising the seriousness of the situation, volunteered. Freeman remembers:

> Attie Roestof was dumb enough to volunteer. He left us his 30-round magazines and, taking just a 75-round cylindrical magazine taken from a destroyed RPK [a type of AK-47] and a single water bottle, he set off down the road in the direction where Echo was supposed to be. Attie hadn't got very far, maybe 80 metres, when he drew heavy machine-gun fire from the same group of buildings in which we were clustered. He went to ground and crawled off the road with bullets flying all around him. Once the threat was cleared, he got up from the scrub in which he'd been hiding and took off at a run. 'I ran for what felt like several kilometres,' he recalled to me recently, 'much further than I should have done. What I hadn't been told was that there was a fork in the road. I took the left fork when I should have gone right.'
>
> So Attie ran some more. 'At one stage I found a little dog running alongside me. It suddenly veered off the road and into the bush. Not knowing why, but trusting his instincts, I followed and lay down in the grass.' A cloud of dust was coming down the road. It was a small herd of cattle that shielded three FAPLA soldiers. 'I was about to open fire on them, but lowered my rifle at the last moment. I'm glad I did – there were another seven or so heavily armed soldiers following behind them. They were deployed on either side of the road, with one group coming directly towards me.' Fortunately, said Attie, the lone Alouette gunship supporting the operation arrived on the scene. Attie got up and started running again. Eventually, realising he was not going to find the Echo reserve, he turned round and started running back to the still-raging battle. It must have taken a hell of a lot of guts to return to the cauldron, but I think it would be a hell of a lot worse to be walking around on your own in FAPLA territory with no map or compass, one magazine and a single water bottle.

Following standard operating procedures, the Alouette gunship pilot, Captain Johan Mertz, and his flight engineer, Flight Sergeant Leon 'Boertjie' Bekker, first had to secure the landing zone before Meyer's Puma could land, guided from the open door by his own flight engineer, Flight Sergeant Siegfried Hoebel. Mertz recalls:

> We were not surprised that after the attack commenced Major Lynch was requested to airlift wounded soldiers from the contact area. As he realised the seriousness of the situation, he tasked the Puma to do the casevac and me to provide top cover during the evacuation. We did not know what to expect, as we were not supposed to get involved in this manner, but based on our experience we were able enough to handle the situation to the best of our abilities. From what I can recall, the landing zone was chosen west of the enemy base and duly marked with smoke.

The helicopters had been waiting at the echelon area where Bouwer had established his casualty evacuation point. The doctor decided to accompany the Puma for the casualty pickup, so he could hand over medical supplies to Van Zyl and help with the wounded. Unfortunately, the Puma overshot the landing zone and had to make a wide turn over Savate. Bouwer explains:

> We heard that there were many casualties and were told to go in and assist because apparently there was some problem at the medical aid station as well. We then took off in the Puma. I was sitting inside with not much view to the front and going towards the field aid post, when suddenly there were severe evasive manoeuvres by the helicopter. We turned around and then we landed. I inquired as to what was going on and heard that we were being shot at by 14.5-millimetre anti-aircraft fire and that the pilot then elected to land in order for the ground troops to silence the anti-aircraft gun.

In the meantime, Nico Groenewaldt and his co-driver, Private Andre Barnard, arrived at the landing zone. Groenewaldt recalls:

> As I stopped, the doctor and some medics were busy helping a wounded guy. It was a tall English-speaking guy [Second Lieutenant John Roberts] and he was wounded high up on the inside of his leg. He was hoisted onto the flat bonnet of my truck. I was busy hooking his drip up to the truck's windscreen wipers when there was a tremendous explosion. Everyone jumped. A Puma appeared and flew low over us. Suddenly, it banked sharp to the left and disappeared. Someone said the enemy had fired a missile at it. I did not see this, but we had to take the wounded guy to another spot for the chopper to casevac.

It was the 14.5-millimetre gun at the airfield that was still active. FAPLA had not fired at the gunship initially, but when the Puma overshot the landing zone, it turned near the gun's position and the crew started to fire, though not accurately because of the distance. Meyer, keeping his instructions in mind, could not risk the Puma being hit. Because of the same restrictions, the gunship could not engage the anti-aircraft weapon. Ferreira called on the mortars to silence the 14.5-millimetre gun. Anderson recalls:

> C.B. distinguished himself as an excellent mortarman during this bombardment. He was a civil engineer and thus had a head for calculations. Willem Ratte gave a correction and within seconds the calculations were done and relayed to the group. The enemy 14.5 was chased around by C.B. and Willem with mortar fire until we eventually silenced it. If it was not for these two, we would have bled much more. The people from Echo can vouch for that: Dave Thompson, Russell Organ and Billy Faul.

Second Lieutenant William 'Willie' Botha from the Recce Wing had the task of controlling the ground-to-air radio communication for the recce group. He remembers how Ratte controlled the mortar fire:

> Whiskey Romeo [W.R., or Willem Ratte] would pick up the dust and smoke from the recoilless and anti-air weapons being used in the counter-fire role, and the fire control instructions would go something like this: '100 up and 150 left from last shot, one round smoke'; then a pause, then 'eight rounds, fire for effect'; pause as the rounds went in, '50 down and 200 right from your last shot, one round smoke'; pause for the smoke to show, then 'six rounds, fire for effect', and so on.

With the 14.5-millimetre gun silenced, the Puma landed at the evacuation point. Bouwer took medical supplies to Van Zyl and because of the situation decided to accompany the Puma, which would just offload the casualties at Omauni base and then return to the battlefield. I was still inside the Puma assisting Bouwer when it suddenly took off, not allowing me to jump out. Bouwer explains:

> At the time they told me that I would probably stay with the field aid station and then let the medic take the casevacs back, but on landing, Richard van Zyl came to me quite upset and shocked. While anticipating about 10 casualties, we now had many deaths and more than 20 casualties. He had used some of his drip needles on soldiers who had died while lying waiting for us to get there, but had run out of drips and drip fluid a long time before we arrived. That meant that most of the soldiers who were lying there injured had not had any drips in them, nor had they been given any antibiotics or painkillers. They were just lying there waiting for us for about four to five hours. In medicine we have a rule, the 'golden hour', which is also known by the troops in the field. You have to do something to get wounded troops

treated as soon as possible within an hour, as their survival rate would then drop dramatically.

These guys had a serious risk of dying either with us or in the helicopter going back to Omauni. I quickly gave him a few things and we started loading all the casevacs into the Puma. I recall about 13 wounded, all lying and sitting squashed together with Piet Nortje, the flight engineer and myself in the back. I told the medic to wait with Richie. I just grabbed as many drips and needles as I could and threw them into a bag. I told them that I would rather go back with them, as they had not had any drips to counter their blood loss, and no painkillers or antibiotics, and this is way beyond the scope of a medic. I also took injection syringes, needles, antibiotics and some pain medication, and left Richard with packs that I had packed and I then rushed back. Putting up drips in an overcrowded chopper with a limited number of needles was also going to be challenging on shocked troops because of their collapsed veins and shocked state.

Those people who know me will know that I am famous for being airsick and this was of great concern to me getting into the helicopter, realising that most of us had not had any water for a few days and with the smell of blood in the helicopter. The minute I got in I started working on putting drips into the troops and giving them shots of antibiotics and some pain medication. I was very surprised to see how quiet and stoical these troops were, just lying there staring at me, even helping me. Piet Nortje held all the drips and stuff ready for me and as I required them he handed them to me, basically being my nurse while I did the work on all the troops. I recall vividly the face of the same Rhodesian, who had got the hole in his forehead during our move into Savate, tapping me to ensure that I did not bump him, as he was in quite a lot of pain. He had a large entry wound in the lower abdomen area. He died in the helicopter. This was exactly what I was worried about, with them having been left alone for so long on account of our inability to get to them in time.

Later, after the battle, Bouwer had the opportunity to find out from Van Zyl a little more about what had happened at the first-aid station:

> While travelling back I spoke to Richard van Zyl and asked him to tell me what had happened on his side. Richie told me that while they were trying to look after all the wounded people, the front line of this battle sort of deteriorated and there was a group of FAPLA that came through on the flanks and then eventually behind, and attacked the first-aid station as well. There was a chappie, John Roberts, who shared a tent next to my tent at Omauni. He was shot through the femur and I remember I put a drip in him, in the helicopter, as well.
>
> When the first-aid station was attacked, he grabbed the AK-47 off Richie van Zyl, threw him on the ground, and then lay down on top of him and started shooting back at the guys attacking the first-aid station. The wounded that were able also started shooting back, and thus they deterred the flanking manoeuvre and FAPLA then made off into the bush. This undoubtedly saved everybody who was there. I thought that he did quite a brave thing. Despite having a fractured femur, he covered the doctor with his body while he fought back.

When the helicopters flew onto the battlefield, the FAPLA commander, who was still in the trenches on the eastern side of the base, must have realised that they were under attack by South Africans. It was reported to Ferreira that Muller and some other men were missing. At 16:20 Ratte reported nine FAPLA vehicles accompanied by many troops on foot leaving the base going north. At Ferreira's request, Chisholm and Viljoen took off from Omauni to be air observers. Ferreira also called the four Buffels under Gregory's control, each mounted with a 7.62-millimetre Browning machine gun, to his command post. There was no chance that Ferreira would allow the enemy to escape, in all likelihood taking the missing 32 Battalion soldiers with them.

It was now almost seven hours since the attack had started and the

		TOP SECRET/UITERS GEHEIM	DD1991
		OPERATIONS WAR DIARY/OORLOGSDAGBOEK OPERASIES	
		OF/VAN	
			BAND/VOLUME............
			MAAND/MONTH............
PLEK PLACE.........................		TYDPERK VAN PERIOD FROM......................TO	TOT ....

Reeks no. Serial no.	Datum en tyd Date and time	Opsomming van voorvalle en informasie Summary of events and information	Verwysing Reference
4	21/1450/6	Moose must come into the air as ø (INHQ) are being attacked with mortars. Moose (Bosvd) must help with radio comms.	Informal
5	21/1620/6	Nine enemy (MPLA) vehicles moving north from the southern position. At this moment ± 4 - 4½ km from Savate. The AIM vehicles travelling very slowly - almost at a walking pace. gunship (doubtful) following the vehicles but drawing fire. Pair of air can ø uffib to be sent with this vehicle; brownings on Buffel to be mounted and mants mounted	Informal

OPS/1/32 BN   TOP SECRET/UITERS GEHEIM

recce teams encountered a huge group of fleeing FAPLA. John Botha, from behind his anthill, saw the enemy approaching:

I was leaning against the anthill in the shade of the small tree when I saw 12 or more trucks surrounded by many troops making their way out of Savate base. Some of the trucks were still invisible in the bush perimeter surrounding Savate base, as we discovered later. At first I was excited that the fight was over and it was 32's vehicles approaching us. Then, with a shock, I realised that the trucks had tarpaulin covers on the back and thus could not be our trucks. The trucks were surrounded by not less than an infantry company moving in a box formation around the vehicles. They had sent a forward patrol out in front that had made contact with one of the recce team stopper groups, that of Sergeant FitzGerald, which was closest to the river. Fitzy's team made contact with a platoon-strength group of FAPLA soldiers who were reconnoitring an escape route along the banks of the river.

De Abreu recalls:

FAPLA escaped from Savate to Caiundo on the secondary road between the main road and the river. I was still asleep until a mortar bomb fell in front of us. I woke up and asked my troop what was happening. He looked at me and said, '*Isto é guerra*' [This is war]. I realised that he had also been sleeping and then my A72 radio was calling me in Portuguese, '*Kota Ta, Kota Ta, por favor vem nos ajudar nos aqui estamos mal o Alberto apanhou no estomago, os pulas...*' [Kota Ta, Kota Ta, please come help us, it is chaos here, Alberto took a hit in the stomach, our pulas...] [The Portuguese-speaking men's nickname for a white person was '*pula*'. Kota Ta was De Abreu's nickname.]

I took the handset and asked who was talking. Jojo Viera answered and gave me a quick sit-rep. I explained the situation to Lieutenant Swannie and we moved toward another stick to regroup in order to go and help Jojo. We picked up the team closest to us. Lieutenant Swannie briefed the white men and I briefed the black men and we moved to the other team. When we reached the next team the guys were still lying down facing Savate, but before we could put our force into formation I saw enemy behind the team lying down, approximately 20 metres away. They saw us, but luckily our camouflage uniforms confused them. I gave the enemy signal and lay down with my RPD. It was impossible for us to open fire because our other team was between the enemy and us. Only God knows how I managed to arm my M72 and shoot at the FAPLA man while shouting '*Inimigo a retaguarda!*' [Enemy at the back!]

I remember old man Kabinda Cunene was the last man on this team facing Savate; he quickly turned around and opened fire and we moved closer. We shouted to FAPLA, '*Camarada, nao mata nos mesma!* [Comrades, do not kill us, we are the same!] We are the reinforcement to help you!' It gave us enough time to start our battle drill. 'Buddy, buddy, *avançar* and kill the idiots!' My RPD was working 100 per cent but I missed my 60-millimetre mortar pipe. Riflemen Belchior, Mario Hongolo, Horacio Cruz (with his PKM) and others with RPDs opened fire. Only the stick leaders had AK-47s. We felt so sorry for them [the enemy] in the chana and we started calling them to surrender, even counting from one to ten in Portuguese, telling them to stop running or they would get a bullet.

Lipman recalls the contact with the FAPLA advance patrol:

We were split into three-man teams, each with a machine gunner, an M79 40-millimetre grenade launcher, our own rifles and loads of ammunition, white phosphorus hand grenades and Claymore mines. Fitzy and myself had the river as our boundary and the other teams extended from our right side away from us. The opening salvo of the attack on the base was something to be heard – everything the battalion had was fired and launched on the base.

During our attack, our machine gunner, Rifleman R. Alberto, was shot in the chest and we had no firepower from his machine gun. Fitzy and myself were under a tree on the edge of the river bend in a natural depression, firing all we could with our rifles and M79. We were covered in leaves and bark from bullets hitting the tree above us. Fitzy leopard-crawled to summon help and in the process discarded his mochila. We tried to help our machine gunner and had to summon a chopper to casevac him, as we were only allowed air support for a casevac. However, our machine gunner, Space Monkey, nicknamed by Gavin 'Doiby' Monn (I will not elaborate as to why he was called Doiby), died before the chopper could get to us.

A convoy headed north through our stopper-group line right into us. It was precarious as we opened up on the convoy with some resistance while the enemy troops were trying to disembark and run for any cover they could find. After the contact we were talking and sharing our experiences, when Fitzy could not find his mochila. We later discovered small pieces of his kit and sleeping bag in a treetop, as his mochila had caught alight in the bushfire that had started during the firefight.

Garret instructed the other teams not to engage in the contact at the river but to start with a flank attack on the enemy, with the vehicles breaking out on the eastern side. This would give FitzGerald's team a chance to make a clear breakaway. Botha recalls:

We all started running over the open grassland in an easterly direction and were initially not seen by the FAPLA troops making their escape. As we started running along, we first waited for the team on our western side to arrive before falling into the line. If I recall correctly, we were the second or third team and were soon joined by the others running in the direction of the FAPLA soldiers. As we passed the other teams they joined in the running.

After running for several hundred metres, I remember clearly Lieutenant Swannie picking up his AK and firing on automatic in the direction of FAPLA. Then all hell broke loose and we all hit the deck. The return fire from FAPLA was so intense that we could not move, and grass seeds fell all around us. The ground was a flat plain, so it was very hard. We were physically pinned down and could not move. Zack Garret was lying a little way behind us and took command of the situation, relaying to Commandant Ferreira that the majority of the recce group was pinned down. He then summoned the only support he could legally muster with the Alou pilot, who had volunteered to come and help. It is important to take into account that the pilot was breaking all rules, regulations and standard operating procedures, and that due to his actions he would put himself, his crew and aircraft in harm's way.

FitzGerald and Lipman broke away from the contact and joined the attack. FitzGerald remembers:

> The first day, when Mike and I were running up and down the corridors packed with FAPLA soldiers and ammunition, there might have been a group of five of us, but Mike and I were leading the charge. We literally had our AKs on automatic and we just fired and struck vehicles as we ran, just spraying them. I remember the one vehicle kept on going around in circles. The driver was dead behind the wheel; obviously the wheel had jammed in a clockwise direction. I am not kidding you, it was going right, clockwise, and this yellow smoke was pouring out the back – a bullet had lodged in an RPG projectile and this yellow powder, I suppose the igniter for the RPG, was pluming up in the air. Eventually, we jumped onto the vehicle, chucked the driver's body out, and disengaged the vehicle and brought it to a stop, and we looted huge tins of tuna that came out of Japan, 2.5-kilogram tins of tuna, tons of the stuff.

Opperman recalls:

> We all grouped together and we took on all the FAPLA groups, as we were in the stopper groups and we realised then that they were not going to use the road and we went down that way. By then they were streaming by in their hundreds and as we went down that way we started shooting. Daisy [Sergeant Dirk Laubsher] stayed behind for some reason; I think we left a skeleton group behind in each location and he went and saw two guys running and he shot the one from far off, and he said, 'I got one' and we said 'Ja, ja, ja!' … Botes and I, we saw the two guys so we split off from the main group and went in to look for the one that he had shot. He was talking us into the location where the guy dropped, so we wanted to go and get him. There was

another one that went into the grass, so Botes and I, we were about 40 metres apart, he was on the far side and I was on the near side, and the main group then swept up the riverbank, and suddenly this one guy popped his head out of the reeds and I shot at him, but my rifle was on automatic and the second shot actually landed right in front of Botes' toes. I had nearly shot Botes and he was the moer in [angry] with me; he said, 'Hey, you nearly shot me,' and I apologised. Then I ran up to the guy; the first shot had actually got him and he was wounded and lying there. And so I ran and jumped on him so he could not shoot us, but in the meantime Swannie in the main group set fire to the veld there.

Sergeant Cornelias 'Tabo' Maree recalls:

What had happened there, we were sitting and three guys walked up to the two Viera twins, and I was on the side. At that point in time my bowels said it was time to get emptied, so I was actually having a crap when these three guys walked up, and I spoke to Viera, because I was still trying to pull my pants up and get my rifle. They thought I said 'fall' so they lay down and I was pulling my pants up and grabbing my rifle and shooting and whatever. They then got into the reeds and that's when we threw the white phos [white phosphorus grenade] to try to get them out, and that caused the initial fire.

Once again, Ferreira approached Lynch to help stop the fleeing enemy. Mertz was subsequently told to do whatever was necessary to slow down the escaping FAPLA convoy, and allow the reserve Buffels to reach Ferreira and catch up with the retreating FAPLA. Mertz did not waste any time trying to delay the convoy. At 16:50, after he had shot out most of the trucks, breaking the FAPLA formation apart, his gunship was hit by enemy fire. He explains:

As there was only one gunship available, my briefing also entailed not putting the helicopter in undue risk and in the case of being forced to do an emergency landing to stick to the eastern side of the river, where Willem Ratte was. When we got to the river I noticed the size of the withdrawing FAPLA forces on their vehicles. I decided to climb higher than the normal 800 feet, thinking that small-arms fire would be less effective and hoping that they did not employ 12.7- or 14.5-millimetre anti-aircraft guns on the back of one of their vehicles. The problem was that our 20-millimetre cannon was not that effective from a greater height, but after the first exchanges of fire we noticed that the vehicles in front actually stopped and the soldiers disappeared into the reeds alongside the river.

As it was our aim to slow down the enemy retreat to the north, we withdrew to the north until we could not hear massive small-arms fire emanating from the convoy on the ground. As soon as we were out of range the FAPLA soldiers got back into their vehicles and proceeded north again. Once again, we engaged them until they dismounted and took cover in the reeds. I cannot recall for exactly how long this pattern continued, but at one stage, when we decided to engage the dismounted soldiers among the reeds, the Alouette was hit by various rounds. By this time I had established that the 32 Battalion soldiers had reached their vehicles and were on their way in pursuit of the FAPLA convoy. As my fuel was getting low and we were not certain of the extent of the damage suffered by enemy fire, I decided to return to Omauni, refuel, assess the damage and return in support of our ground forces if required.

Willie Botha communicated with Mertz on the radio:

The gunship passed overhead headed for the convoy, and moments later it sounded like someone was tearing a huge sheet of cloth apart in the sky as a couple of hundred AKs opened up on the chopper. 'Tell me when I

TOP SECRET/UITERS GEHEIM

DD1991

OPERATIONS WAR DIARY/OORLOGSDAGBOEK OPERASIES

OF/VAN

BAND/VOLUME...............

MAAND/MONTH...............

PLEK
PLACE.................................. TYDPERK VAN
PERIOD FROM.................... TOT
TO ....

Reeks no. Serial no.	Datum en tyd Date and time	Opsomming van voorvalle en informasie Summary of events and information	Verwysing Reference
6	21/1650/6	Gunship has been hit and will have to return to base.	Informal.
7	21/1803/6	The MPLA vehicle fleeing north with road turned off into the bushes and headed	
		eastwards towards the river, with our own	
		forces chasing them. The enemy rushed	
		into the river, trying to swim for safety.	
		A lot of the enemy reached a small	
		island in the river. Our forces preparing	
		to throw mortars on them. Some enemy	
		tried to swim to the other side of the river,	
		when this happened and at least two (2)	

OPS/1/32 BN   TOP SECRET/UITERS GEHEIM

TOP SECRET/UITERS GEHEIM

DD1991

OPERATIONS WAR DIARY/OORLOGSDAGBOEK OPERASIES

OF/VAN

BAND/VOLUME..............

MAAND/MONTH..............

PLEK
PLACE.................................. TYDPERK VAN
PERIOD FROM.................... TOT
TO ....

Reeks no. Serial no.	Datum en tyd Date and time	Opsomming van voorvalle en informasie Summary of events and information	Verwysing Reference
		enemy were caught by crocodiles.	Informal.
8		Our own forces met with strong resistance when attacking	
		Savate. Apparently our information was not exactly right	
		as there appeared to be more enemy than was esti-	
		mated at first. Losses of our forces were as follows:	
		24 wounded (of which 21 were SP's) and twelve (12)	
		dead (of which 4 were white).	
		The white killed were: 1) Capt Grearman (Sch INT)	
		2) 2 Lt + S Patnck (INT OFF) – A HQ COY	
		3) 2 Lt J.M.H. Muller of F16 pl leader	
		4) L/Cpl Fachie also F16	

OPS/1/32 BN   TOP SECRET/UITERS GEHEIM

TOP SECRET/UITERS GEHEIM			DD1991

PLEK PLACE......		TYDPERK VAN PERIOD FROM......	TOT TO ......

OPERATIONS WAR DIARY/OORLOGSDAGBOEK OPERASIES

OF/VAN

BAND/VOLUME..............
MAAND/MONTH..............

Reeks no. Serial no.	Datum en tyd Date and time	Opsomming van voorvalle en informasie Summary of events and information	Verwysing Reference
		The three (3) whites wounded was: *DEFENCE INTELLIGEN.* *DECLASSIFIED*	
		1) LL Cpl D. Cline of A₁ *2 3 NOV 2009*	
		2) Cpl J. H. Nell	
		3) 2Lt J.M. Roberts of F-Coy. *SMIT*	
		Missing still at 21/1900/1 May 80 is	
		Lt C. Muller, Coy Cmdr of A Coy.	Informal
		who missing is Rfn E. C. Langenhoven of F-17	
9	21/1645/B	A Puma lift Omauni for Cunene with six casualties of which two (2) are quite serious. ETD = 21/1645/b May 80	Informal

OPS/1/32 BN   TOP SECRET/UITERS GEHEIM

start picking up small-arms fire,' came from the pilot. 'You're picking up a lot of small-arms fire,' was my immediate response. He would orbit at a precise 300 feet (so his gunner would have a good shot) [it was 800 feet, according to Mertz] and allow the gunner to take out one or two engine blocks with a couple of well-placed rounds. He would then break out of the orbit to confound the ground fire, and re-enter at a different point, asking me all the time to confirm that he was attracting his fair share of attention. I became tired of answering in the affirmative.

At one stage this came over the radio: 'Okay – she's been hit, let me just go check if this girl still flies.' Shit, my mouth went dry; if the chopper went down, that would mean no top cover for the badly out-numbered teams chasing down the cornered enemy, no casevac and who exactly would have to go fetch his ass out of the wreckage? Before long, however, he returned with his dry, just-another-day-at-the-office tone: 'Tell me when I'm picking up small-arms fire.' My answer was, once again, positive.

From monitoring the FAPLA-brigade radio network, it became evident that the brigade commander was busy with a full-scale withdrawal, leaving Savate in the hands of 32 Battalion. Viljoen, in the Cessna, also reported the column of troop-carrying vehicles engaged by the gunship leaving the base area. Viljoen was concerned about the whereabouts of Muller, and instructed Rolf Heiser and his few men to search for him.

In the meantime, the four Buffels reached Ferreira's headquarters. Heap, Ferreira, Taylor, Ueckermann and Ross, with some Charlie Company troops, mounted the vehicles and gave chase, arriving at the convoy the moment the gunship broke away to return to Omauni. Heap explains:

Falcon ordered the Buffels to the front. Falcon, Jim Ross, myself and, I think, Sergeant Major Ueckermann were in command of a Buffel each. We travelled through Savate town and turned north following the flee-ing FAPLA soldiers. The road and river run parallel with each other with a strip of about 500 metres between the river and the road. We could see how the FAPLA soldiers, on foot, were fleeing to the north, running through the grassland.

The recce group, which was deployed in ambush positions to the north, started to report successes as they shot out the enemy convoys that entered their ambush positions. Myself and another Buffel (I think it was Jim's) turned towards the river and started a duck shoot. The fleeing FAPLA were shot from the Buffels while trying to escape or hide in the long grass. We later stopped at the dead enemy to pick up their ammunition, as we were quickly running out; the hunt continued!

Charl was the unit's adjutant and one of the very few members in possession of an AKM. There were simply not enough AKMs in the stores at Buffalo. The entire leader group envies an AKM instead of a normal AK-47. I collected an AKM for myself from one of the dead FAPLA while collecting ammunition from his body. I used the AKM in the chase. We were called back to Savate after Charl's body was discovered in a trench. It seemed that he was wounded in the arm and had jumped into a trench to put on a bomb bandage, when he was shot from the back through his head.

We were getting out of the Buffels when Sergeant Pedro from Charlie 7 platoon accidentally discharged a shot. The bullet ricocheted from the Buffel's side and a piece of shrapnel hit me in the cheek, my only wound in my three years' service with 32 Battalion.

From the Cessna, Viljoen directed the Buffels towards the fleeing enemy, who were running over the floodplain. In the meantime, more enemy vehicles had left Savate. Fierce fighting continued. At 18:03 Viljoen saw some enemy vehicles turning off the road heading towards the Cubango River, across which some of the fleeing enemy tried to escape but either drowned or were taken by crocodiles. From the Cessna Chisholm witnessed the FAPLA troops' attempted escape:

During this period Deon Ferreira came on air to inform us that Charl Muller plus a number of other 32 personnel had been killed; this really made E.V. upset at the time. With the enemy travelling in a convoy of trucks northwards along the riverbank, E.V. called the chaps on the ground to jump into the Buffels and head the enemy off by going along the road that was coming to a bottleneck at the river a few kilometres up the road.

The enemy by now could see they were going to be in the shit at the bottleneck, so they jumped trucks and waded into the river to an island one-third of the way across. Our chaps began knocking them off while they were trying to get to the island. I cannot remember how many managed to make it to the other side of the island, which protected them from our chaps on the main bank. The enemy realised they were in shit street now and so they began to wade into the river, which was about 80 metres across to the open plain.

Most had by now dropped their AKs and were just managing to stay afloat in the reasonably deep water – you could see they had no idea how to swim. At this time, E.V. was pleading with me to shoot them from the side door of the Cessna, but I was under strict instructions not to allow this. By this time the enemy (about 30) were about halfway across when … one was taken by a huge crocodile (similar to the *Jaws* movie): he did not even have a chance to put up a fight. We were by now flying at 200 feet and you could see the enemy were not worried about us in the air or our guys on the ground – their main concern now was the crocodiles.

Anyway, about a minute later number six in line was attacked by another crocodile, which was not as big as the other one, and this enemy put up quite a good fight with the crocodile for about 50 metres down the river before he also disappeared. The rest of the enemy were really frantic now and were trying to hide behind one another while making a beeline for the open plain. E.V. decided we should let the rest go, as they had had enough excitement for the day, and so we flew back to the enemy camp to help coordinate the cleaning-up operations, which took another couple of hours. I flew 11 hours that day.

There were fears that Ferreira would lead his convoy towards the mines that the recce teams had planted on the road, so Viljoen directed him away from the road and over the floodplain. Taylor remembers getting involved in the shooting before returning to Savate:

Finally the call from Echo Victor (E.V., or Eddie Viljoen) came and we cut off the road into the bush, heading for the river. We came up against a seemingly impenetrable line of bushes as high as the Buffel. Echo Victor told us that what was left of the convoy was on the other side and to our right. We paused, not sure. My suggestion was to send some-one on foot to check it out, lest we get taken out by an RPG as we burst through into who knew what on the other side. In addition, we couldn't be sure the line of bushes didn't conceal a bank, over which we could somersault, spilling out of the overturned Buffel in full view of the enemy.

Commandant Ferreira looked at me, then at the bushes, then back at me before deciding not to heed my advice and shouted to the driver to smash through the bushes. His gamble paid off – no bank and no RPGs. Sure enough, the lead vehicle was barely 80 metres off to our right. As we charged towards it, I stood up and turned to fire over the driver's head, twisting my rifle so that the ejecting cartridge would spin up and not into Commandant Ferreira's face. I heard my first round hit the windscreen with a distinct crack and the door flew open as the driver jumped out. I saw these white takkies, which looked very out of place below his camouflaged uniform, appear on the step of the cab, before he fell out onto the ground. I fired two or three more rounds into him and he lay crumpled in a heap. I looked across at Sergeant Major Ueckermann and saw that he had also pumped a few shots into him ... he hadn't stood a chance. Almost in slow motion, with its driver's door hanging open, the truck continued forward, rolling down into the ravine and smashing into the bank.

We continued towards a batch of about five abandoned trucks parked one behind the other. The guys behind us were firing at something when I heard a loud bang. A bit dazed, and feeling something warm and wet, I looked down to see blood flowing from the back of my hand. 'Commandant, I've been hit,' I said to Commandant Ferreira sitting next to me. He was talking to Echo Victor over the radio and without a pause he said, 'Justin's hit, Justin's hit', and went right on with what he had been saying before. I felt no pain in my hand and so started checking the rest of my body, to find that I had been hit in my upper arm as well. It must have been the fragments of a bullet that had hit the inside of the Buffel, spraying me like a shotgun. We bandaged my hand as best we could to stop the bleeding.

We circled the abandoned vehicles and then headed back, as it was now getting late and we didn't have long before the sun set. We passed the body of the driver and with my emotions welling up I said, 'Commandant, I shot that fucking cunt for Tim.' I had never used language like that in front of the commander and no sooner had I said it than I thought what a stupid thing it was to say. He didn't reply, but looked off into the middle distance. It had been a long day and I suppose there was nothing more to be said.

The stopper groups and the mounted group could not stop all the fleeing columns, but made sure that FAPLA had left all their vehicles and many dead behind before the rest fled north. Botha was glad that he had made it through this extremely tough engagement. He explains that his end-of-service date was constantly in his mind:

> One of the things I remember was that, coincidentally, many members were killed on their last operation, such as Sergeant Ben Gerrike. Ben joked when he went on his last operation, and was teasing that he was going to dig waist-deep trenches to ensure that he would survive. Sadly, Ben was killed on his last operation when a mortar round exploded between his legs during a contact. Naturally, I was also concerned about my last operation, as I had resigned. During the fire and movement, after running several hundred metres at full speed, my chest was starting to burn. As we approached the river, small pools of water could be found in the grass.
>
> Once when I went down during the shooting I started to sip water from such a pool. As I was soaking wet from sweat, I thought it wise to cool my head. While on the ground in between fire and movements I put my weapon down and stuck my hands into the water. When I got up for my next fire and movement I slipped. With my one hand still on my head I was pouring water and with the other hand holding

my rifle to stay in sequence with the fire-and-movement drill. When I fell some of the other members thought I had been shot in the head, looking at how I went to the ground. From the recce members and to Willem and Piet, monitoring the radio, the message went out that I was wounded.

In a makeshift emergency room in a tent in Omauni, Bouwer treated the wounded as best he could after they had been offloaded from the Puma. When the Cessna landed with Viljoen, he arranged for the evacuation of the critical cases to Rundu military sickbay. It was decided that the Puma, accompanied by Dr Breedt, would take the more serious casualties to Rundu, leaving no available means for Bouwer and me to return to Savate. Bouwer explains:

> I managed to get everybody dripped, climbing over all the troops in that cramped space, without getting airsick. By the time we landed at Omauni I had one drip left to do on one of the troops, which I then did on the tarmac. We quickly did a triage between myself and Dr Breedt, who then immediately loaded the worst guys back onto the Puma to go to Rundu. I took the less seriously wounded ones and put them in a little tent that we had set up for them in our camp in anticipation of bringing back the wounded from the operation.
>
> The Cessna crew that landed in the interim went to the mess while I started working on the wounded. During the work-up, I found that one of the soldiers also had a chest wound that had not been noticed and he ended up having a pneumothorax [collapsed lung] on the left-hand side. I put an underwater drain on him there in the little tent. The rest of them were just minor gunshots through muscles and legs, and they were then all removed the next morning to Rundu by vehicle.
>
> I went to the pub to find something to eat, and Piet and I got quite a rev from Major Viljoen for coming back with the troops. But under

113

the circumstances, I was responsible for the casevacs, who had not had any medical treatment since they had been shot earlier in the day. I managed to get something to eat, shower and get into clean clothes.

5

Consolidation

The fighting was over and consolidation could now begin. Grobler remembers making a horrific discovery:

When FAPLA fled we swept the base. We were very thirsty and hungry. Many of us swept through the town back to the base where the trenches were, with a mug in one hand and rifle in the other. It became a drill: when you see a water drum, you shoot at it, fill up your mug and drink the water. At some places FAPLA had been preparing food. Some of the troops, when there was time, stood in a circle around these places and ate. By that time it was safe to.

I remember when we reached one place I smelled braaivleis [barbecued meat]. Me and a few troops got the wind direction and walked towards the smell. When we arrived there we found that it was not braaivleis but somebody from 32 Battalion who had been burnt to death. The person lay on his stomach; we could not determine if it was a white or black guy. I tried to turn him over with my foot. I did not want to touch him because it looked very bad. His upper leg muscle came loose. When we turned him on his back we still could not determine who it was. I noticed his radio (think it was an A72 with a black handset) and then realised it was Tim Patrick. He was the only one that had ground–air communication. What apparently happened was that he had tied his white phosphorus grenade to his webbing. A bullet must have hit the grenade, it exploded and the rest is history. If he had not been carrying that thing there, it would have been a clean shoulder wound! [It was later determined that Patrick was walking behind to control the company assault line. They missed one of the bunkers and, as they passed it, the enemy in the bunker opened fire, hitting Patrick's WP hand grenade, which exploded.]

We started to look for Charl. We swept back (another reason why we went back after the fight was over was that some troops were missing) to find the wounded, give first aid and gather the dead bodies. I still remember Lance Corporal Kaumba. He had no mark on his face, but I did not recognise him. He looked so calm. He was a very good NCO [non-commissioned officer], a true pillar one could trust. That is why he was dead – he fought. Just shows you what facial expressions do.

All of a sudden, 122-millimetre mono-Katyusha rockets began exploding all around them. Grobler continues:

The next moment there was a hell of a bombardment. Troops ran around looking for cover. Everybody ran to the trenches, of which there were more than enough. I am unsure what they shot at us with, but it missed. The loose sand and trenches made it ineffective. Nobody was wounded. Myself and Attie Roestof were sitting in the same hole, laughing nervously.

We had to take stock. We counted and re-counted, and could not believe the calculations. We could not believe that so many people were not with us any more. Dave Hodgson stripped his moer [became angry] and told the troops to 'Formatura trez trez' [Form up in three lines]. After much bitching and saying 'the white guys are now really mad, as you do not do such things in the bush,' they formed up. We got the answers and sent through the figures. Two blokes from Foxtrot were still missing, Corporal Engelbrecht (we called him Engel) and a troop. We thought they had been captured.

Fortunately, nobody was injured during the bombardment, which, it turned out, was not an enemy counter-attack at all. Ratte admits he was responsible:

> They discovered a big cache of mono-Katyushas next to the airstrip. We had a sergeant from England called Ron [Gregory], a good guy, older than most of us – in his 40s but very fit and a good NCO, respected by all of us. Ron always told me I was wasting explosives. It always stuck in my head. That day when I saw the mono-Katyushas, I thought, well, put all these mono-Katyushas in a trench, make a pile of them and then put wood on it, light the wood and then the heat will sort of explode all these rockets. So we did that and some guys said to me, 'Hey, Lieutenant, watch it.' I did not listen to anybody.
>
> We stacked the rockets, put wood on top, then we cleared the area and went back to the middle of the town and waited for the big bang. I was waiting, still sitting in the Buffel. I warned everybody not to go close, waiting for the explosion. The next moment there was this woossshhh bang, woossshhh bang. The heat of the fire ignited the booster charges of the rockets and they took off in all directions. It was the worst half hour in my life. I thought to myself, 'If anybody gets killed today, I will be court-martialled.' Sitting in the Buffel, I did not know where the next rocket was going to explode. They fell north, east, south, west, all over the town. It was a miracle that nobody got killed. It lasted for half an hour then calmed down. I never tried to explode rockets by lighting a fire again.

The mortar platoon was called in to Savate and redeployed to give support in case of a counter-attack and to help mop up the base. They too experienced the 'counter-bombardment'. Johan Anderson remembers:

> The mortars were the last group to arrive at the base and helped with the cleaning-up operation. We were still busy when more 122s went off.

117

We all took cover, as we thought it was an enemy counter-attack. It was, however, the veld fire that detonated the rockets. The fire was a result of the destroying of the bunkers by Coenie Nolte. There were lots of PKMs and RPDs that we could use.

There were no reports of enemy movement in the direction of Savate, neither from Caiundo nor Cuangar. The FALA guerrillas to the west of Savate, who had been instructed to move towards the town to take control of large stores of military clothing and tinned food, and also to take over the administration of the civilians who had fled the town, had not arrived by last light. There were only the two or three FALA who had travelled with CSI's Francisco from the beginning – that was it.

Leaving the recce group in position as an early warning in case FAPLA reinforcements were sent from Caiundo, Ferreira called the rest of his force away from the battle area and laagered for the night near where his head-quarters had come under mortar bombardment. Grobler remembers the initial chaos in the dark:

> Some monkey then decided that we must collect our backpacks. What he did not realise was that you cannot see anything in the dark. The whole story was one big confusion. Bags were just distributed. One could not see which bag belonged to which company. They were marked with pens, but in the dark you could not see the marks. When I received my backpack the next day it was empty; many others had the same experience. Hell, that asshole could not think!
>
> We lay down in the cold using scrap blankets and rags to cover us. Through the night there were many bangs, many! I don't know if it was FAPLA or the exploding ammunition stores. In any case, one could not sleep.

Rifleman Gilbert Everlett was attached to Echo Company. He had not accompanied the platoons to the mortar positions, but helped clear the base during the consolidation phase. It was his first deployment and he remembers the death all around him:

> For the Savate operation I had been temporarily attached to Echo. Echo Company did not take part in the main assault that morning – we were kept as a reserve. I would later participate in mopping-up actions around the base as volunteers were gathered.
>
> Later during the afternoon, when I entered the main base, my first impression was 'this must have been a tremendous fight'. There was that smell of death everywhere, genuine! I saw with my very own eyes a young lieutenant (the name I do not remember) giving mouth to mouth to one of his black troops, who had been shot through the liver.
>
> The day went by, going from hut to hut searching for documents and [there was] sporadic fighting. At one stage we had to pull out from the main base, as across the river FAPLA started to shell the main camp, but it did not last long. Also, we heard rumours that FAPLA tried to cross the river in order to escape; apparently some of them had been taken by the crocodiles (I never saw it myself).
>
> At the end of the day I was totally wrecked and wanted only one thing: to get some food and sleep. Darkness fell and I could not find my mochila anywhere. Monrevel and myself started to go from truck to truck in search of sleeping bags. We found several all right. The next morning we discovered that we had slept in sleeping bags that were used as body bags.

Earlier in the afternoon, the platoon commander sent the trained Rhodesian medic, Andy Falcus, to take some of the wounded to the evacuation post. On the way there Falcus was wounded, but managed to make it to the post. Unfortunately, he died of his wounds later in the helicopter on the way back to Omauni. Anderson remembers:

That evening when I arrived where the blokes had gathered around the fires they could not believe that I was alive. They'd heard over the radio 'Andy is dead'. Luckily for me, that was Andy Falcus, who had only joined the unit some weeks before.

Most of the captured equipment and vehicles were removed from the town to the overnight laager. Oelschig describes the feeling in the laager and confirms the spirit of the 32 Battalion leader group:

The night after the battle was spent in a cold, dark bivouac. No lights or fires were permitted. Despite a comprehensive victory over the defenders of Savate, there was a feeling of despondency, even gloom, among the soldiers. There is no doubt that the effect of the large number of casualties was sorely felt. The troops were grieving. It was also apparent that the losses sustained were keenly felt at higher headquarters. During the night Deon Ferreira received a personal message from General Viljoen instructing him to return to Rundu in order to make a full report on the operation. He was also instructed to send the battalion back to the battlefield to find and recover the bodies of the missing people. Deon Ferreira requested that he be allowed to return to Savate to personally command the battalion in its search for the bodies. He proposed that I return to Rundu in his stead to report on the operation. Shortly after this I received an instruction by radio from my own higher headquarters instructing me to do exactly that.

As we lay resting in the cold bivouac, one of the young officers came around and offered us (Deon and me) some tinned smoked mussels and caviar. Proof, if ever that was needed, that these men were hard, tough, skilled and professional fighting men, but that they also had a touch of class.

It was also in this bivouac, and this is not hearsay, that Deon admitted to me just what a close-run action it had been. He told me that his mortars had used up all their ammunition except for a handful of bombs, including the ammunition set aside for use in the event of a counter-attack. He agreed with me that the appearance over the battlefield of the helicopter had been the turning point in the battle.

Kevin FitzGerald also vividly recalls that first night after the battle:

I can still picture the moment, just before sundown at the end of that first day of battle, when Peter Lipman came over to me. He and I, together with [Rodriques] Alberto, had formed one of the 10 Recce Wing stopper teams that had been deployed north of the Savate base. My backpack, or mochila as we used to call them, and all my kit that had been squeezed into it had been blown to smithereens by a veld fire earlier in the day. I had been carrying a sizeable amount of explosives. Given that it was winter, a number of the guys had packed their sleeping bag 'inners', which they very kindly lent to me to fashion a sleeping bag. Because my attention was focused on making my sleeping bag, I only noticed Pete when he tapped me on the shoulder. When I looked up, he leaned in towards me and whispered in my ear, 'Fitzy, whatever you do tonight, remember to pray to the Lord and thank him for sparing our lives.' I must have looked a little bemused because Pete leaned forwards once again and said, 'Seriously, Fitzy, remember to pray to God and thank him for saving our lives.'

At the time, in the heat of battle, the thought of meeting my Maker had never entered my mind. Pete, Alberto and I had, at times, faced what appeared to be hordes of FAPLA troops of almost biblical proportions. Throughout the day, we engaged the enemy. Sadly, we lost Alberto when we were pinned against the Cubango River, and it was just Pete, a new lieutenant who had just joined us (whose name, unfortunately, I do not recall) and I shooting it out with what appeared to be an ever-growing mass of enemy troops. Even then, I was so focused on maintaining a constant rate of fire from my 'snotneus' [an effective close-range 40-millimetre grenade launcher] that I paid no heed to our dire situation. Even after I had exhausted my stock of 40-millimetre rounds and I had to go scratching about in the reeds to find my folding-butt AKM, all I could think about was getting back to Pete to help them keep the FAPLA hordes at bay. Fortunately, by that time our situation had become known, and the two Gavins – Monn and Veenstra – and a couple of the other sticks came to our rescue by launching a flanking attack against the relentless tide of enemy soldiers.

Pete's words have lived with me every day of my life since. They will always be linked to the events of that day and how that battle came to affect me, my fellow comrades in arms and, ultimately, our unit – 32 Battalion.

At 22:12 it was reported by radio to Omauni that Muller's body had been found lying face down in a trench, but there was still no sign of Corporal Eduard Engelbrecht or the other missing troop. There are a few versions of how Muller was killed. The most plausible, however, is Bouwer's:

The morning after the Savate battle the bodies of the dead 32 Battalion members were to be repatriated to Rundu. They were all placed in line in the shade next to a clump of little bushes next to each other. I was preparing everything to put them into the body bags so that they could be flown down by the Puma, and Ron Gregory and myself went through all the wounds that we saw on everybody to assess what had happened to them.

One of them was Charl Muller's body. He had a wound in one of his legs, in one of his hands and also an entry wound at the back of his head and the exit wound through his face. At the time we were surmising how these guys had actually been shot, looking at the wounds, and Ron Gregory told me that he was told by somebody who was close to Charl that both Charl and a comrade were wounded and both fell down while they were in the open. The other person, I do not know who it was, could not move. Charl grabbed him by his uniform behind the neck and started dragging him back to the trench or depression that they were sheltering in from the continuous fire they were under. In the process of turning his back towards the front, dragging his comrade, a shot came from behind, hitting him in his head and exiting through his face. This is what killed him. When he was hit in the hand I can't say, it could have been during the same fusillade that killed him. [The hand wound was sustained earlier in the battle, according to Taylor.]

While the men laagered for the night, in Rundu Colonel Gert Nel and Chaplain Gerrit Theron prepared to inform the wives of the two resident white soldiers about their husbands' deaths. It was a difficult task, as Nel recalls:

It was no easy task and very emotional. The most difficult for me was to inform Zelda, Charl Muller's widow. I [had] met Charl's parents long before he started at 32. His father and I built up a significant friendship from the beginning. With Charl at 32 and his later marriage to Zelda, our relationship became much more than that of unit commander and troop. Zelda and my wife, Dina, clicked, and therefore Dina was more than just the colonel's wife.

That morning, very early (I think it was just after six in the morning on 22 May), I went to inform Zelda about Charl's passing. The chaplain went with me. When she opened the door she immediately started to keen, even before anybody could say a word. She then shouted, 'He is dead, I know he is dead.' She repeated it a couple of times and then started to cry.

It transpired that the night before the attack, Zelda and Charl had (illegally) made radio contact, and since then she had the feeling that

		TOP SECRET/UITERS GEHEIM	DD1991	

OPERATIONS WAR DIARY/OORLOGSDAGBOEK OPERASIES
OF/VAN

BAND/VOLUME...............
MAAND/MONTH...............

PLEK
PLACE........................ TYDPERK VAN PERIOD FROM................... TOT TO ....

Reeks no. Serial no.	Datum en tyd Date and time	Opsomming van voorvalle en informasie Summary of events and information	Verwysing Reference
10	21/1640/b	c/s 90 (New grp under command of 2Lt Ganith) got another contact gang No more info received yet about this	DEFENCE INTELLIGEN DECLASSIFIED 27 NOV 2009
		It is impossible to say how many terr men killed at this stage.	
11	21/2212/b	Body of Lt C.Muller found. Lt Muller was the key commander of A company during the attack launched at Savate.	Informal.

OPS/1/32 BN   TOP SECRET/UITERS GEHEIM

she would never see him alive again. That's why when she heard us knock on her door she was scared to open it. When she saw me, she knew her premonition had come true.

The following day, Lieutenant Frans Fourie arrived at Rundu Air Force Base from Recce Commando selection, which he had successfully completed. Here he witnessed the sorrow of a wife who had lost her husband in Savate:

It was strange; I was the only passenger on the Dakota that left for Rundu that afternoon. On arriving at Rundu airstrip and stepping down from the Dakota, I could see Impala jet fighters parked. On the airstrip standing by a few Avtur drums I saw a lonely figure. At first I did not recognise who it was. I then recognised Major Eddie Viljoen as he came walking towards the Dak. I saluted a man I had much respect for. 'Welcome,' he said. 'Congratulations, I am proud of you.' He went on to say: 'With joy, there is also great sorrow. It is the blackest day in the history of 32, we lost a lot of soldiers at Savate.' It was 23 May, two days after Operation Tiro-Tiro, the attack on Savate. As he was talking, I saw Zelda, Charl Muller's wife, walking towards us. Four Impalas were rushing down the runway on a mission take-off. As they climbed and banked away into the air, Zelda shouted, 'Kill the bastards', and broke down in a great sob and embraced Big Daddy.

There were no chaplains at the Buffalo base and so the base commander had to convey the sad news to the families.

On 22 May at 07:45, Bouwer and I were back at Savate. The Puma also brought in Viljoen. While the dead were being put into body bags, the force continued mopping up Savate and searching for the two missing soldiers. Bouwer saved a child's life. He recalls:

Of interest is that once we loaded all the dead troops, Richard [van Zyl] showed me a little black girl who was found lying among some dead civilians. She had a huge hole in her left lung and they did not anticipate that she would live. They then left her there for the locals to find and look after, but I elected to bring her back in the Buffel with us, as we knew the chopper would come and get the bodies later and we could then take the girl to the hospital as well. We put her on the Buffel with us and I still recall how she was lying on her side hiding under a tarpaulin but holding my hand all the time. Every time I moved away she grabbed my hand and did not want me to let go of her, babbling away all the time in her language, which I could not understand. We carried on towards Omauni, and eventually the Puma returned after dropping off the bodies and picked up the two bodies that we had for them and also the little girl, who was then taken to Rundu. We went back to the base and by that time my medics had looked after the wounded well, and they were all taken to Rundu.

TOP SECRET/UITERS GEHEIM

DD1991

OPERATIONS WAR DIARY/OORLOGSDAGBOEK OPERASIES

OF/VAN 32 BN TACT HQ

BAND/VOLUME...........

MAAND/MONTH...May 80..

PLEK PLACE....Omauni....... TYDPERK VAN PERIOD FROM...22/0800/B...TOT TO....23/0800/B..

Reeks no. Serial no.	Datum en tyd Date and time	Opsomming van voorvalle en informasie Summary of events and information	Verwysing Reference
1	22/0730/B	Tiger (Puma) + messie (Bosbok) leave this base for Savate to pick up twelve (12) wounded and transportation of the following: 1) 6 drums of diesel 2) 8 cases of AK rounds 3) D4 explosives 4) Thirteen cases of R1 rounds 5) 6 boxes of 60 mm mortar bombs.	Informal
2	22/0945/B	Mission clearance requested for ump coming from Ondangwa to Omauni. Dr Murray coming to pick up Lt Dunlop — granted	Informal

OPS/1/32 BN

TOP SECRET/UITERS GEHEIM

TOP SECRET/UITERS GEHEIM

DD1991

OPERATIONS WAR DIARY/OORLOGSDAGBOEK OPERASIES

OF/VAN

BAND/VOLUME............

MAAND/MONTH............

PLEK PLACE........................ TYDPERK VAN PERIOD FROM.................TOT TO.............

Reeks no. Serial no.	Datum en tyd Date and time	Opsomming van voorvalle en informasie Summary of events and information	Verwysing Reference
3	22/1015/B	± Twelve (12) dead ± ± 5 survivors left for Rundu at 22/1015/B May 80, by Tiger (Puma). ETA at Rundu 22/1100/B May 80. Rundu 32 BN HQ to tell Blue Dop	Informal
4	22/1100/B	Fifty cases of 14,5 mm bombs found in Savate when going through the base. Also found a whole lot of 122 mm bombs and a TNT dump. Own forces busy destroying all these ammo.	Informal.

OPS/1/32 BN

TOP SECRET/UITERS GEHEIM

The recces also received instructions to return to Savate from their ambush positions. It was much easier for them to drive the enemy vehicles they had captured than to walk all the way. De Abreu remembers the experience of driving them:

During the consolidation and reorganisation funny things happened. We got lots of enemy equipment and vehicles, however, the problem was driving them to headquarters or Savate, because only a few of us knew how to drive, especially the Russian vehicles. I took one Mercedes-Benz truck loaded with new AK-47s. Horacio Cruz did the same and the white leaders also tried their best to start and drive the trucks. Horacio and I gave a few of the black recces who had driven before some vehicles to take back to Savate. There was one Russian IFA truck parked under a tree and Horacio told me that once in Angola during the civil war he and other FNLA troops had driven one, and that he and I must try to take it. The key was in and he started the vehicle. It was full of new AK-47s and cans of food. We were just driving away when I saw a FAPLA coming out of the bush where he had been hiding and he jumped on the back of the vehicle. My RPD was between me and Horacio, who was driving. I shouted to Horacio, 'Stop, stop!' He stopped and I told him that there was a FAPLA on the back of our vehicle. Horacio said, 'Sergeant, why do you wait? Kill him!' Horacio did not realise I was without a weapon. I told him that I was going to capture the enemy. I called out to him, *'Camarada, vem afrente!'* [Comrade, come to the front!] He jumped from the truck and I opened the vehicle door. He gave me his AK-47 and I allowed him to sit between me and Horacio. I then did a safety check on his AK-47, took out the magazine and gave him back his weapon. I asked him how he felt. He answered, 'Okay, with the grace of God we survive these UNITA commandos. They are very dangerous.' While we were talking the FAPLA realised something was wrong and asked me, *'Chefe,* why are we going back to

127

Savate? Enemy took over the town and the base.' I asked him his name and who the enemy was and who I was. He answered, 'I am Vasco, you are Cuban or mulattos from Luanda come to reinforce the brigade.' I asked him where he came from and what language he spoke. He was from Gamba and spoke Umbundu. I spoke to him in Umbundu. Gamba is the small town where I had started my primary school in 1960. He was surprised and asked me not to kill him. I asked him why he thought I was going to kill him, as we were the same people. We reached Savate where I met E.V. and handed over the FAPLA to him. In those days communication was zero, but E.V. knew me very well. He said, 'Abreu, *kuluma* [Fanagalo for come here], what happened?' I told him, '*Lo prisioneiro kamina lo FAPLA*' [The prisoner is mine, he is from FAPLA]. He called over a white man and told me, '*Kuluma lapa* [Come over here], Major Oliveira speaks Portuguese.' This Oliveira, it was the first and last time I met him. I tried to introduce myself before explaining about the capture. All he asked was who the prisoner was. I showed him the man and, without asking anything, he started beating the boy straight away in front of all of us and the boy started shouting, 'Please do not kill me!' in Umbundu. I asked Oliveira not to beat him because he wanted to talk, but Oliveira did not stop. I spoke to E.V. in my broken Fanagalo: '*I kona i kona, lo prisioneiro kamina*' [No, no, the prisoner is mine]. I then left them and went back to Horacio. Another man came out from the grass and I stopped him. Horacio asked this guy, about 45 years old, who he was and he answered in the Kwanyama language. Because of the language, Horacio told me this was a SWAPO. When he was about 10 metres from me, I asked the guy if he was SWAPO. [There was never any evidence that there were SWAPO in Savate.] He replied 'yes' and Horacio give me a hand signal to kill him. End of story.

Two enemy soldiers were found wandering around Savate and were captured. At 10:15 Viljoen, the captured enemy, the child, the dead and the last five lightly wounded were airlifted out by Puma and transported to Rundu.

The post-battle clean-up in Savate was harder for some than others. The attack on Savate was the first time since 1976 that the old Bravo Group, now 32 Battalion, had gone into combat against FAPLA. When they fled to South Africa in 1975 and 1976, the former ELNA guerrillas left behind relatives with whom they lost contact. Many of these relatives continued their lives in Angola and it is probable, although one will never know for sure, that some became conscripts in FAPLA or voluntarily joined the Angolan military. During and after the attack, some of the 32 Battalion men discovered their relatives serving with FAPLA in Savate. The effect on these men was tragic and profound. Grobler remembers:

> Corporal Almeida (according to witnesses) during a house-clearing shot his own brother, who was a FAPLA officer. He was sitting behind a desk when Almeida opened the door and started to shoot. Before this incident he was a good soldier, afterwards he became bossies [*bosbefok* – bush-crazy, i.e. traumatised]. Captain Lotter took him out of the company and he started to work in the stores.

By afternoon on 22 May, the mopping up was complete, but the two missing persons had still not been found. Also, no FALA force had yet arrived. Ferreira decided to withdraw to Omauni, but at 19:00 Viljoen radioed to say that higher headquarters, in the name of someone called Liebenberg, had ordered that they return to Savate and stay in position for at least 72 hours, and that Engelbrecht had to be found at all costs. It was never confirmed whether this decision to stay longer was made to allow time for FALA to occupy the town.

Ferreira knew that FAPLA was by now aware that 32 Battalion had attacked, and not FALA, and was obviously concerned about his men's safety and a possible counter-attack from Caiundo. The following war-diary entry explains Ferreira's concerns:

> Commandant Ferreira replied that the battalion had little ammunition and rations left at this stage, and that he was not happy, as there may be a counter-attack from the enemy if they stayed there, which could cause a lot more casualties. He also said that he had the vicinity of the attack searched through five times and that there was absolutely no trace of either Corporal Engelbrecht or Augusto (an SP [Special Project] member), who was also missing. Air support had to be arranged if they had to stay there longer.

Meanwhile at higher headquarters there was concern over a possible FAPLA air retaliation on Ferreira's forces and on the military base in Rundu. Four Impala strike aircraft were sent from Ondangwa to Rundu as a show of force. Oelschig was airlifted by Puma to Omauni and from there by light aircraft to Rundu. He and Eddie Viljoen had some explaining to do. Oelschig recalls:

> Upon my arrival I fielded personal telephone calls from Generals Viljoen and Geldenhuys, and from Admiral Putter, the CSI chief. There was understandable anger and dismay at the large number of SADF casualties, but once I had reported the initial inventory of vehicles, weapons, ammunition and equipment captured there was more recognition for and understanding of the nature of the Battle of Savate. It had become clear that, instead of attacking a small town believed to be defended by no more than a battalion of FAPLA, 32 Battalion had engaged and over-run a major defensive position held by no less than a FAPLA brigade.

At 21:20 on 22 May, from the Rundu headquarters operations room, Eddie Viljoen plotted Ferreira's overnight position as 10 kilometres south-west

TOP SECRET/UITERS GEHEIM

DD1991

OPERATIONS WAR DIARY/OORLOGSDAGBOEK OPERASIES

OF/VAN

BAND/VOLUME.............

MAAND/MONTH.............

PLEK
PLACE...

TYDPERK VAN
PERIOD FROM...................

TOT
TO ....

Reeks no. Serial no.	Datum en tyd Date and time	Opsomming van voorvalle en informasie Summary of events and information	Verwysing Reference
5	22/1900/6	Major Viljoen at c/s ØC (Mundu) informed Cmdt Ferreira at c/s Ø (BN HQ) that they have to return to Savate, and stay just there for at least seventy-two (72) hours. In that time they must be certain to find Cpl Engelbrecht of FN who is still missing since the attack on Savate 21/5/80 May 80. Major Viljoen received this message from a person Liebenberg who got the message from General CO Viljoen. Cpl Engelbrecht must be found at all costs.	

OPS/1/32 BN

TOP SECRET/UITERS GEHEIM

TOP SECRET/UITERS GEHEIM

DD1991

OPERATIONS WAR DIARY/OORLOGSDAGBOEK OPERASIES

OF/VAN

BAND/VOLUME.............

MAAND/MONTH.............

PLEK
PLACE...

TYDPERK VAN
PERIOD FROM...................

TOT
TO ....

Reeks no. Serial no.	Datum en tyd Date and time	Opsomming van voorvalle en informasie Summary of events and information	Verwysing Reference
5 (continued)		Cmdt Ferreira replied that the battalion have little ammo and rats left at this stage and that he is not happy as there may be a counter-attack from the enemy if they stay there - that could cause a lot more casualties. He also said that he had the vicinity of the attack searched through five (5) times and that there was absolutely no trace of either Cpl Engelbrecht or an Engote (SP member) who is also missing. Air support was arranged if they had to stay there longer.	

OPS/1/32 BN

TOP SECRET/UITERS GEHEIM

of Savate. The next morning, Ferreira informed his men about the instructions to stay in the area and sent Charlie and Foxtrot companies back to look for the missing men. At 10:20 their bodies were found about 800 metres from the original medical-evacuation point, where they had dug a trench in anticipation of the battle's end and their evacuation. Heap was with the search party:

> We had already been travelling for an hour or two when Falcon informed me that myself and Jim Ross had to turn around and look for the two missing persons, both of whom were from Jim's company. Needless to say, we turned around heavy-hearted, following our own tracks. We formed up the troops at Jim's original advance line, and carefully and systematically searched every bush and possible hide. Soon we found both bodies under a bush, where they had most probably bled to death after being wounded.

The handwritten operations war diary form:

TOP SECRET/UITERS GEHEIM — DD1991
OPERATIONS WAR DIARY/OORLOGSDAGBOEK OPERASIES
OP/VAN 32 BN TACT HQ
BAND/VOLUME......
MAAND/MONTH...May 80..
PLEK/PLACE......Omauni......
TYDPERK VAN/PERIOD FROM...23/0800B...TOT/TO...23/0800B.

Reeks no. Serial no.	Datum en tyd Date and time	Opsomming van voorvalle en informasie Summary of events and information	Verwysing Reference
1	23/1020B	The two bodies of Cpl Engelrecht + Augrato (SP member) was found this morning, when searching through the area of the attack. They were missing since the day of attack i.e 21/±1000B May 80. Td a dead = 15 ; Td wounded = 25	
2	23/1300B	Ø (Bn HQ) send us (Tad. HQ) a signal to say that the convoy will be returning to this base any moment.	Informed
3	23/1715B	Message received from Rundu that al captured equipment must be sent to Rundu A.S.A.P. — including Sam 7 and radio equipment	Ops/325/May80

Mr Lopo must accompany equipment confiscated.

OPS/1/32 BN   TOP SECRET/UITERS GEHEIM

DEFENCE INTELLIGENCE DECLASSIFIED 23 NOV 2009

As Ferreira had predicted, the enemy conducted an air reconnaissance. Anderson remembers:

> We did not sleep well that night. The next morning we left for Omauni, but had to turn around to look for Engel and another troop. While sweeping through the FAPLA trenches, an FAA [Angolan Armed Forces] aircraft flew over us to see what we were doing. Gavin Veenstra was just too late to mount a 14.5 to give the pilot a scare.

CSI reported that FAPLA had also sent two helicopters to the area and that UNITA had shot down one somewhere between Caiundo and Savate. The helicopter burnt out and the crew and passengers were killed.

Alpha Company was tasked with driving out some of the captured vehicles. In fact, because of the shortage of drivers, most of the white leader group who could were driving vehicles loaded with captured equipment.

Grobler continues:

> Alpha was tasked to drive out the captured vehicles. I still remember how the vehicles that were left behind were destroyed. Willem Ratte put some dry grass in a vehicle and without any ceremony set it alight. The Russian mobile bridge was destroyed with PE4 explosive.
>
> I remember that myself and Rod Howden sat on the back of a Kwê with some troops; we had no food because of the stupid decision to distribute the backpacks at night. We had nothing. Some of the troops had FAPLA food with them. The leader group (like us) had too much work to do to be looking for food. Therefore we basically had nothing. Rod Howden got hold of a case of tinned pineapple rings. While driving back to the cut line he asked with a typical American drawl, 'Leon, would you like some pineapple pieces?' Hell, then we started to eat and eat. Every time he asked the question we laughed, and we ate. We finished the case on the way to the cut line. My tongue was raw. To this day I still do not eat pineapples!

Lipman, driving a captured diesel tanker, followed Veenstra, who was also driving a captured vehicle. Lipman recalls:

> We brought many vehicles and weapons back with us from Savate and destroyed plenty as well. I remember driving behind Fitzy and the late Gavin Veenstra, who was in the vehicle in front of us. As we rounded a corner we saw something falling out of the door and tumbling into the sand, only to discover that Fitzy was leaning on the door when it opened going around a corner and he was flung from the truck. I laugh every time I recall this incident.
>
> Doiby [Gavin Monn] and myself brought a diesel tanker back and we had a medic who was detached to us whose name I cannot recall. He was sleeping on the rifle rack behind our seats when I hit a concrete

cattle trough with the tanker as we were driving using the moonlight only and I did not see that the track turned right until it was too late. Sparks were coming out of the exhaust, which was in the front of the cab. The medic took one look and ran for cover as he thought that the tanker was going to explode into flames. Fortunately, there was not too much damage to the tanker and we slowly proceeded back to Omauni.

By midday on 23 May, the FALA occupation force had still not reached Savate. The 32 Battalion men were not aware that UNITA had trained semi-regular battalions and took it for granted that the guerrillas they encountered along the route would occupy Savate. Hodgson recalls:

Probably halfway back to Omauni, we stopped at a ragtag, ill-equipped, hungry, desperate group of UNITA guerrillas. Their clothes were in tatters. Between three or four guys they had one AK-47 and one magazine of ammo each. They cheered us and were ecstatic. None more so than when they realised that we were going to leave some of the vehicles and equipment with them. They were so enthusiastic that a Kwêvoël truck rode over one guy's foot. We dished out equipment as if we were Santa Claus. The guy's foot was treated (luckily the sand was soft) and we continued south. There was no way they would have been able to conquer Savate.

At 22:00 on 23 May, Ratte and the recce group driving captured vehicles arrived at the Omauni base, and by 05:00 on 24 May the total force was back at base. At 11:00 the first vehicles transporting the force back to the Buffalo base left Omauni. After some delays and breakdowns, the last of the companies arrived back at Buffalo on 26 May. During the day a FALA semi-regular battalion arrived at Savate to dominate the area.

TOP SECRET/UITERS GEHEIM

DD1991

OPERATIONS WAR DIARY/OORLOGSDAGBOEK OPERASIES

OF/VAN

BAND/VOLUME..............
MAAND/MONTH..............

PLEK
PLACE...................................
TYDPERK VAN
PERIOD FROM................
TOT
TO ....

Reeks no. Serial no.	Datum en tyd Date and time	Opsomming van voorvalle en informasie Summary of events and information	Verwysing Reference
4	23/1800/B	Sitrep no 3 ~ Period 20/1700/B — 23/1700/B May 80 ~	Ops/217/May80
5	23/1920/B	Small service informed us this side that their present log stat is BXC and that they are moving out to this base tonight.	Informal.
		2 Lt G Taylor (Sig Off) ~ Lt H Heap who sustained shrapnel wounds during the attack on Savate were flown in to this base today for medical attention. 2Lt Taylor had shrapnel wounds through the left hand. He returned to Rundu today by air. Lt Heap got shrapnel in the chin but remained with convoy.	Informal.

OPS/1/32 BN

TOP SECRET/UITERS GEHEIM

TOP SECRET/UITERS GEHEIM

DD1991

OPERATIONS WAR DIARY/OORLOGSDAGBOEK OPERASIES

OF/VAN

BAND/VOLUME..............
MAAND/MONTH..............

PLEK
PLACE...................................
TYDPERK VAN
PERIOD FROM................
TOT
TO ....

Reeks no. Serial no.	Datum en tyd Date and time	Opsomming van voorvalle en informasie Summary of events and information	Verwysing Reference
6	24/2430/B	Find convoy arrive at Omauni.	Informal
7	24/0500/B	Lost vehicle at this c/s ~	Informal.

OPS/1/32 BN

TOP SECRET/UITERS GEHEIM

6

Debrief and result

I vividly remember that Wednesday, the 21st of May 1980, as if it
were yesterday: moments that will forever be etched in the minds of those
involved in this epic conflict. This was the first day of the battle that came to
define our unit, 32 Battalion. It served to establish the unit's reputation as
one of the finest combat units in the history of the South African Defence
Force and, arguably, as the most effective unit in the Border War.
 – Sergeant Kevin FitzGerald, Reconnaissance Wing, 1978–1981

On the morning of 24 May 1980, a newspaper headline in South Africa
declared: '81 terrorists killed in SWA'. According to the report, security
forces walked into an enemy ambush on the border and five soldiers were
killed. It named five of the six white men who died at Savate, but made no
mention of the black Portuguese-speakers who fell.

Neither was there any mention of the many acts of bravery displayed
by the men of 32 Battalion on that day, actions that to this day have never
been recounted in public – actions that under normal circumstances would
have earned the highest decorations for bravery. As this was a 'UNITA'
operation, there would be no pomp and ceremony, no medal parades. Only
the SAAF recommended their pilots for bravery awards, and Johan Mertz
therefore received a well-deserved Honoris Crux decoration.

In all, 15 men of 32 Battalion were killed, five were very seriously
wounded, eight seriously wounded and 13 lightly wounded – up to then
the highest casualty count in any attack. The men who were killed, whose
biographies are given in Chapter 10, were:

Captain A. Erasmus

Lieutenant C. de J. Muller

Second Lieutenant T.S. Patrick

Second Lieutenant J.M.H. Muller

Corporal E.C. Engelbrecht

Lance Corporal J. Kaumba

Lance Corporal A.J. Falcus

Rifleman R. Alberto

Rifleman B. Albino

Rifleman A. Caliango

Rifleman M. Augusto

Rifleman C. Marcelino

Rifleman A. Livingi

Rifleman J. Matamba

Rifleman S. Angelo

The following is a list of the wounded:

Second Lieutenant J.M. Roberts

Second Lieutenant J.S.W. Taylor

Corporal C.J.H. Nell

Lance Corporal D.R. Cline

Rifleman G.P. Agostinho

Rifleman A. Antonio

Rifleman P. Antonio

Rifleman J. Augusto

Rifleman M. Baca

Rifleman M.D. Borges

Rifleman A. Casule

Rifleman T.F. da Cunha

Rifleman Z. Eduardo

Rifleman P. Elias

Rifleman J. Francisco

Rifleman R. Gabriel

Rifleman N. Gomes

Rifleman R. Irmao

Rifleman G. Karimbue

Rifleman M. Keoa

Rifleman J. Martins

Rifleman J. Quissueia

Rifleman J. Rafeal

Rifleman F. Shipo

Rifleman P. Vika

Rifleman M. Vuti

Radio intercepts presented by CSI revealed 558 FAPLA killed, wounded or missing (most were probably missing). While there are official lists of captured and destroyed vehicles, weapons, ammunition and equipment, I disagree with the numbers of captured vehicles specifically: there were many more vehicles parked on the Omauni base airstrip than recorded. Nevertheless, for historical purposes, below is the destroyed and captured list, as it appears in the Chief Army Memorandum 20/80, dated 29 May 1980:

Captured			Destroyed		
Type	Description	Amount	Type	Description	Amount
Weapons	AK-47 rifles	458	Weapons	14.5-mm anti-aircraft guns	3
	RPD machine guns	8			
	G3 rifles	12			
	HK21 light machine guns	4			
	RPK rifle	7			
	60-mm mortar tubes	3			
	B10 recoilless guns	6			
	122-mm Grad-P rocket launchers	5			
	14.5-mm anti-aircraft guns	2			
	RPD machine-gun drum magazines	40			
	G3 rifle magazines	10			
	AK rifle magazines	100			
	75-mm recoilless gun tripods	1			
Ammunition	RPG7 rockets	347	Ammunition	122-mm rockets	12
	RG5 hand grenades	660		82-mm rockets	40
	TA grenades	4		4 × 2 m ammunition dump with anti-personnel mines	1
	stick grenades	24			
	7.62 × 51-mm ball rounds	6750			
	7.62 × 54-mm ball rounds	2160			
	7.62 × 54-mm tracer rounds	7040			
	7.62 × 54-mm armour-piercing rounds	2649			
	7.62 × 54-mm hard-nose rounds	29920			
	7.62 × 39-mm AK rounds	24640			
	14.5 × 114-mm ball rounds	70000			
	3.5-inch rockets	82			
	60-mm HE mortar bombs	30			
	82-mm HE mortar bombs	6			
	TM46 landmines	5			
	cheese mines	2			
	82-mm recoilless HEAT	18			
	7.62 × 39-mm RPD machine-gun 100-round belt	17			
	122-mm rocket-nose fuses	77			
	82-mm rocket-nose fuses	100			

139

Captured			Destroyed		
Type	Description	Amount	Type	Description	Amount
Equipment	periscope	1			
	mine detector	1			
	RPG sight	1			
	TB33 radio	1			
	travail radio	1			
	power generator on trailer	1			
Vehicles	IFA 5-t trucks	2	Vehicles	different types of cargo/	
	IFA 3.5-t trucks	1		personnel	45
	STAR 3.5-t trucks	1		amphibious pontoons	2
	Mercedes-Benz 3.5-t trucks	1		BRDM armoured cars	1
	STAR mobile workshops	2			
	motorbikes	2			
Uniform	groundsheets	100			
	shirts	40			
	trousers	40			
	boots	20			

Major W.A. Dorning, the official SADF biographer for South Africa–UNITA relations, wrote:

> The large number of own-force casualties, coupled with the adverse reaction to the incident in the international media, created something of a furore in South African military and political circles at the highest level, and Chief Army [Constand Viljoen] was instructed by Chief SADF [Magnus Malan] to convene a detailed inquiry into the circumstances of the Savate debacle.

On 26 and 27 May, the chief of the South African Army, Lieutenant General Constand Viljoen, attended the debriefing at Rundu. The investigation concluded that the attack had 'failed' as a result of faulty intelligence regarding enemy strength and the size of the target, insufficient support firepower, poor aerial-photograph interpretation and faulty communications. It was also discovered that the attack had never been authorised –

the message to proceed that Ferreira had received had been incorrectly sent. The message that the staff officer in the operations room in Bastion had given to the signaller was '*Gaan voort met die verk*', '*verk*' being an Afrikaans abbreviation for '*verkenning*' (reconnaissance). As it was standard operating procedure that abbreviations were not allowed in top-secret and operational messages, the signaller had apparently thought that the word '*verk*' was not an abbreviation but was wrongly spelt and should have been '*werk*' (work). So he sent the message '*Gaan voort met die werk*' (Proceed with the work). In his memorandum to Malan, Viljoen wrote:

> The fact that South African troops were used to support this attack against an MPLA-only target made it imperative to get State Security Council authority. Army headquarters or CSI did not know about this attack. GOC SWA did not ask authority for the attack; GOC SWA only authorised the recce. GOC SWA said that, if the recce was reported to be positive, he, in any case, would have given instructions to proceed with the attack.

From Viljoen's memorandum it is evident that instructions had been received from higher headquarters, or maybe even from government, that somebody had to be held responsible. He, however, did not agree:

> The price in human lives during this battle makes it not economical, and the consequent diplomatic and political risks worsen the situation. At this stage, there would not be much aim to take further disciplinary or legal action. GOC SWA was present in Rundu during my discussions and this matter was fully discussed with him. I thus recommended that we, except for rectifications to directive, now let this case rest.

The only action taken was therefore a complete review of the operational command-and-control doctrine governing SADF participation in UNITA operations based on the principles of avoiding, where possible, the use of SADF/SWATF troops against purely FAPLA targets and obtaining State Security Council authority when to do so proved unavoidable.

Despite the heavy casualties, the capture of Savate altered the military situation in the southern part of the Cuando Cubango Province. With the threat against Cuangar removed, the major military objective of the SADF/ UNITA strategy for the province had, in fact, been achieved by securing the Okavango River on the border with South West Africa and thereby preventing the opening up of a possible SWAPO infiltration route. Even though Mpupa remained in FAPLA's hands, it was not seen as a threat because of its isolation.

By the end of May 1980, FALA had five trained and fully equipped semi-regular battalions, with two more in training at the new Tiger base. With the capture of Savate, FALA forces could be released for operations, already in the planning stage, against Mpupa, Rivungo, Luengue and other towns in the interior of the Cuando Cubango Province. On 14 July, three semi-regular battalions of about 2 000 men successfully attacked Rivungo on the Zambian border.

By early August it had become apparent from SADF and UNITA intelligence sources that FAPLA intended to recapture Savate. With a view to warding off the attack, FALA reinforced the battalion already in Savate with one of the semi-regular battalions from the Rivungo attack.

As predicted, during their dry-season offensive FAPLA tried to retake Savate. On 16 August, a FAPLA helicopter-borne force surprised the defenders at Savate and succeeded in taking the town. The FAPLA follow-up occupation force, travelling by vehicle from Caiundo, however, was ambushed three days later before reaching Savate. The occupation force fled, leaving behind 30 dead and 38 brand-new vehicles. The FALA victory forced FAPLA to abandon the area completely and they retreated to Caiundo. After this, two additional FALA semi-regular battalions were deployed in the Savate area to conduct follow-up operations against the demoralised FAPLA forces.

Encouraged by the ease with which Rivungo had been captured in July and the manner in which FALA had beaten off a FAPLA attempt to recapture Savate in August, UNITA demonstrated its new-found conventional capability by attacking and defeating the FAPLA battalions at Luengue and Mavinga. Their success, however, was short-lived. In October, FAPLA launched Operation Red May. With massive air support, FAPLA not only recaptured Mavinga, Luengue and Rivungo, but, between 1 and 2 November, they also retook Savate. They did not, however, move beyond Savate, leaving the towns along the Okavango River in UNITA's hands.

In January 1981, FALA recaptured Savate (by then they had also captured Mpupa) and, until the Border War ended in 1989, retained control of the area and prevented any SWAPO infiltrations.

7

The founding father
throws punches

32 Battalion's founding father, Colonel Jan Breytenbach, did not hesitate to speak out when it came to 32 Battalion matters. His dislike for UNITA and some individual former intelligence operatives is well known and explained in his publications. He laid the blame for what happened at the Battle of Savate at the door of UNITA and individual CSI operatives. He unfairly put much of the blame on FALA intelligence chief, Brigadier Huambo 'Wambo' Kassito, and CSI's Colonel Flip du Preez. Kassito had successfully completed the first intelligence course presented by the French at Camp Delta just months before the Savate attack and, as a captain, was only appointed FALA chief of intelligence in June 1980. Kassito, now a practising attorney in Luanda, answered questions regarding his role in the Battle of Savate via email:

> After our training, I was sent to the office in Rundu because I was the best student on the course. In the office, I updated maps and also gave information that I received from higher levels. By the end of June 1980, I was appointed chief of intelligence and I left for Mucusso.
>
> QUESTION: Did you give intelligence briefings while you were working in Rundu?
> ANSWER: No, it was not my task; I only conveyed messages from higher levels.
> QUESTION: Did you attend the planning for the 32 Battalion attack on Savate?

ANSWER: I was there but other officers did the planning. I only gave them the information I received from higher levels.

As for Du Preez, he was transferred from the CSI Rundu field office in November 1978 and was not involved in the Savate planning. The attack was planned and recommended by the Rundu coordination committee.

The following is an account of the Battle of Savate, as told by Colonel Breytenbach in an email to former 32 Battalion members:

'The late Deon Ferreira, also known as "Falcon", had taken over from Gert Nel as commanding officer of 32 Battalion. I remember meeting up with him in the Southern Cape during the 1979 to 1980 holiday season. He informed me that he had been transferred to 32 Battalion, in the New Year, as commander. He had been advised by the Chief of the Army to adopt an operational philosophy halfway between the unorthodoxy of Jan Breytenbach and the orthodoxy of Gert Nel, which seemed to work pretty well, although it appeared to me that, subsequently, he too was rather leaning towards the unorthodox.

'I had advised him to earn his spurs in the eyes of the black troops by proving his mettle in actual battle. All commanders at all levels had to pass this litmus test, in the eyes of the black troops, and that particularly included the unit commander. Fortunately for Falcon, therefore, the war was beginning to heat up sufficiently for him to make his mark in the near future. Unfortunately, he was not only to be tested as regards his conduct under fire, but also whether he was capable of turning near disaster into triumph in the heat of a battle, when his own design for battle was beginning to unravel alarmingly.

'As usual, the blame can be fairly and squarely laid on the shoulders of Military Intelligence (MI) and their own "surrogate" army, namely UNITA. Flip du Preez had been approached by Savimbi to organise a SADF attack on Savate in order to destroy the FAPLA unit in situ there. He was asked to do this because they were located firmly and squarely astride UNITA's logistics line to UNITA guerrillas, who were operating in the Cunene Province further north, and also west of the Cubango River. Flip assured Deon that there was only a battalion of FAPLA deployed at Savate, which was about 300-men strong with nothing much in support. A three-company attack would easily see them off.

'To reassure Deon, Flip organised an intelligence briefing by Brigadier Kassito, the chief intelligence officer of Savimbi. I attended several briefings by this individual and it provided me with much amusement to see, and experience, the mutilation of real facts while delivered with an incredible manner of lily-white integrity. He always used to kick off with a double statement that: "The morale of the UNITA troops is very high. The morale of FAPLA is very low." This was accompanied by a pitying shake of the head. I always half-expected, just by looking out the window or door, to see droves of FAPLAs descending on us with their hands thrust skywards in a mass token of surrender. He was a "smoothie" all right; an advocate, under Savimbi's tutelage, of a counter-philosophy that an intelligence officer's sole task is not to provide a factually true picture of the enemy, even if unpleasant. Instead, he would tweak facts in compliance with Savimbi's desires to create an enemy picture that would mislead the stupid "Boers", or any of their other supporters. The row of skeletons in the UNITA cupboard also had to be carefully hidden from the gullible MI operators, who had all become totally enthralled by the charismatic Savimbi.

'Thus, Du Preez, a seasoned intelligence operator himself, should have seen through this posturing facade, which was blatantly obvious even to me as a clod-hopping infantryman.

'Savimbi thus always presented an enemy picture, via Kassito, that would cause the SADF, as counselled by MI, to react in a way that suited Savimbi's aspirations. This was not in accordance with a real enemy situation which was, therefore, often out of step with the overall South African national strategy of successfully countering the enemy threat. In fact, Savimbi had an unholy and a totally counter-productive influence on the South African strategy underpinning the so-called "Bush War". This was precisely because of the way intelligence was "doctored" by Savimbi through the likes of Kassito and the MI sycophants who had become part of his "bush court".

'Thus, the SADF was successfully coerced into attacking a "battalion strength" FAPLA location in Savate in order to open up supply lines to the UNITA guerrillas, which were deployed in the north-eastern Cunene Province. It coincidentally also opened up access to the substantial elephant herds still found in the area and created a real potential to also get at vast additional sources of Angolan teak. By this time, Flip du Preez, as the willing agent of both MI and Savimbi, had already put in motion the eventual mass slaughter of more than 100 000 elephants in the Cuando Cubango, as well as the total stripping of Angolan teak throughout the south-eastern parts of the province. The Cuando Cubango was to be mercilessly plundered by Savimbi, with the unholy encouragement of MI, to such an extent that it finally became a lifeless desert.

'But Deon was not aware of these unsavoury truths. He trusted Kassito and Flip du Preez implicitly, not having had intimate experience yet of the undercurrents in what surely was a hot-bed of intrigue. This was definitely not conducive to above-board relationships between the SADF and UNITA. He eagerly grasped the opportunity to command his battalion for the first time in actual battle. Thus, Deon formed a combat force consisting of three rifle companies and an 81-millimetre mortar platoon, which was ample combat power to take on and destroy about 300 FAPLAs. He also deployed Willem Ratte and a reconnaissance team to check out FAPLA combat power and deployments. This recce team would deploy in advance of the main force to ensure that Deon was kept up to date as regards FAPLA and to confirm the information provided by Kassito.

'Lopez, right-hand man to Flip du Preez and the chief ivory smuggler in all of Africa at the time, was to take Willem and his team to a drop-off point north-west of the target, from where Willem and his team would deploy to check out FAPLA's dispositions in and around Savate. Lopez, according to Flip, knew the area like the back of his own hand, but he still managed to drop Willem off some distance south-south-east of Savate.

'Afterwards, Lopez would fulfil the same mission for the battalion by guiding them to a drop-off point west of Savate, from where the assault would be launched. He managed to cock that one up too by dropping them north-west of the target. Fortunately, 32 Battalion found a track leading south-eastwards to the target and could make some progress to be in position by 21 May 1980 for a first-light assault.

'Meanwhile, Ratte and his team were trying to make up for lost time in order to get in a decent reconnaissance of Savate during the night of 19 May. But, because of Lopez's inability to find his way around this particular bit of miombo forest, Ratte could only close with Savate during the day of the 20th, which would have been suicidal under the circumstances. He was thus forced to cross the Cubango River to find a safe lying-up place during the daylight hours of the 20th. They heard much vehicle movement, which seemed to indicate that Savate contained much more than just a single run-down battalion.

'They, however, crossed over to the west bank during the night of the 20th to do a close-in recce of the FAPLA deployments and to confirm current intelligence about FAPLA. What they found was alarming and a certain indication that Savate was occupied by much more than a weak battalion of 300 men. There was a battalion deployed in the vicinity of the airstrip, north of the town, including some dreaded 14.5 AA [anti-aircraft] guns, which can also be used, devastatingly, in the ground firing role. There also were 82-millimetre mortar positions in the same area. In the town, there were positions manned by most probably another two battalions. It was confirmed later that the total FAPLA deployment amounted to 1 080 men, somewhat more than the 300 predicted or, rather, presented as gospel truth by "Smoothie" Kassito.

'So while 32 Battalion marched towards a confrontation with FAPLA, they were unaware of the fact that they were vastly outnumbered and out-gunned. They were also running way behind schedule because of MI's much vaunted Mr Lopez, who had no idea where the hell he was in the first place – nothing new for MI generally, of course, because they rarely knew where the hell they were supposed to be in the first place, especially as regards "military intelligence".

'They had this marvellous tendency to rely on dodgy outsiders, such as Lopez, rather than proven experts from our own ranks. Eddie [Viljoen], of course, could have recommended some excellent South African or 32 Battalion guides, who had spent months in Savate, at the beginning of my tenure as OC of 32 Battalion. But then MI always preferred the exotic solution rather than the true and tested South African way of doing things. Hence, the trust in a dodgy ivory smuggler, who was in cahoots with Flip du Preez, rather than trusting the likes of Geraldo, Zaire and other black troops who had proved their reliability in battle on numerous occasions and who knew the west bank of the Cubango River intimately – certainly much better than Lopez, Flip du Preez or any UNITA.

'Because of misplaced trust in MI's capability in the bush, the unit had a longer distance to cover while weighed down with heavy kit, as well as the mortar bombs carried by every man for the mortar platoon. The mortar platoon, of course, had to carry base plates, bipods and barrels, as well as their personal kit. Thus the unit, as a whole, could not be in place for a first-light attack on Savate. Another "buggerance" factor intruded when a GAZ lorry, coming up from the rear along the track that was being used by 32, got shot up with some survivors escaping into the night and, pre-sumably, to Savate, where the FAPLA brigade was warned that something dreadful was on its way to sort them out. The surprise factor was lost and, consequently, the initiative principle of war became badly compromised through the ineptness of MI and, specifically, their much vaunted "Senhor" Lopez. The FAPLA defences had been alerted well in advance of the attack and were therefore on the alert.

'Ratte and his patrol had slipped back across the Cubango after their recce, to act as FOO/MFC [forward observation officers/mobile fire controllers] for the mortar platoon. The base-plate positions would be to the south of the target. Ten three-man recce teams were deployed north of Savate and the landing strip. They would act as cut-off groups, if and when FAPLA decided that they had had enough of this blood-spilling nonsense, which could lead them to take the gap northwards to get away from very angry "Buffalo soldiers".

'The attack on Savate would be executed with two rifle companies, while another rifle company, minus one platoon, under the command of Sam Heap, would be attacking the FAPLA positions around the airstrip. Two rifle platoons would protect the mortar platoon base-plate positions while the four Buffels would be moved up in good time to exploit a "break-through". Eddie Viljoen would take off in the back of a Bosbok reconnaissance aircraft from Rundu Air Force Base in good time to be overhead to assist Deon Ferreira in taking and maintaining control of the battle.

'The mortars started shelling the FAPLA positions at 09:00. Two rifle companies moved into an extended line to attack Savate base itself, while Sam Heap and his understrength company attacked the airstrip. The latter ran into heavy 14.5 AA fire used in the ground role, and the attack stalled. The other two companies got into the defensive positions around and in Savate itself, and a hand-to-hand melee developed in the trenches. It had become cruelly obvious by that time that, instead of tackling a mere battalion of FAPLA infantry, Falcon and his men had, unwittingly, got hold of the tail of a very angry tiger; a whole FAPLA brigade in fact. So the battle swung to and fro with the 32 men refusing to let go, being acutely aware of the fact that there was no other choice but to go forward in order to win the battle. The whole unit had become so totally embroiled, and were in such close contact with the enemy, that any attempt to break off the fight would have led to certain disaster. Victory for the 32 depended on dogged tenacity ("vasbyt" in Afrikaans) and strong nerves on the part of Falcon, as commander, to see it through. It had become a contest of willpower between him and his FAPLA opponent.

'The 32 was beginning to suffer casualties, however. Meanwhile, the four Buffels had closed up from the rear to be available for the next phase of the battle. But a FAPLA detachment had infiltrated between the Buffels and the battalion, still furiously clearing the trenches inside Savate, so that another battle developed to regain contact with the main body of the 32. The drivers managed to beat off FAPLA with their mounted machine guns, but incurred the loss of one of the second lieutenants.

'It was about midday when FAPLA's nerve began to crack. They began to vacate the battlefield, first as a trickle but then in an ever-increasing flood, as panic inevitably set in when fellow FAPLA soldiers, still in contact, began to experience a sudden thinning of ranks all around them. Eddie (E.V.), aloft in his Bosbok, could see that what was rapidly beginning to develop below was a brilliant opportunity for the 32 to exploit, although maximum speed would be required, in order to turn a defeat for FAPLA into a massive annihilation of the whole brigade. He informed Falcon, who then ordered the Buffels to close up immediately. Each Buffel quickly took some 32 Battalion men on board and started up the road at great speed to catch up with the rear of the panic-stricken FAPLAs, under the direction of E.V.

'The gunners on the mounted Browning machine guns went wild as the Buffels caught up with what had become a panic-stricken mob, some in vehicles but mostly on foot. The open and wide Cubango floodplain became a killing ground par excellence. The Buffels eventually caught up with the fleeing FAPLA vehicles and shot them up in passing, which caused the escaping FAPLAs to bail out; at times they even took to the crocodile-infested Cubango River in a mad attempt to put the river between them and the marauding 32 Battalion. The crocs said, "Thank you very much for instant lunch," and grabbed whatever snacks came their way.

'The Buffels finally overtook the fleeing, disorganised convoy and Falcon pulled his own Buffel across the road to force the whole lot to an abrupt stop. To underscore the 32's serious intention, unit RSM Ueckermann shot the driver of the lead vehicle out of his seat with a single shot from his trusty FN rifle. FAPLA finally abandoned all intent on withdrawing in an orderly fashion in accordance with a laid-down drill, and abandoned all vehicles to seek refuge in the bush, the swampy floodplain, anywhere else while on foot. They were desperately trying out any means to get away from the marauding Buffels and their 32 Battalion crews. Thus, the FAPLA brigade ceased to exist. But then the scavengers moved in. UNITA, on whose behalf the battle had been fought by 32 Battalion in the first place, appeared from nowhere to lay claim to all the spoils and also to 32 Battalion's well-deserved battle honours. Something like 39 enemy trucks were captured and handed to UNITA; the 14.5s and other machine guns and weaponry became war loot for UNITA and anything else that could be of use went to the inventory of, presumably, Savimbi's quartermaster, Bock. UNITA then rubbed salt into the indignant feelings of 32 Battalion by claiming the whole Savate episode as a magnificent victory for UNITA.

'UNITA, however, never came near the battlefield but, like vultures, hovered in the wings to claim the spoils. They, therefore, suffered not a single casualty while the 32 had some grievous losses, not so much in quantity but definitely in quality. The unit lost more men in this single engagement than in any other battles past – Ebo excluded of course, and battles still to come. From a total of 15, seven were killed as leaders at company, platoon and section levels, indicating that leadership in 32 Battalion was always from the front. Falcon himself led from the front in this, his first battle as unit commander, and, consequently, he made his name, no doubt under critical scrutiny from the black troops, as a worthy commander of 32 Battalion.

'Because this terrific battle was fought in the name of a UNITA force that was totally absent from the battlefield, 32 Battalion is, to this day, not allowed to display "Savate" as a battle honour on our own unit colour.

That, too, should be rectified but how to do this remains a problem because, as far as the present government is concerned, 32 Battalion no longer exists. This is in spite of the fact that its legacy will live on long after the last ex-32 Battalion veteran has gone on to pastures much greener and far beyond human reach.

'A splendid battle was won, but it nevertheless still occurred way outside the spectrum of war I had envisaged for 32 Battalion. General Viljoen, quite rightly, was most upset during the after-battle debrief. He quite rightly reminded General Geldenhuys and CSI, most forcibly, that 32 Battalion was, "My guerrilla battalion. It is not a conventional infantry battalion."

'Unfortunately, this timely reprimand did not sink in. 32 Battalion was fated to become more and more conventionally orientated as the years marched on. It fought the conventional battles forced on it most successfully, it should be admitted. However, it would have produced strategically and vitally decisive results out of all proportion to its size if it had remained a "guerrilla battalion". This would have been particularly true if it had been deployed on the type of missions I had envisaged for it, after in-depth discussions with Delville Linford, and which I had described in detail in the "Strategic Mission" chapter in *The Tempered Sword*. [Breytenbach's latest book, published in August 2011.]

'Taking up arms on behalf of UNITA became standard procedure. In 1985, 32 Battalion, its combat power greatly boosted by attaching an anti-tank squadron of Ratel 90 tank destroyers, a troop of MRLs [multiple rocket launchers] (Valkyries) and a troop of mounted 20-millimetre AA guns, stopped the advance of FAPLA mechanised brigades on the Lomba River. Severe casualties were inflicted on the enemy.

'In 1986, 32 Battalion backed the futile attempt by two badly trained and worse-led UNITA brigades to take Cuito Cuanavale.

'In 1987, the battalion repeated its 1985 performance by again stopping a multi-brigade advance by FAPLA on Mavinga via the Lomba River, with 61 Mechanised Battalion also becoming involved. One and a half FAPLA brigades were wiped out. Basically, 32 Battalion was used by SWATF HQ, as demanded by the Special Tasks Division of MI, to pull Savimbi's chestnuts out of the fire, while, had they been used as guerrillas, they could have restored the strategic initiative to the SADF. Only once was such an attempt made and that was during Operation Forte when the 32, under E.V.'s command, was deliberately deployed, Chindit-style, deep inside enemy-dominated territory. Large parts of the strategic Cunene Province fell under the domination of 32 Battalion, but then somebody got cold feet and the unit was withdrawn. This obviously made it easy for SWAPO to move back to reclaim the entire Cunene Province, in the absence of 32 Battalion domination, to again be utilised as their restored guerrilla base area.

'One way or another, the modern South African generals, who were the top-level inheritors of guerrilla warfare traditions as developed by the likes of Generals Koos de la Rey, Christiaan de Wet, Louis Botha and Jan Smuts, just could not or would not utilise this style of war. This is despite it having been proved to be extremely cost-effective with regard to lives and equipment, while also guaranteeing the restoration of the strategic initiative to the SADF, which at the time, had become caught up in a spider's web of going nowhere; marking time in one place so to speak. The SADF was fatally giving our opponents the time and space to escalate the war until we could no longer sustain its constant drain on our own limited resources in manpower, finances and equipment. We never regained the initiative, which we could have done by being better guerrillas than SWAPO. And, in the absence of the "INITIATIVE" principle, no war has ever been won.'

8

Information vs. disinformation

Operation Tiro-Tiro is the most talked-about operation in 32 Battalion's history, but it is also the one with the most unanswered questions and myths. Until recently, the enemy strength in the base and surrounding area on the day of the attack, and the number of enemy casualties previously published, had never been questioned. Since 2010, though, these have become points of debate. An extract from a 2010 publication, *Anderkant Cuito: 'n Reisverhaal van die Grensoorlog* by Louis Bothma, in which enemy strength and casualties are questioned, reads as follows:

> According to one source, information from 'intercepted radio messages' indicated that 558 FAPLA soldiers were killed at Savate. Another source gives the total as 400 ... This does not add up. How is it possible that Blackie and the others during Operation Super, where they had the element of surprise and where there were at least four gunships that, for the day, helped to shoot 201 PLAN guerrillas (the true total was probably closer to 160), but at Savate, where there was no surprise and no air support, 400 FAPLA soldiers were killed? This, while the enemy at Savate were dug in and were better and heavier armed than 32 Battalion? PLAN was a tough enemy in comparison to FAPLA, but still the calculations do not add up. [Operation Super was a military confrontation in March 1982 to prevent SWAPO guerrillas infiltrating into South West Africa through the kaokoveld.]
>
> Many years later, I approached Eddie Viljoen, the second-in-command of Operation Tiro-Tiro, by email on 21 May 1980. [He was

not, in fact, the second in command of the operation, but of the battalion.]... Eddie's answer: 'This figure is totally exaggerated and wrong. There were not even 400 FAPLA at the base. The enemy started to flee north and there was no proper head count. Because there were so many whites and blacks killed, the operation had to be justified. Therefore these [are] ridiculous numbers. Nobody will ever know how many enemy were killed, but the figure of 81 (the number reported in newspapers) could be looked into. This is more realistic for me.'

On 20 May 2012, in a conversation about enemy strength and casualties, the FAPLA commander on the day, Daniel Rufino, had this to say:

We had a brigade. It was a brigade in name only ... We had about 100-something people, because in the sister units we had one battalion, but it was also not complete and was operating here in Mucusso [this cannot be correct, because Mucusso was under UNITA control] ... We had about 120-something men between Savate and the border ... We had a battalion of 200-something men that was operating there in Cuangar ... So there were only base-maintenance people. The worst was that we had many losses. Those cowards, they attacked; we were losing and were in no position to attack. We had about 600-something men but they were all scattered. Inside, we had only about 180. Late in the afternoon, after getting in the cars and wanting to leave, tanks and helicopters surrounded us, and we were bombarded. The troops lost morale and each went their own way.

In a Battle of Savate briefing to Memorable Order of Tin Hats (MOTH) members, a former 32 Battalion commander paints a rather different picture:

Let's come to the enemy that was killed and so on. In all my time, and I have been there for quite a few years, with air force, with artillery, with multiple rocket launchers, with G5s, etc. Those are massive numbers of people to kill: 699 that are dug in. Nobody that was in that battle can tell you exactly how many kills there were.

I then spoke to those guys afterwards. They confirmed there were lots but they were more angry about the guys who ran away. These guys were gapping it to live another day.

Many weapons were captured. They just left ammunition, even the bridging vehicles – you know, what you use to cross the river or something and various other items, even gas masks. What they were expecting us to do, I don't know.

The following extract about enemy strength and casualties appears in the 29 May 1980 memorandum sent by army chief Constand Viljoen to defence force chief Magnus Malan:

> Instead of the projected battalion (about 300 troops) in Savate, there was a brigade, thus about 1 000 troops ... on the concurred right hand objective, 41 dead bodies were counted and it is expected that more enemy were killed by the gunships and the three Buffels filled with troops who did the cutting off of the fleeing enemy. Conservatively, I guess the enemy casualties to be between 100 and 150.

While the above extracts raise many questions, it is possible to answer at least four: What was the base strength on the day of the attack? How many enemy casualties were there? Did the enemy anticipate an attack? And, if yes, did they know it was 32 Battalion from the start?

Base organisation and strength
So, how many enemy soldiers were in the Savate base on 21 May 1980? About 100 to 180, as claimed by Rufino (although at times in conversation he mentioned 600)? Or 400, as suggested by Eddie Viljoen? Or 1 000, as

written in the Chief Army Memorandum? Or was it 1 050, according to the radio intercepts presented by CSI at the Rundu field office? After his reconnaissance, Willem Ratte reported that 'we went all the way around until we got to the airstrip and then walked down the airstrip back to the river. In the process we established the extent of the base, which was far bigger than we expected and also that they must have some heavy weaponry there ... it was not just a normal little garrison.'

FAPLA's force reorganisation after 1976 was based on Soviet military doctrine. One of the newly formed and trained BRIL (light infantry brigades) designated for counter-guerrilla operations was 60 Brigade, the defenders of Savate.

A fully staffed BRIL had a strength of 1 260 soldiers of different ranks and appointments. Because 60 Brigade was new, it is generally accepted that it was fully or close to fully staffed, and had most of the weapons and vehicles typical of a BRIL.

In a February 2013 email, Rufino wrote that 60 Brigade arrived at Savate sometime in February 1980 and stayed there for three months before withdrawing from the area. Besides Savate, 60 Brigade had forces deployed at Cuangar, Calai, Dirico and Mpupa. While the FAPLA commander claims not to remember deployment strengths and who was deployed where, because of the UNITA threat, 60 Brigade had probably deployed at least a company (127 infantry) plus support elements to each of its bases along the Angola–Namibia border, leaving the balance to defend Savate, conduct area patrols between the Cubango and Cuito rivers, and to keep an eye on FALA guerrilla activities west of Savate.

We know from Rufino that there was 'a battalion of 200-something men' at Cuangar. A brigade is organised so that if an element, for example a battalion or a company, deploys to work independently of the brigade, not only will the battalion support weapons be deployed, but brigade headquarters will also provide anti-tank, anti-air and artillery elements in support, which remain under their direct command. In an area occupation

FALA BRIL ORGANISATION

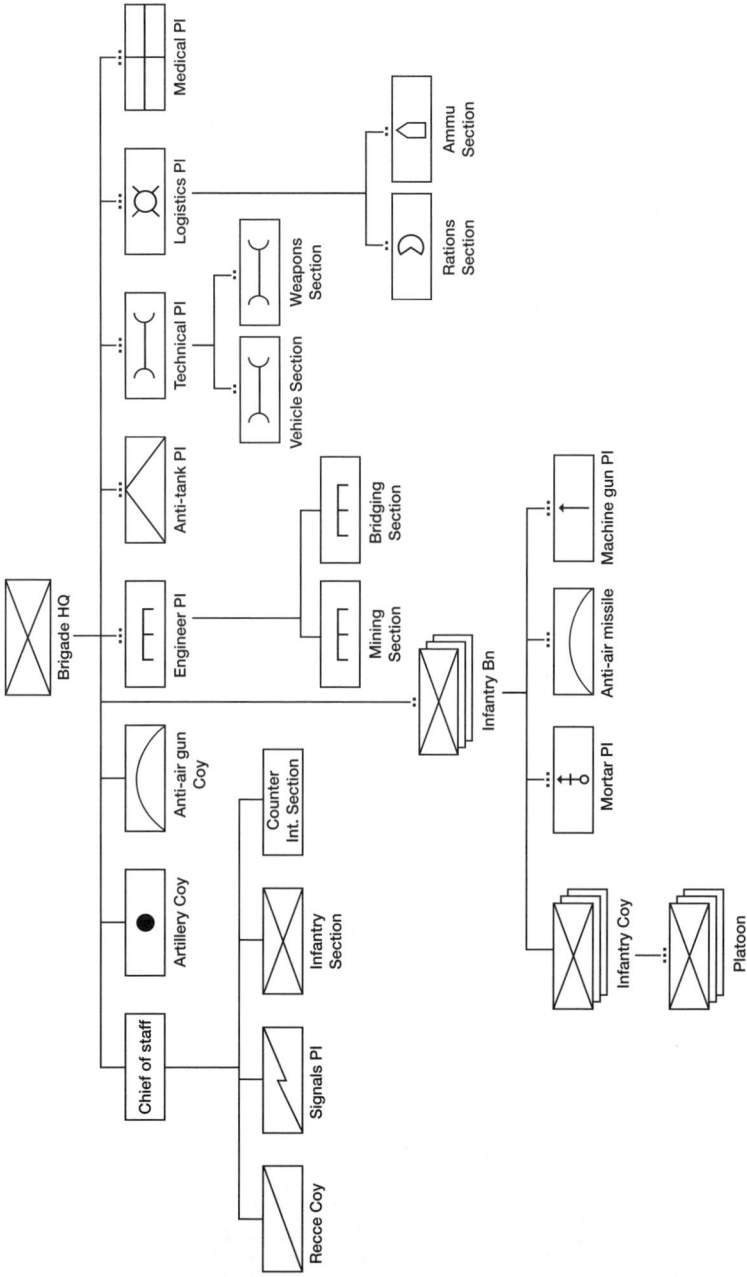

The organisation of a typical BRIL in the early 1980s, according to SADF records

Organisation	Personal	Weapons								Vehicles			
		LMG	60mm mort	82mm B10	82mm mort	RPG7	122mm Grad-P	14.5mm ZPU	SA7	TMM Bridge	BRDM 2	BTR 152	Pers/Cargo Truck
Brigade headquarters													
Recce company	35					3					3	3	1
Sign. platoon	14												1
Infantry section	10												1
Counter-intelligence	9												1
Other	4												
Total	72					3					3	3	4
Battalion													
Infantry Company (x3)	351	4	3			18							9
Mortar platoon	20				3								3
Anti-air-missile section	12								4				1
Machine-gun platoon	12												1
Total	359	12	3		3	18			4				14
Total 3 battalions	1 053	54	9		9	54			12				42
Artillery company	24						4						2
Total	24						4						2
Anti-tank platoon	12			5									2
Total	12			5									2
Anti-air-gun company	30							6					6
Total	30							6					6
Engineer platoon	24									1			2
Total	24									1			2
Support services	25												10
Total	45												10
Total brigade	1 260	54	9	5	9	57	4	6	12	1	3	3	68

Typical BRIL personnel, weapons and vehicle strength in the early 1980s, according to SADF records or domination role, such as 60 Brigade had, it is likely that these brigade support weapons would deploy to positions where they could assist in the support and defence of bases or towns. That 60 Brigade support weapons were provided to sub-units is confirmed by Mateus Timoteo, a former 60 Brigade anti-tank platoon member, now living in Cuangar. In a September 2013 interview, he said:

> I was with the forces from Cuangar. My responsibility was to fire the B10 cannon. I was sent from Savate to Cuangar with many others and we stayed there till we were attacked by the bandits and then we went back to Savate.

The B10 recoilless gun is an anti-tank platoon weapon generic to the brigade organisation, and not the battalion organisation. Although Timoteo could not remember how long they stayed in Cuangar, he said it was for some months. Another man, Batista Moreira, confirmed that the Cuangar defenders fled to Savate after the 14 April attack:

> About nine comrades who were in Savate when the racists attacked us live in Cuangar; others are still in Savate and other places. This is my town and I was here when the bandits attacked us. We fought fearlessly, but after some time the young ones started to run and then we all went to Savate ... I was shooting with the rifle. I was a soldier. [After the young ones started to run], we fought, but then we got into the vehicles and we left for Savate.

Strangely, Rufino denies any FALA attacks on his bases, while Timoteo and Moreira both speak of an attack on Cuangar.

It is a known fact that by the middle of May 1980 the Dirico, Calai and Cuangar bases were deserted. Where did the defenders go? Chances are slim that they went to Mpupa, the only base still occupied. The most likely scenario is that the Cuangar defenders consolidated at Caire, because it was the only crossing over the Cubango River, and from there withdrew to Savate.

The intelligence intercept presented by Oelschig at Rundu stating that 'the enemy positions at Savate complain that the general shortage of food, ammunition and weapons makes it impossible for them to defend the position against an attack' is a possible indication that the full brigade was present in the base and that this had not been planned for, and therefore they were running out of food and other supplies.

The list of enemy weapons and vehicles destroyed or captured that appears in the Chief Army Memorandum of 29 May 1980 is also an indication that the total brigade was present in and around Savate on the day of the attack. Only the presence of a full brigade could account for the large amount of equipment and goods at the base that day.

Weapons								Vehicles			
LMG	60mm mort	82mm B10	82mm mort	RPG7	14.5mm ZPU Grad-P	14.5mm ZPU	SA7	TMM Bridge	BRDM 2	BTR 152	Pers/ Cargo Truck
54 (12)	9 (3)	5 (6)	5 (6)	57	4 (5)	6 (5)	12 (1)	1 (2)	3 (1)	3	68 (53)

Typical BRIL weapon and vehicle allocation. The figures in brackets show the amounts either destroyed or captured by 32 Battalion, as reported by Chief SA Army to Chief SADF

In addition to the figures given in the table, a GAZ truckload of 458 AK-47 rifles was captured. I can confirm this because I oversaw their offloading at the Omauni base store shortly before they, the B10 recoilless guns, the one SA-7 surface-to-air missile and the vehicles were collected by the 32 Battalion staff sergeant, Mike Rodgers, and CSI Francisco, and taken to the CSI base in Rundu on 3 June 1980.

Moreira said that in Cuangar they had personnel and cargo trucks, which they used to evacuate the base. A number of these vehicles would therefore have been present in Savate. Assuming the brigade was fully equipped, the balance of 15 trucks that were not captured or destroyed might have been at Mpupa on the day of the attack, as no vehicles escaped past the Recce Wing stopper-group positions.

Why more weapons than the generic brigade allocation (see, for example, the 122-millimetre Grad-P, the 82-millimetre B10 and the 82-millimetre mortar) were captured or destroyed remains unexplained. There could have been reserve weapons kept in stores, or maybe more reinforcements from Caiundo had been deployed earlier in the towns along the Okavango River. Instead of TMM bridging equipment, there were two GSP amphibious pontoons. The presence of the pontoons, together with landmines found in the storerooms, indicates that an engineer platoon was on the base. And photographs of vehicles taken in Savate point to the presence also of a reconnaissance company, an inference confirmed by Daniel Jorge Ernesto in an interview in September 2013. From eyewitness accounts and from the list of destroyed or captured weapons, one can confidently judge that a total brigade support-weapon grouping was present at Savate.

G3 rifles (leftovers of the Portuguese Army when they left Angola in 1974/5) were also found at the base, indicating the possible presence of armed Organização de Defesa Popular (People's Defence Organisation; ODP) militia. The ODP had been formed in September 1975 as an adjunct to FAPLA, to defend towns against Portuguese-settler resistance and anti-MPLA insurgents. After the civil war, it kept its territorial-defence and counter-guerrilla supporting roles, and was placed at almost every FAPLA-controlled town as a reserve force.

Taking into account all the mentioned facts, as well as possible losses during attacks, understaffing and other inevitable personnel issues, such as those on leave, those absent without leave and those hospitalised at the time, I believe the CSI figure of 1 050 enemy soldiers in and around Savate on 21 May 1980 is accurate.

Those who planned Operation Tiro-Tiro did so using information from the 24 April 1980 aerial reconnaissance and the UNITA intelligence report, and failed to update their plan to take into account any subsequent UNITA and enemy actions that occurred between 24 April and 21 May.

Death trap

The town of Savate was not a brigade defence position, but a base area from where forces could be deployed to occupy border towns with the aim of conducting counter-FALA patrols. This is evinced by the differences in layout between the Savate base and, for example, FAPLA's 11 Brigade defence of Cuvelai during Operation Askari in 1983. Before 1980, there was no need to defend Savate because the FALA guerrilla threat was relatively low.

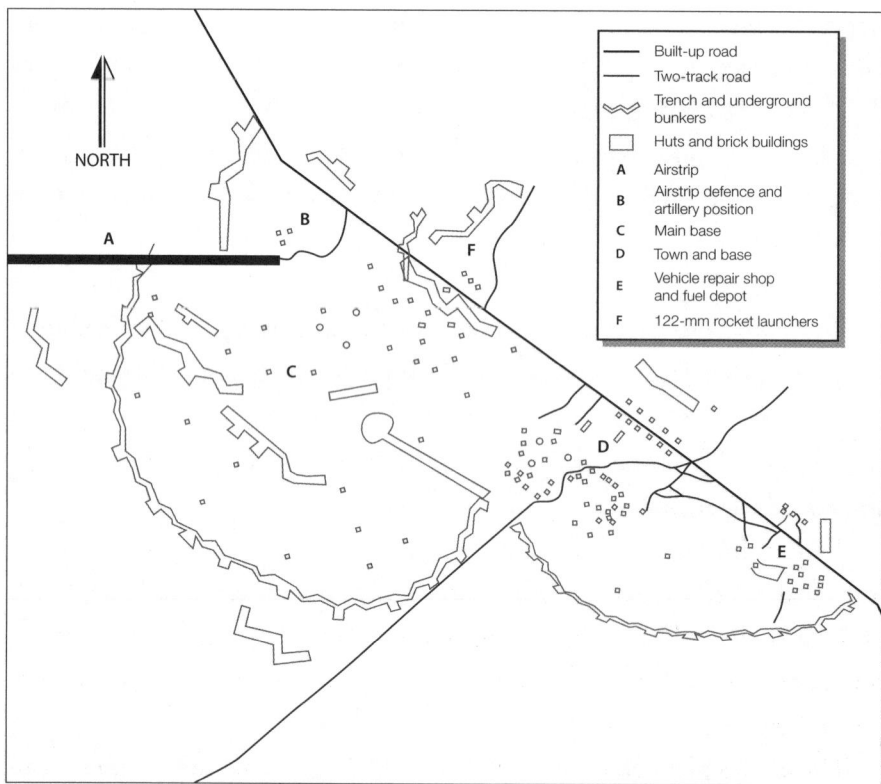

Savate trenches and defence positions

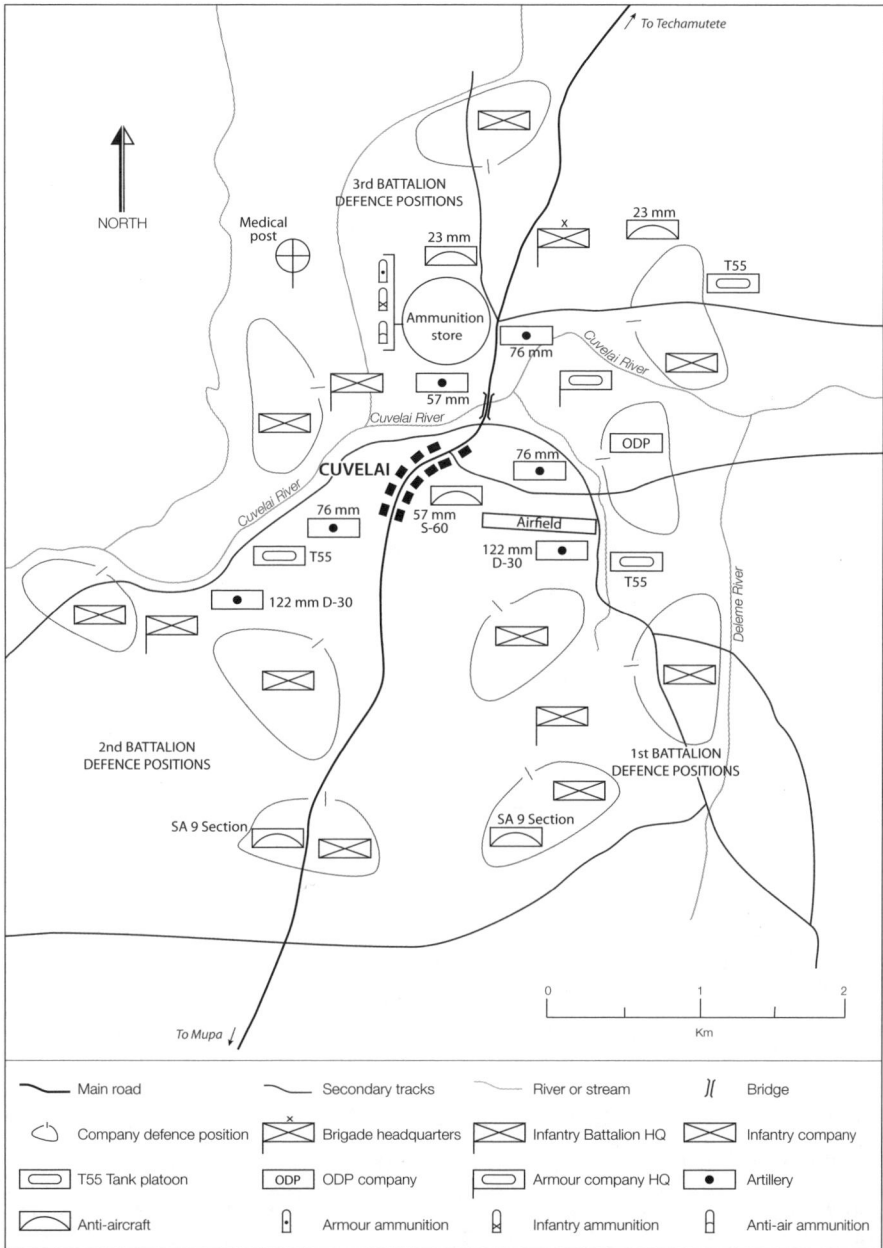

NORTH

To Techamutete

3rd BATTALION
DEFENCE POSITIONS

Medical
post

23 mm

23 mm

x

T55

Ammunition
store

76 mm

Cuvelai River

T55

57 mm

Cuvelai River

ODP

CUVELAI

76 mm

Cuvelai River

76 mm

57 mm
S-60

Airfield

Delerne River

T55

122 mm
D-30

122 mm
D-30

T55

122 mm D-30

2nd BATTALION
DEFENCE POSITIONS

1st BATTALION
DEFENCE POSITIONS

SA 9 Section

SA 9 Section

0   1   2
Km

To Mupa

Main road	Secondary tracks	River or stream	Bridge
Company defence position	Brigade headquarters	Infantry Battalion HQ	Infantry company
T55 Tank platoon	ODP company	Armour company HQ	Artillery
Anti-aircraft	Armour ammunition	Infantry ammunition	Anti-air ammunition

11 Brigade at Cuvelai, showing battalion base and defence areas

During a veterans' visit to Savate in 2012, Leon Grobler and his companions were shown around by a former FAPLA officer. Afterwards, Grobler said:

> He took us to the airstrip, pointing out trenches and gun placements. There were lots of them. I then understood why Sam [Heap] decided to pull the two Charlie platoons back. It was plain suicide and obviously the correct decision at that point in time. What amazed me was the number of trenches north of the runway. We missed the bulk of the base in 1980.

Their guide, however, did not explain to the tour group that what he showed them were actually the FAPLA defence positions after the October 1980 offensive. They were therefore not part of the original May 1980 base.

The layout of the base in May 1980 had a direct influence on the number of enemy casualties on the day. It is clear that the base was designed to house only the brigade headquarters and protection elements, and not the full brigade. The Savate base was overcrowded on the day of the attack: around 1 000 men were present, some of whom had temporary shelter and no allocated trenches or underground bunkers. According to Moreira, he was 'sleeping behind the holes [sleeping bunkers] in a grass house and not in the big holes'. It would seem that when the defenders of Dirico, Calai and Cuangar arrived at Savate, no underground bunkers were available. Instead, small grass shelters had been built all over the base to accommodate the temporary influx of soldiers, who were expected to return to their captured bases sooner rather than later. When the bombardment started, they took to the trenches and bunkers for protection. The 32 Battalion mortar bombardments concentrated on the trench system, in the knowledge that the enemy would take cover there. Imagine the effect of an 81-millimetre HE mortar bomb exploding inside an overcrowded trench or gun position. If a mortar bomb, or even a hand grenade, explodes in a trench or gun position, the chances that everyone inside will be killed, or at least severely wounded, are high. The 32 Battalion platoons fired many mortar rounds into the Savate base and threw countless hand grenades into the trenches. Whereas during Operation Super, the enemy scattered the moment the gunships opened fire, as there were no trench and gun positions to retreat to, in Savate the enemy was concentrated inside the trench system, making it easier for the attackers to take aim and fire on them.

The attack was planned around the belief, based on aerial-photograph interpretation, that the Savate base had a single trench system, and not the typical Soviet system consisting of two lines of trenches: once you cannot defend your position from the main trenches (the first line), you fall back to the second line of trenches.

The year 2013 was an exceptionally dry one in Angola, which meant there was not much foliage. For the first time, satellite images of the Savate area revealed the May 1980 base layout. A typical Soviet trench system is clearly visible, proving that the attack planners were working under an incorrect assumption. Most of the mortar bombs would have fallen inside the base, missing the outer line of trenches. The 32 Battalion mortar section, however unwittingly, probably killed or wounded most of the enemy in the inner line of trenches, where most of the non-resident soldiers would have taken shelter.

Until the publication of *The Terrible Ones* in October 2012, few people were aware that the attack force had a helicopter gunship at Savate and that it actually took part in the battle. The gunship engaged many of the escaping vehicles approaching the cut-off positions. The Recce Wing men would report vehicles packed with enemy and those with infantry protection walking beside them, and the gunship would open fire. Chances are good that should a gunship fire a salvo of 20-millimetre cannon rounds into the back of a truck packed with people, most, if not all, would be killed. Second Lieutenant Steph Naude, a recce group member, recalled seeing a bus filled with passengers being shot out in this manner by the gunship.

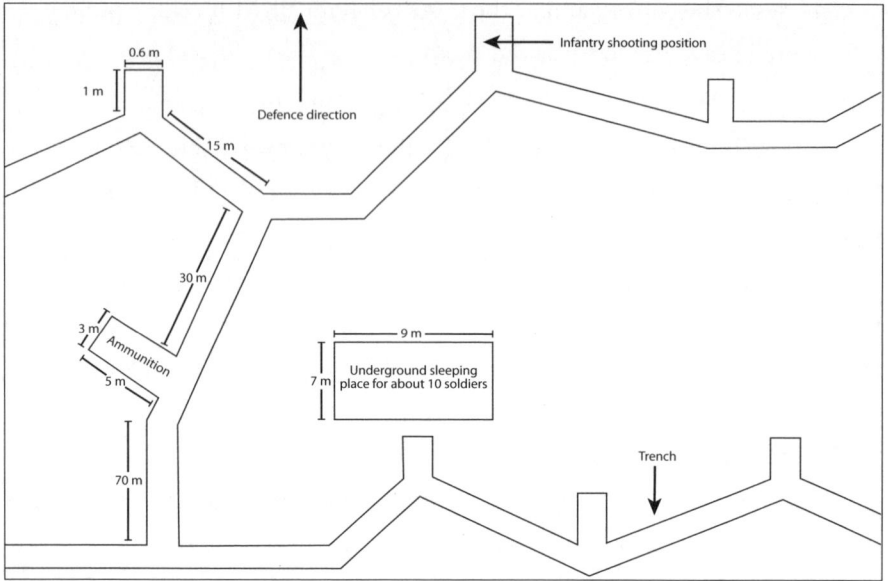

Typical Soviet trench design, as used by FAPLA in the Savate base

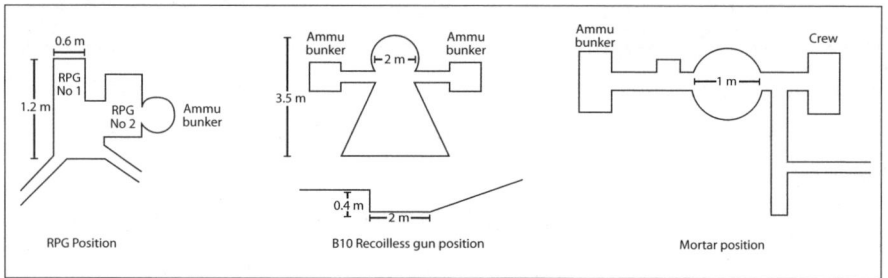

Typical Soviet support-weapon positions, as in the Savate base

And the gunship was not the only threat to the retreating enemy. Corporal Rick Lobb remembers:

We very cautiously advanced closer to where the vehicles were driving and at the same time Gavin and I quickly assembled and armed our M72 LAW [light anti-tank weapon] disposable rocket launchers. On the count of three, we activated the rockets straight towards the nearest vehicles in the convoy and at the same time our PKM machine gunner initiated heavy fire towards the enemy.

The effect of an anti-tank rocket hitting a troop-carrying vehicle at the same time as a machine gunner sprayed the vehicle with bullets is not hard to imagine.

It is misguided to compare the results of Tiro-Tiro with those of other operations like Super. Operation Super had an attack force of 45 men facing a scattered enemy. At Savate, there were almost 250 men firing at a concentrated enemy contained in trenches. This involves a massive amount of firepower in comparison to that of 45 men.

So just how many enemy soldiers were killed at the Savate base on 21 May? Forty-one dead were counted on the objective south of the air-strip alone, killed presumably at the hands of Foxtrot Company, because they had an 'easy' target, according to Jim Ross, and would have had time to properly sweep and clean the objective while Alpha Company took on the bulk of the enemy. The FAPLA commander's comment that 'the worst was that we had many losses', leads me to believe that the figure of 558 enemy dead, wounded or missing, as reported by CSI, is the most realistic.

Surprise or not?

There is no question that the defenders of Savate were expecting some action. However, they did not know it would come from 32 Battalion. According to Rufino, he only became aware of his attackers' identity some days later, when he arrived at Caiundo.

Until he was interviewed in September 2013, Daniel Jorge Ernesto, a sergeant in what he called the specialist company (after more explanation, it was determined that it was the reconnaissance company), was still under the impression that it was a UNITA attack. He remembers:

There was a control point between the wood [referring to the thick bush west of the base] and the camp. We heard an aeroplane flying behind the woods but it went away. Later that day, the people at the control reported cars behind the wood. Sorry, we had a control point on the road going to the woods. The lieutenant sent me and some men to the control to help. When the noise stopped, I reported it to the lieutenant. Later, he said I must send people to go and see where the noise had stopped. Five people went in a truck, but had an accident when the bandits shot at them. We, all in a hurry, went back to the base. We then started to prepare the base for an attack.

Ernesto cannot remember the second truck that Heap found in the bush and is unsure if anybody from the shot-out truck survived and returned to the base. He does remember that, as part of the preparation, at least one company was sent by vehicle south of the base to take up an ambush position there.

The men at Savate defended their base only because they believed it was a UNITA attack. If they had known it was 32 Battalion, they probably would have fled much earlier and suffered far fewer casualties.

Missing Voices

While much of the confusion over numbers of casualties and battle manoeuvres can be attributed to human error, the passage of time and poor memory, some of it has more sinister origins. After the South African Special Forces, which is still in existence, 32 Battalion is the most talked-about unit of the former SADF. It is common knowledge that, due to the unit's later deployment in the townships in the early 1990s, there are individuals with their own political agendas seeking to discredit and criminalise 32 Battalion. The Portuguese Angolans were branded mercenaries by the African National Congress (ANC), who wanted them out of the townships and the country, and they were accused, among other things, of brutality and of being biased towards the Inkatha Freedom Party. Even today there are those who believe 32 Battalion committed atrocities in South Africa and are trying to prove their allegations. It is particularly distressing when some of these individuals come from within the battalion's own ranks.

Between July 2004 and June 2008, the History Papers Archive at the University of the Witwatersrand undertook a project called *Missing Voices: The Untold Stories of Apartheid's War.* In her article 'Missing voices: Border War memories, meanings and archival musings', Michele Pickover, curator of manuscripts and archives at the university's William Cullen Library, gives the aim of the project as follows:

> *Missing Voices* chose to engage with the messy apartheid past and its memory traces through oral interviews precisely because it is a powerful tool for discovering, exploring and evaluating ... how people make sense of their past, how they connect individual experience and its social context and how the past becomes part of the present, and how people use it to interpret their lives and the world around them.

The university contracted freelance employees to collect the personal experiences, perceptions and stories of former members of the ANC Self Defence Unit (SDU) from Thokoza and Katlehong on the East Rand of Gauteng, and former members of the SADF, including Permanent Force members and conscripts.

Angela McIntyre's involvement in the project focused predominantly on former members of 32 Battalion, particularly the Angolans. She also interviewed members of Koevoet, the police counter-insurgency unit, and veterans of 31 Battalion (later renamed 201 Battalion). She produced in the region of 120 interviews, of which 42 are with former 32 Battalion men. Pickover writes:

The military units chosen for *Missing Voices* were concealed in secrecy during the time of the apartheid regime and beyond. The little information available to the South African public on 32 Battalion, 31 Battalion and Koevoet and their role in the 'Border War' has cloaked their activities in mystique. The controversial nature of the South African Defence Force's 32 Battalion made this research project particularly fraught. From the beginning, many colleagues doubted that *Missing Voices* would be able to obtain any meaningful information from a group of people that constituted the sharp end of South Africa's apartheid-era foreign policy stick in Southern Africa in the 1970s and 1980s.

There are a few recollections of the Battle of Savate, but most are vague and allude simply to the battle's difficulty. However, one interview in particular caught my attention – not because of the recollection of the battle itself, but rather the lies it contains. There is a distinct difference in viewpoint between the former white leader group and this specific Angolan interviewee. While the leader group praises the courage of the Angolan 32 Battalion troops and regards the Battle of Savate as a major victory, this soldier claims that the intelligence supporting the attack was a lie.

Why do I include this particular interview here? The *Missing Voices* project is available to the public and while use of the ANC SDU interviews in the collection is restricted, there are no such restrictions on the usage of the 32 Battalion interviews. This interview provides exactly the kind of ammunition the 32 Battalion naysayers are looking for.

The interview was with Joaquim Manuel, at Pomfret in March 2005.

MCINTYRE: Can you tell me your name, first of all?

MANUEL: My name is Joaquim Majita Manuel. I am Angolan, from Malange Province, Massango District. In 1974, I quit studying and left for Zaire, where I undertook terrorist training. Before becoming a terrorist, I was in the Portuguese regular forces. I am 53 already. I am a father of six children, as my wife said.

[Manuel relates how he ended up in 32 Battalion.]

MCINTYRE: But can we talk about Savate? What happened there? I have heard that there were some intelligence problems, and I have been told that the Generals, the South Africans, were very close to Savimbi, and it was Savimbi who asked to go to attack Savate, and that there were – what did they say, that you met several battalions of FAPLA, when the intelligence services reported that there was a garrison with a few hundred? And you arrived with three platoons and met two brigades, and ended up losing 16 members of 32 Battalion, and the enemy lost 500–600?

MANUEL: At the time, the leader of the battalion was Col Deon Ferreira.

MCINTYRE: The Falcon.

MANUEL: Yes, and the reconnaissance men – my late brother was one of the reconnaissance men, the man with the most courage. They had divided the intelligence zones – he brought – what he brought, Major Ratte brought, was false information, as you heard. They lied that there were 200 soldiers, when there were six battalions. That is what happened. What happened was this: Savimbi was trying to get Savate. He attacked it twice and did not succeed. There were prisoners, a lot of them, in Luanda. There was a competition between the big men, the Para Battalion, 1 Recce, 2 Recce and 5 Recce, said that they were the best at defending the interests on the South West border. And Ferreira said, 'I am the one who is protecting the border best,' and there were also the integrated Namibian forces ...

MCINTYRE: The South West African Territorial Force?

MANUEL: Yes, the Territorial Forces. They also said they were the best. There was a competition, and we were divided. The Recces, one to five, went to attack Ondjiva and the SWATF went to attack Menongue, and the Koevoet attacked Mulembe [Mulemba], and we were chosen to go to Savate, the one we would win. There would be a prize, but we did not know what kind of prize.

MCINTYRE: Like a game?

MANUEL: Yes.

MCINTYRE: And so you lost 16 brothers in a game.

MANUEL: Colonel Ferreira, who passed away, said at [the] time, 'I believe 32 Battalion will not need any heavy weapons,' and so we went with 60-millimetre and 81-millimetre mortars.

MCINTYRE: And no air support – why was there no air support or heavy weapons? I have had trouble understanding this.

MANUEL: They don't want to tell you.

MCINTYRE: Did they tell you this was a covert operation? South Africa could not be seen doing this operation?

MANUEL: No, no, Angela, Ferreira said we did not need it. As you know, Angela, a combat operation costs money, it costs money – medicine, transportation, fuel, drinking water, insurance for the soldiers, all of it counts. But Ferreira said, 'I will do this battle. I will only take transport, fuel and material for light weapons, and I will show you how 32 fights, that they are better than the Special Forces.' It was like this Angela, no one should tell you otherwise. By then Carpenter, Samanjimbu, [Colonel Jan Breytenbach] was in Kwando, helping UNITA. There at Jamba where there was a Battalion, I don't know if you have heard this, he was there, leading that force in the Caprivi, near the border with Zambia. We brought four 81-millimetre mortars and 60-millimetre mortars, and our light weapons, R4s and R5s that we had liberated. They did not tell us there were six brigades, or we would have been afraid. They said there were only 200 enemy, and we went with that idea of 200, and the way we could fight, we said 'Let's go!' And we went. Charlie Company. Alpha Company, Foxtrot Company went; Echo went to cover the mortars. And the forces of my deceased brother were the stopper group, where the enemy would retreat, on the north side, near Mavinga, and we went, we left at 15:00 and travelled the whole night, when we were about 20 kilometres away, we had to hide the cars and go on foot. Angela, that is where I felt, a human being feels, smells the raw blood ... the weight – the packs we carried were normally 130 kilograms and were now 160 kilograms. You have a pack on your back and a kibuto on your head – they were mortar bombs that we had to take. When 05:00 arrived, we rested and planned and waited for the mortars – the Recces would give us the coordinates. Angela. We began the war at 10:15, and it stopped at 19:00.

MCINTYRE: Were the enemy warned in advance? Didn't the Recces meet them on their way? Weren't some of them killed and others got away, and warned them about your mission?

MANUEL: No, Angela, those people are not telling you the truth. I was there, on that operation. Where we left our vehicles, when we went on foot, was where we met the enemy forces. They were hunting – killing animals to eat – and we met them. And we shot at them, but they fled and no one was killed. It was at night and they returned to their camp on foot. But they did not know it was 32 Battalion forces with South Africa; they thought we were UNITA forces.

MCINTYRE: Were you wearing UNITA uniforms?

MANUEL: No, we were wearing South African uniforms. Don't let them tell you otherwise; we were wearing South African uniforms.

MCINTYRE: But some people told me that you were wearing UNITA uniforms there.

MANUEL: No, they are liars. They don't want to tell you the real story; they are liars! We were there with our brown uniforms, and Angela, when we returned we got the Sjambok, beating, what happened to us – when we left Omauni, near Rundu, where we departed from, where Ovamboland meets the Kuvango, where we entered, we earned 300 Rand per months. If you returned, you were paid 800 Rand; if you died, it was your coffin. That was a part of the politics – that we used our uniforms.

Before we left there, there was an accident at my house and every-thing burned. If not, Angela, I would show you. And when we returned, after we did that clean-up, the one who was leading – that was the late Col Ferreira. He was very strategic in that war, Angela.

MCINTYRE: But he was a bit of a joker – you did that operation as a game.

MANUEL: Yes, it was a game, really. There we lost a captain who was to be promoted to major, and a lieutenant who was to become a captain – he was just married, and he was killed. He was burned. Ferreira gave us a promise: the one who got the communications person of the MPLA, with the radio, alive, that man would get something. And we were all with that captain, and he died trying to get the communications man from the MPLA, to bring him to Col Ferreira so he could rise up. And he did not succeed. He was just a man, Angela … they got him, our captain; he burned. That was a fire, Angela!

The language was a problem, Angela. Don't let them tell you that we dressed in UNITA uniforms. We dressed in the uniforms of the Angolan Government, of the MPLA, their own camouflage. We were mixed up with their forces…

MCINTYRE: You wore the same uniforms as the enemy?

MANUEL: Yes, we copied them, to confuse the enemy. Don't let anyone tell you otherwise, Angela. Where the enemy was, they were calling us, 'Comrade, comrade, how are you comrade, I am over here!' The prob-lem was that they used a sign in their army, and we did not know it, you see, so they would know who was the enemy, if the uniform was the same. The language was the same; some were speaking my dialect. I answered, you see …

MCINTYRE: But how could you fight against your own people, who spoke your own language?

MANUEL: They were communists; we were democratic.

MCINTYRE: But these ideas of communism and capitalism are the ideas of outsiders, from other countries. How did you think about these terms?

MANUEL: You used the language, Angela. These things, as I said before,

Angela, there are some things, we can't endanger our old leaders, our ex-leaders ... many things happened, and we can't bring them out.

MCINTYRE: How did you feel after Savate?

MANUEL: After Savate, I am telling you here, Angela, I had those papers and those photos of my nephew; I changed my ideas. It took me an hour or so before I could get my ideas together, and I said, 'No, I am a soldier.'

MCINTYRE: You were in shock?

MANUEL: Yes, I got that feeling that I had lost family. If I go back tomorrow, who will I tell? That is why we are here. They brought us here; they abandoned us, they knocked on our doors, and when they rose to higher positions, they abandoned us, and this is why, Angela, you must do what is possible. We have nothing to pay you, to save us. We are on an island ... we are like slaves.

In light of my research and countless other eyewitness accounts, as related in this book, Manuel's account is worthless and full of blatant lies. But, unfortunately, the uninformed will take interviews such as this as truth.

9

Savate Day

After Founder's Day (27 March), Savate Day (21 May) is the only remembrance day still marked by 32 Battalion. The first annual Savate Day service was held in 1981 at Buffalo. On 25 May 1985, the Tree of Honour – a stump cut from a leadwood tree in the Buffalo base's training area and on which appeared the names of those battalion members who had died – was officially declared 32 Battalion's memorial of the dead at a special parade held at Buffalo (the tree had been moved from its original position, where it had stood since 1983). For as long as the unit existed, the Tree of Honour served as the pivot for all memorial services. And so, from 1985 the annual Savate Day service and parade took place wherever the Tree of Honour was situated: at Buffalo until the unit was moved to the Pomfret military base in 1989; at Pomfret until the unit was disbanded in 1993; and once at 2 SAI Zeerust, on the 32nd anniversary of the unit's founding. In October 2009 the Tree of Honour was moved to its final resting place at the Voortrekker Monument heritage site in Pretoria to form part of the SADF Wall of Remembrance, which was inaugurated on 25 October 2009. The following year's Savate Day service was held at this new location for the first time.

The 32 Association, which started as an informal reunion of sorts before being formalised, held unofficial Savate Day memorial services in and around Pretoria. After 32 Battalion's disbandment, the association continued to hold an annual service until the organisation, too, was dissolved. The newly established 32 Battalion Veterans' Association held its first formal Savate Day service in Pretoria in 2004. The 'Ride to Agadir' (a funeral dirge requested by Lieutenant Charl Muller before his death, see Chapter 10) was played at the end of the service for the first time, establishing a new tradition that would extend to all future Savate Day memorial services. Thereafter, the organisation's various regional branches took turns to host the official annual Savate Day service on the Sunday closest to 21 May.

In 2006, a former 32 Battalion member residing in Belgium, Jean Louis Maximillian Winand (known as 'Frenchie'), visited the Delville Wood South African National Memorial in France where, in his private capacity, he laid a wreath in memory of the fallen at Savate. His action eventually sparked the idea for a Savate Day service in Europe, to be held annually at Delville Wood. Political red tape among other things, however, resulted in Europe's Savate Day being shifted to an alternative venue. A few former 32 Battalion men residing in Europe still attend this service annually. Kim Zocher, now living in Germany, explains how it all came about:

> In 2008, I got involved after meeting up with Frenchie in Luxembourg. We then organised to meet up at Delville Wood and lay a wreath and hold a small medal parade as we had received Frenchie and George's [George Coetzee, residing in the Netherlands] medals from South Africa.
>
> I decided to do everything correctly and seek permission to lay a wreath at Delville Wood. I then wrote to the curator, seeking permission and explaining Savate Day, our regiment 32 Battalion and who I was, only to be turned down as this memorial is only in memory of WW1 and WW2 and has nothing to do with the South African 'Border War'. I accepted that and then wrote seeking permission to lay a wreath 'in memory of all South African soldiers killed in all wars' and permission was granted.
>
> We had a wonderful weekend, all meeting up for the first time.

Frenchie, George and myself were also joined by Jose de Sacadura (an ex-Rhodesian intelligence guy), and then we were surprised by a guy who stood watching our small service from a distance, dressed in bike leathers. After our small memorial service which included the last post and 'Ride to Agadir', he walked up and introduced himself as Charles Evans [living in the UK]. The next day, we revisited the Delville Wood Memorial, the Museum and the surrounding area.

The visit to one of the most beautiful SA War Museums unfortunately left us with a bad taste in our mouths. First, let me say again what a stunning museum in the shape of the Cape Town Castle with the history told in the most beautiful murals telling the history. The centre court is all blocked off by full wall glass panels with engraving/sandblasting on them and a cross in the centre of the court.

It is worth a visit, but please do not let the last exhibit as you are about to leave the museum upset you as it did me. 'The History of the African National Congress (ANC) and their struggle' is displayed on the wall on a few panels. I have no problem with it, but I hate double standards and if I was told that we could not lay a wreath for our Brothers in Arms (which we did indirectly) as this monument was only for WW1 and WW2 and nothing to do with the 'Border War', then please tell me what the hell the ANC had to do with either World Wars?

This then got us so upset that we started looking for an alternative venue to lay our wreath on Savate Day in memory of our Brothers who lost their lives from 32 Battalion. And that is how the town of Ypres came to light. As I told Frenchie, I had heard there is a town in Belgium where there are many South African graves. Then, on his research for this town with the South African graves, he found Ypres and we decided to try it out and the rest is history, as we now meet there for Savate and for the last 2 years on Remembrance Day on 11 November each year as well.

Because of their combat experience, many former 32 Battalion members later served in other conflict areas. So, informal Savate Day gatherings have been held in Iraq and, in 2005, Johannes 'Groenie' Groenewaldt initiated the first informal Savate Day gathering in Kabul, Afghanistan. It was formalised in 2006 and attended by former 32 Battalion men as well as a large contingent of expatriates. Over time it grew in numbers and was even attended by individuals from allied military forces deployed in Afghanistan. In 2011, the former chief of the SADF, General Jannie Geldenhuys, was the guest speaker. Unfortunately, when Groenewaldt and most of his former comrades left Afghanistan, the services stopped.

As time progressed, changes were made to the Savate Day service. In 2005, 'Savate' was done away with, making it an annual Remembrance Day for all those who died while serving in the unit, despite the fact that 11 November exists precisely to remember all fallen soldiers and that an annual remembrance service is held within two weeks of Savate Day at the Wall of Remembrance at the Voortrekker Monument, a more appropriate occasion to remember the rest of 32 Battalion's fallen. The chairman of the 32 Battalion Veterans' Association, Stefanus van der Walt, recalls his feelings on the matter:

> During an Annual General Meeting of the 32 Battalion Veterans' Association in 2005, the use of the name Savate Day was debated, as certain members thought that it one-sidedly stressed only the losses at Savate while neglecting the others. As chairman, I took a strong position in favour of keeping the name due to its symbolic meaning, based on two elements. The first was the fact that the unit had suffered its greatest loss in a single battle at Savate, and the other was its example of the unit's characteristic 'vasbyt' and determination against unexpected resistance, and in spite of its own heavy losses.

The change was made regardless.

Then, in 2011, instead of 'Remembrance Day', the official programme called the occasion 'Skouer Skuur', the Afrikaans term for an informal get together (translated as 'rubbing shoulders'). This was done in error, however, and was rectified the following year.

'Ride to Agadir' was a song about Moroccan Arabs fighting ('for Mohamed and Morocco') the French colonial power ('the infidels of France'), and at a 32 Battalion Veterans' Association meeting complaints were voiced against the nature of the lyrics and its links to Islam, which led to a resolution that only the music, without the words, would be used in future. Van der Walt was instrumental in resolving this issue. He explains:

> In order to create an instrumental version without the lyrics, I asked my wife, Corlea, who is well qualified in music, to transcribe the song for us. After listening to it several times, she was able to write it down in note form. We then had to record it from scratch, and for this went to a friend who had his own recording studio. From the sheet music, the two of them were able to orchestrate and then, with me as attentive listener in the back ground, record the instrumental version of the song. This version was then used at several Savate Day commemorations.
>
> But I felt that the song had definitely lost some of its impact, and started toying with the idea of writing new words for it that could really resonate with the character of 32 Battalion – a song that eventually could also be sung by members.

'Ride to Agadir' remained a contentious issue until the 2011 Savate Day held in Port Elizabeth, when Van der Walt went to work on writing new lyrics. He explains how 'Proelio Procusi', which replaced 'Ride to Agadir' from 2012, came about:

> In 2011, during the Savate Day held at Port Elizabeth, Reverend Ernst Endres also asked me why we couldn't write our own words for the

song, and recommended someone in his parish who could help with it, as well as a group of vocalists who could then sing the new words for a recording. But it transpired that this person was a young musician without military background, who would have to get his knowledge of 32 Battalion from books. This caused me to reconsider the matter. So I listened to the gripping music again, and was soon left convinced that this song was too special and too personal to leave to an outsider. I had to do it myself.

On our farm near Brits, we have a mountain which I used to cross three times a week with the dogs. These solitary moments in the mountain now became filled with the music of *Agadir* that kept turning through my head. Especially the second verse of my wife's rendering, where the dramatic bass enters the music, aroused feelings that just had to be expressed in words. I started putting the words on paper, and in my mind sang them every time I went up the mountain. While climbing, I would shuffle and test new angles and words that grew primarily out of my personal experience with 32 Battalion, and write them down when I reached home. Then I would let it lie to ripen and after some time look at it again.

I considered writing a verse in Portuguese, but realised that many people would not understand it, so only a few well-known expressions were incorporated. There also was a third English verse, but in recognition of the fact that Afrikaans, in effect, was the principal language of the unit, I decided to write an Afrikaans one in its place, and eventually had it all on paper. I was contented that in the result we had something of enduring value, reflecting something of 32 Battalion's true essence. I then put it before the VA [Veterans' Association] committee for their opinion, and did this by playing the music while reading the words aloud. They endorsed it and gave the go-ahead for the recording, which I then intended to be ready for the 2012 Savate Day commemorations, which were fast approaching.

Now we had everything needed for Ernst's singers to work on, music and lyrics. But the question of copyrights still had to be addressed, and Marius Scheepers volunteered to handle it. He explained our request to [the songwriter] Mike Batt's agent, as well as the relevant authorities in South Africa, but when there was no response from either of them, it was decided to simply continue with the project.

I very much wanted to be present when they did the recording, as I knew exactly what I wanted and had to make sure the true spirit of the song was captured. But work dictated that I was away at Steelpoort at the time, and I had to manage the recording by email 'remote control'. I was really surprised with the first results. The music was well adapted for voices; the singers were really good, and every word was clearly pronounced. After a few adjustments regarding the instrumentation and, of course, also a few voice notes clarifying the Portuguese pronunciation, it was ready for the final editing. Timewise, things were cut very fine as the departure date for the Angolan expedition was very close. In the end, there wasn't even time for me to pick up a compact disc with the song, but when we departed on the tour, it was with the first MP3 version of our new song freshly received on my BlackBerry.

On our way in the Overlander, I circulated the phone with the recorded song as a trial, and only got positive feedback. On our return, it was also ratified by the AGM, and the next day officially played for the first time at the special 32 year Savate Day Commemoration at the Tree of Honour on 26 May 2012.

32 Battalion Proelio Procusi

I

Savate, Op Super,
In Angola they would dare,
With the blooded sand as witness
Killed the lion in its lair.

Marching on into contact,
Or to battle at first light,
They have faced the brink of darkness
Breathed the cordite in the fight.
Friends have crossed the brink of darkness
And their souls have taken flight.

II

Yes, Proelio Procusi,
In the flame that forged us all,
In the battles of the Bush War
Some were scorched and some would fall.
In our memories of comrades
They will tower straight and tall,
We salute our *camaradas*
True in death to Three-two's call.
We salute our *camaradas*
True in death to Three-two's call.

III

Oor die helder Kavango,
In die lug bo Buffalo,
Rys die beeld van 'n buffel
Trots en aan sy trop getrou.
Dan verskyn nog getalle,
Staan daar bonkig sy aan sy,
Straal die gees van egte vegters,
Kon Ate o Fim dit bly.
Pryk nou met hul kamerade
Op die kamoefleer beret.
Pryk steeds met hul kamerade
Op die kamoefleer beret.

(Stefanus van der Walt, 2011)

188

In 2012, the 32nd commemoration of the Battle of Savate was held at the Tree of Honour in Pretoria. At that year's 32 Battalion Veterans' Association annual general meeting, it was decided that all future official annual commemoration services would be held at the Tree of Honour, but that the regional representatives could also hold services in their regions.

While it is still called Remembrance Day, for most of us former 32 Battalion men who took part in the battle, it will always be Savate Day.

10

Let us remember

Sunday 23 May 2010 was the first time the Savate Day service was held at the Voortrekker Monument near Pretoria, the final resting place of the Tree of Honour. Colonel (retired) Stefanus van der Walt, chairman of the 32 Battalion Veterans' Association, delivered an address that brought tears to the eyes of many hardened former and serving soldiers. He said:

Right at the beginning of our proceedings on this bright new Sunday morning, I wish to reaffirm our view that not only this one, but every Sunday is special, if we keep in mind that it was on a Sunday that our Saviour arose from the grave. However, on this Sunday, we are here also with the purpose of commemorating our fallen comrades.

As an introduction to our main event, I would like to present to you a short review from our mutual past. Although it is, of course, in time and place bound to a certain period in the bush war, I am sure that every veteran here will be able to recognise elements which he can really identify with.

Do you remember the broad, flowing water of the Kuvango River as it turned south past Buffalo, towards the training area? And Botswana, with the tall, cool trees on its sandy banks with the variety of buildings scattered underneath? The messes, stores, troop lines and the Kimbo near the graveyard that for many made our home away from home?

Can you, in your mind's eye, see the platoons marching through the early morning freshness to morning parade? Do you hear their vibrant singing? Do you feel their pulsating energy?

Can you still feel the sudden entry of quiet excitement and methodical preparation when a new operation was in the air?

Can you ever forget the long drive on an open Kwêvoël, sitting in the glaring sun while the swirling white dust settled over everything, or the perpetual clinging to a swaying, bundu-bashing Buffel, while sticks and leaves and all sorts of fauna showered down your neck?

Do you remember how, initially, three days' rat packs were actually enough for the first five days in the bush, and you could afford to discard stuff like dog biscuits and mixed veg? Do you remember filling your water bottles with welcome rain water caught from your bivvie, or in chana-marshes smelling of cow dung?

Can you still smell the sweet, oily vapour of avtur, and hear the high-pitched whining of an Alouette, slowly swinging its sweeping rotor blades into action, the black muzzle of the 20-mil cannon thrusting from its side?

Can anyone forget the incredible weight of a mochila freshly packed for days of action, which you had to carry through that loose sand of southern Angola? Can you still feel the close, personal sanctuary of your foxhole in the night, seeing the pensive moon, and the same Southern Cross that was also shining over your loved ones down in the States?

Will you ever forget the sudden eruption of a contact, the tightness in the throat and the intense focus during the firefight, the sharp, somehow muffled reports of rifle and machine-gun fire in the bush, the hollow, sucking thumps from mortar tubes, and the subsequent crash of their bombs exploding in the sand around you? Do you hear 'Avançar!'? And afterwards, the dry, smoky smell of battle, the excited, often sobering, stocktaking of casualties – on both sides?

Can you recall the heart-warming clapping beat of a Puma's rotor blades, as it banks in the air towards the smoke that marked your position, bringing fresh ammo, rats, and life-giving water in plastic bags – or to lift out a casualty; a young friend, a comrade?

Can you still experience that feeling of tired fulfilment that surged through you at the end of a mission, settling yourself on the floor of an overloaded Puma, looking at the black, sweaty faces of the others in their dirty camos, to be lifted out of the ops area to Eenhana, Elundu or wherever, for the first wash in weeks, and that indescribable taste of the first two gulps of cold Castle?

Do you remember the return to Buffalo, weary but contented; smiling and greeting but inwardly reflective, gathering in the mess that evening for robust celebration of life, acutely aware of death?

Do you remember the knocking out of bottoms from the empty tankards of those comrades whose lips would never touch it again, who had forever fallen silent, while outside the setting sun turned the flowing waters of the rushing river the colour of blood?

Do you remember? Do you remember them…?

> Those comrades, still silently waiting for the
> Bright Morning Star
> to herald that grand last Sunday
> that will dispel the black velvet of death
> to reveal the serenely flowing River of Eternal Life?

If this contribution has succeeded in transporting you for a moment back to the realities of that unique time in our history, which you and I have had the privilege to participate in, I thank my Creator also for this privilege.

67280552PE Captain Andre Erasmus
*19 November 1951 †21 May 1980

Andre, the youngest of Warrant Officer Class 1 Jonny Erasmus's three sons, was born in Pretoria. After completing his schooling in Voortrekkerhoogte (now Thaba Tshwane) in 1969, Andre started his compulsory one-year military service in the Signal Corps. He completed the regimental NCO course and was promoted to corporal, finishing his one-year service in June 1972. For the next three years, he worked as a bank clerk. He married Linda Marie Hall on 15 September 1972.

On 12 January 1975, Andre enrolled in the Permanent Force, mustering in the technical and administrative branch of the Personnel Services Corps. After completing his initial training, on 1 October he started Phase 2 training, a six-month officer selection and formative course at the Military Academy in Saldanha Bay. On 27 March 1976 he completed the candidate officer course at Personnel Services School and was promoted to lieutenant. On 29 September he was appointed an officer instructor at Personnel Services School. During 1977, Andre successfully completed Phase 4, young officers training, at Infantry School to qualify for platoon commander level. On 19 December 1977 he was promoted to temporary captain and transferred to the Office of the Chief of the Army, where he became Lieutenant General Constand Viljoen's personal assistant.

Andre applied for a transfer to the Intelligence Corps, which was granted on 22 June 1978. At the end of the year he was transferred to Defence Headquarters, Intelligence Division. In 1979 he participated in Operation Safraan as an intelligence officer and received the Pro Patria medal. On 15 January 1980 he was again transferred, this time to 32 Battalion as intelligence officer.

He was buried with full military honours in the Voortrekkerhoogte cemetery on 27 May 1980. He left behind his wife, their daughters, Tanya (four) and Desiree (three), and a six-month-old son, Mark Andre.

72419369PE Lieutenant Charl de Jongh Muller
*30 June 1956 †21 May 1980

Charl was born in Windhoek, Namibia. After completing his schooling, on 9 January 1974 he reported to the technical and administrative branch of the Personnel Services Corps in Pretoria for his compulsory military service and decided to enrol in the Permanent Force. Still in the Administrative Corps, on 11 February 1974 he started Phase 1, Permanent Force basic training and selection, at Infantry School in Oudtshoorn. On completion of the training on 5 April, he was selected as a potential officer and received a candidate officer rank, the first step in his officer's career.

On 8 April, Charl started Phase 2 at the Military Academy in Saldanha Bay. The day after he completed this training on 29 September, he started Phase 3, a two-year course to qualify for a BMil degree. He graduated on 26 September 1976 with a major in trade and economics. Four days later he was promoted to second lieutenant and was ready to start the final phase of his officer's training.

Charl reported to Infantry School for Phase 4, young officer's training. Not happy with his career choice, in December 1976 he asked for a transfer to the South African Navy, a request that was denied. During career counselling, he indicated that his first choice was the Anti-Air Corps, specifically 10 Anti-Aircraft Unit. Failing that, he could continue in the technical and administrative branch of the Personnel Services Corps but would prefer to be placed in Pretoria. His last choice was the Artillery Corps, specifically Artillery School.

On 13 May 1977, after completing Phase 4, Charl was transferred to 16 Maintenance Unit in Grootfontein, Namibia. During his short stay there, he met Zelda Christine le Roux, who was originally from Otjiwarongo. Up until then, a somewhat rebellious Charl had had a stormy career. His father, Dr D.A. Muller, was a good friend of Gert Nel, the OC of 32 Battalion. Dr Muller decided that serving in a full-time operational unit would soothe his son's rebellious temperament and so he asked Nel to arrange for Charl's transfer to 32 Battalion.

On 10 November 1977, Charl reported to 32 Battalion mustering as platoon commander in Golf Company. His appointment as an officer was confirmed on 1 January 1978 and he was promoted to lieutenant. His service with 32 Battalion was a game-changer; now in an environment that suited his temperament, he excelled and, in December 1978, Nel recommended him for a Chief of the Army Commendation medal.

Charl married Zelda and settled in Rundu. On 15 November 1978, he became the training officer and decided to join the Infantry Corps. His application for a corps transfer was sent to a higher authority on 18 November and approved on 24 January 1979. He continued to excel in the training environment and, on 9 June, Commandant Deon Ferreira, the OC since January, recommended him for another Chief of the Army Commendation medal. On 1 August, during his deployment with Operation Seiljag (15 June to 8 September 1979), Charl was withdrawn and became the adjutant. While fulfilling his duties as adjutant at the Rundu headquarters, he participated in Operation Driehoek (4 to 22 February 1980) as company commander. Three months later he was appointed company commander for Operation Tiro-Tiro, this time with Alpha Company.

Charl was cremated on 23 May 1980. At the request of his parents, his ashes were buried in a traditional full-size grave in the Windhoek cemetery on 25 May 1980. He left behind his 23-year-old wife, Zelda.

Long before the Battle of Savate, Charl had said that if he was killed in the operational area, Mike Batt's 1970s song 'Ride to Agadir' should be played at his military funeral instead of the traditional funeral march. His wish was carried out and from then on the song became part of an informal ritual in the unit's officers' club, where it was played on the occasion of an officer's death. It was eventually adopted formally as the unit's private funeral dirge.

77316404BG Second Lieutenant Timothy Simmons Patrick
*31 August 1961 †21 May 1980

Tim was born in Pietermaritzburg. After matriculating from Michael House in Balgowan, Natal, on 6 January 1979, he reported to 1 South African Infantry Battalion in Bloemfontein for his compulsory two-year national service. He was one of six men from the battalion to pass Intelligence Corps selection and, on 9 February, he became an Intelligence Corps member. A week later, however, Tim was sent to the Infantry School in

Oudtshoorn to start junior leader training. After completing the section leader phase of the training on 2 July, he reported to Army College for a month-long intelligence theory and practical course. While busy with this course, he was promoted to candidate officer.

Tim returned to Infantry School to complete his junior leader training, and was deployed with the school in the Sector 20 operational area between 27 July and 2 October 1979, qualifying him for the Pro Patria medal. He completed his training on 7 December. He and four other Intelligence Corps men on the same course were transferred to 11 Commando in Kimberley. On 20 December 1979, while still a candidate officer, Tim was transferred to 32 Battalion as an intelligence officer. He received his commission to second lieutenant on 7 January 1980.

Tim was laid to rest in a private cremation ceremony in Pietermaritzburg. He left behind his mother, Mrs D. Hindle.

76490556BG Second Lieutenant Johannes Mattheus Heyns Muller
*20 October 1961 †21 May 1980

Johannes, more commonly known as Heyns, was born in Villiers. After finishing school, he reported for his compulsory military service to 3 South African Infantry Battalion on 10 January 1979. On 17 February he began the junior leader course at Infantry School in Oudtshoorn and on 1 July 1979 was promoted to candidate officer. On 31 October he was selected to join 32 Battalion and was made second lieutenant on 15 December.

Johannes was buried with full military honours in the Heroes' Acre of the Villiers cemetery on 23 May 1980. He left behind his parents, Mr and Mrs H.H.M. Muller.

76487503PF Corporal Eduard Coetzee Engelbrecht
*5 August 1960 †21 May 1980

Eduard, known by his friends as 'Engel', was born in Otjiwarongo, Namibia. After finishing school, he reported for his compulsory military service at

3 South African Infantry Battalion on 8 January 1979. On 17 February he began the junior leader course at Infantry School in Oudtshoorn and on 1 July was promoted to lance corporal. During career counselling, he indicated that he would prefer to return to Namibia and so made 32 Battalion his first choice, followed by 41 Battalion in Otjiserandu and 2 South African Infantry Battalion in Walvis Bay.

On 31 October 1979, Eduard was selected to join 32 Battalion and on 15 December he was promoted to corporal. He joined the Short Service System and continued his service as platoon second in command in Foxtrot Company.

Eduard was buried with full military honours in the Otjiwarongo cemetery on 26 May 1980. He left behind his parents, Mr and Mrs P.C. Engelbrecht.

78910528SP Lance Corporal Joao Kaumba
*5 April 1959 †21 May 1980

Joao was from the Thokwe tribe and was born in Kwebe, Angola. He had no formal schooling and worked in a government garage for a year before he joined UNITA in January 1975. He deserted to Namibia in December 1976 and stayed in a refugee camp near Rundu until August 1978. On 1 August 1978, he attested into the South African Army and joined 32 Battalion as a rifleman. His brother, August Francisco, was also a soldier in 32 Battalion. Joao married Rosa Johannes, who stayed with him in Pica Pau.

He was buried on 29 May 1980 in the Pica Pau cemetery, Buffalo base, in grave number 136.

800165230PF Lance Corporal Andrew Jeremy Falcus
*1 November 1959 †21 May 1980

Andy finished his schooling at Ottershaw School in Surrey, England. He went to Rhodesia (present-day Zimbabwe) to join their military and, on

7 January 1979, enrolled in the Rhodesian Light Infantry as a trooper, serving in Sierra Battery Support Commando. Besides the standard infantry courses, Andy also attended a team medic course.

With the Rhodesian war coming to an end, he applied to the SADF and, on 14 March 1980, was enrolled as a lance corporal (with the temporary rank of corporal) under Projek Buurman for one year's service and routed to Pretoria to start his service.

Andy reported for duty with 32 Battalion on 24 April 1980 and, together with 15 other former Rhodesian servicemen, was sent to the training area for orientation training. He was busy with this training when they were withdrawn for Operation Tiro-Tiro.

Because he was a trained medic, Andy was sent by the platoon commander to take some of the wounded to the evacuation post. On the way there he himself was wounded, but he made it to the post, only to die of his wounds later in the helicopter on the way back to Omauni.

Andy's parents were informed of his death by a Church of England minister only on 23 May 1980 and his name did not appear in the media report of 24 May. An SADF document states: 'For security reasons, his name was withheld from the press. South African Army headquarters originally did not plan to couple his name to the external operation in which he was killed because he was not a South African citizen.' After much pressure from his father, David Falcus, and lengthy letters and telephone conversations between the military attaché in London and South African Army headquarters, a newspaper article appeared in *Die Burger* on 5 June 1980, although it incorrectly gave Andy's date of death as 23 May.

Andy was cremated with full military honours on 30 May 1980 in Pretoria, and his remains were sent to his family in the United Kingdom on 3 June. During a private ceremony, he was buried in the St Lawrence Church cemetery in Surrey on 5 June.

76919109SP Rifleman Rodriques Alberto
*3 March 1954 †21 May 1980

Rodriques, nicknamed 'Space Monkey', was from the Umbundu tribe. Born in Silva Porto, Angola, he had no formal schooling. Between September 1969 and December 1972, he worked in Serpa Pinto as a mechanic. In 1973 he joined JPPA Construction in Silva Porto and then the Castille Company. From 1973 to 1974, he stayed at home helping his father before joining the ELNA as a soldier in January 1975. Rodriques had a cousin, Ana Paula, in Pica Pau and a nephew, Jeronimo Jose, at the refugee camp in Rundu. He attested into the South African Army on 12 November 1976 and joined Foxtrot Company. On 18 November 1978 he was transferred to the Recce Wing.

Rodriques was buried on 29 May 1980 in the Pica Pau cemetery, Buffalo base, in grave number 139.

769080292SP Rifleman Benedito Albino
*15 August 1957 †21 May 1980

Benedito was from the Umbundu tribe and was born in Nova Lisboa, Angola. He had no formal schooling and in 1972 started work as a storeman in the shop of Alviera Barro in Caala. He married Fernanda Luzia.

In July 1974, Benedito left his wife in Caala and joined ELNA as a soldier, serving until March 1976. He was one of Kioto's battalion members who was transferred from Pereira d'Eca to the Buffalo base. He officially enrolled in the South African Army on 26 October 1976 and joined 32 Battalion as a rifleman.

Benedito was buried on 29 May 1980 in the Pica Pau cemetery, Buffalo base, in grave number 140.

79830956SP Rifleman Antonio Caliango
*9 August 1949 †21 May 1980

Antonio, from the Kwanyama tribe, was born in Dunyenda, Angola. He had no formal schooling. He joined FALA in 1966 and served until 1972, when he broke his leg and was discharged. He then went to Namibia and worked for Christina's Construction Company in Grootfontein until 1976. Then he went to South Africa to work at a West Rand mine as a miner until 1979. He and his wife, Meli Lorna, moved to Pica Pau where, on 19 December 1979, he attested into the South African Army.

Antonio was buried on 29 May 1980 in the Pica Pau cemetery, Buffalo base, in grave number 132.

77880912SP Rifleman Manuel Augusto
*5 April 1954 †21 May 1980

Manuel, from the Gangela tribe, was born in Serpa Pinto, Angola. He had no formal schooling and, at the age of 19, started work as a painter for Carlos Isquelro in Serpa Pinto. In March 1974 he joined ELNA as a soldier and served until January 1976, when he crossed the Okavango River with other refugees. He left his mother, Christina Chimunma, behind in Serpa Pinto when he fled. He stayed in the Rundu refugee camp until 1 September 1977, when he attested into the South African Army and joined 32 Battalion as a rifleman.

Manuel was buried on 29 May 1980 in the Pica Pau cemetery, Buffalo base, in grave number 131.

76926674SP Rifleman Castro Marcelino
*5 April 1952 †21 May 1980

Castro was from the Umbundu tribe. Born in Dobby Grand, Angola, he had no formal schooling. From January 1968 until July 1970, he worked as a carpenter, first helping his father and later taking an apprenticeship in Dobby Grand. He joined FALA in September 1970, but deserted in May 1976, crossing the Cubango River with other refugees. On 1 July 1976, he attested into the South African Army and joined 32 Battalion as a rifleman.

Castro, who had no relatives in Namibia, was buried on 29 May 1980 in the Pica Pau cemetery, Buffalo base, in grave number 141.

76928886SP Rifleman Abel Livingi
*15 January 1957 †21 May 1980

Abel was from the Gangela tribe and was born in Serpa Pinto, Angola. He had no formal schooling. From January 1964 until March 1974, he worked as a labourer at his father's timber workshop; thereafter, he joined ELNA as a soldier and served until December 1975. He returned to Mpupa and served in Colonel Breytenbach's group, arriving at Pica Pau in March 1976.

Abel, who had no relatives in Namibia, was buried on 29 May 1980 in the Pica Pau cemetery, Buffalo base, in grave number 133.

76910611SP Rifleman Joaquim Matamba
*9 November 1958 †21 May 1980

Joaquim, from the Kimbundu tribe, was born in Santa Comba, Angola. He had no formal schooling. He helped his father at home until he joined ELNA as a driver in January 1972. He was in Colonel Breytenbach's Bravo Group during Operation Savannah and, in January 1976, he returned to Mpupa. He transferred to Pica Pau in March. His wife, Markita Augusta, lived with him in Pica Pau. On 3 November 1976 he attested into the South African Army in Grootfontein and officially joined 32 Battalion as a rifleman.

Joaquim was buried on 29 May 1980 in the Pica Pau cemetery, Buffalo base, in grave number 134.

76907641SP Rifleman Sebastiao Angelo
*3 February 1958 †21 May 1980

Sebastiao was from the Umbundu tribe and was born in Nova Lisboa, Angola. He had no formal schooling and worked as a driver for Agostino Lopes before joining ELNA in 1974. He was one of the men who returned to Mpupa in February 1976 and transferred to Pica Pau with Bravo Group, where he stayed with his brother, Ruben Guayo. They left their mother, Adilaide Chilomeo, behind in Caala Varra Cangote. On 26 October 1976,

Sebastiao attested into the South African Army and joined 32 Battalion as a rifleman.

Sebastiao was buried on 29 May 1980 in the Pica Pau cemetery, Buffalo base, in grave number 135.

Their duty fearlessly and nobly done, we will remember them.

Savate Day, Buffalo base, 1985

The Tree of Honour was relocated from the Palacio Regimental to a site in front of the Trechis mess. A combined inauguration and Savate Day ceremony was held, with Major General Georg Meiring (GOC SWATF) as the functionary. This was the first Savate Day attended by all previous commanders

eft to right: Colonel Jan Breytenbach, Brigadier Gert Nel, Major General Georg Meiring, Colonel Deon Ferreira and Commandant (later Colonel) Eddie Viljoen

Left to right: Warrant Officer Class 1 Faan Joubert (RSM), Warrant Officer Class 2 Koos Kruger, Sergeant Johan Strause and Sergeant Louis Lombard

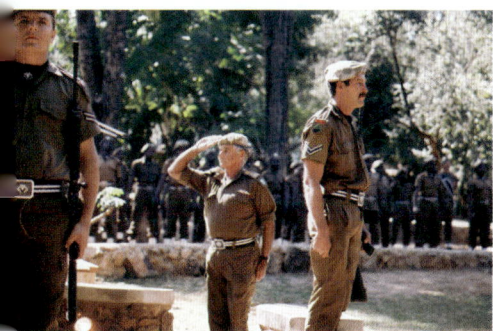

Wreath-laying ceremony: Colonel Jan Breytenbach, commander 1976/77

Brigadier Gert Nel, commander 1977/78

Colonel Deon Ferreira, commander 1979–83

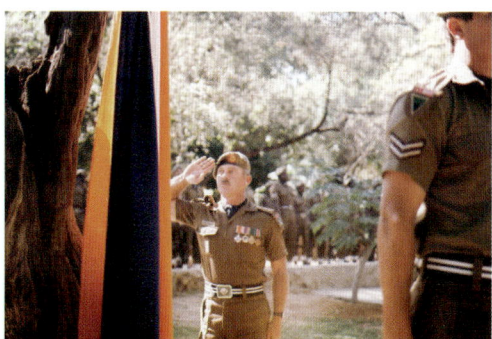

Commandant Eddie Viljoen, commander 1984–86

Savate Day, Buffalo base, 1986

Above: Guests at the ceremony included Elise Smit (left), Buffalo base commander Major Tom Barron (front and centre) and Sergeant Harry Hollander (right)

Left: Lieutenant (Rev.) Paul Prinsloo delivers his sermon. The sentry in the foreground is Sergeant Louis Lombard

Colonel Eddie Viljoen, Officer Commanding

Warrant Officer Class 1 Piet Nortje, Regimental Sergeant Major

Savate Day, Buffalo base, 1987

Left:
Sentries at the Tree of Honour

Far left:
The flagman after hoisting the national flag. The officers' club building can be seen in the background

Above: Sentries at the Tree of Honour
Left: Sergeant Eduardo Joao

olonel Mucho Delport, Officer Commanding, delivers
is message

Lieutenant (Rev.) Herman Herman gives his sermon

uests at the ceremony

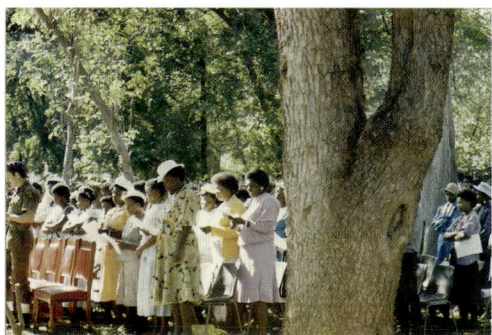

Savate Day, Pomfret military base, 1991

Wreath-laying ceremony: Donny Brown, chairman of the 32 Battalion Veterans' Association (above); Colonel Mucho Delport (top right); and Lieutenant Joao Appolinario on behalf of the officers (right)

Savate Day, Roy's Lodge, Pretoria military base, 2004

Reverend Stephanus 'Oppies' Opperman reads the names of the fallen

The purposely made memorial shows a photo of the Tree of Honour and also displays the Roll of Honour

Nico van der Walt hands over a wreath for the wreath-laying ceremony

Savate Day, 4 Reconnaissance Regiment, Langebaan, 2005

Wreaths were laid at a specially designated place

Left to right: Gert Nel, Johan Anderson, Barry Roper, Lubbe Heroldt, Stefanus van der Walt and Nico van der Walt

Savate Day, Kabul, Afghanistan, 2005

The first gathering was informal and only attended by former 32 Battalion men. Left to right: Rowan Pridgeon, Lourens du Plessis, Eric Rabie, Martin Venter (kneeling), Charles Loxton and Johannes Groenewaldt

Savate Day, Delville Wood, France, 2006

Jean Louis Maximillian Winand pays his respects after laying a wreath in remembrance of the fallen at Savate

Savate Day, Kabul, Afghanistan, 2006

The wreath laid at the memorial

Billy Faul reads the Roll of Honour, while Heinrich Rademeyer looks on

Savate Day, Roy's Lodge, Pretoria, 2007

Barry Roper, Jean Louis Maximillian Winand, Andrew Olivier (guest) and Johnny Mendes

Former 32 Battalion men and guests who attended the ceremony

Savate Day, Kabul, Afghanistan, 2007

The conflict in Afghanistan had taken its toll and already South Africans had paid the highest price helping to protect and build that nation. A memorial plaque with the names of South Africans killed in Afghanistan was unveiled during the ceremony. Lourens du Plessis, a former 32 Battalion soldier, was added to the plaque

Unveiling the memorial plaque

Wouter de Vos (left) and Kobus Human

Former 32 Battalian men. Kneeling, left to right: Wouter de Vos, Johan Louw, Gert Kitching (5 Recce) and Peter Bowls. Standing, left to right: Villiers de Vos, Patric Rolf, Martin Venter, Heinrich Rademeyer, Stephanus Opperman, Billy Faul, Johannes Groenewaldt

Savate Day, 2 SA Infantry Battalion base, Zeerust, 2008

The 32nd commemoration of the founding of 32 Battalion. Not all 32 Battalion men received their medals before leaving military service. The 32 Battalion Veterans' Association went to great lengths to get these outstanding medals. After the Savate Day ceremony, medals were handed out by the guest of honour, former chief of the SADF, General Jannie Geldenhuys

The chairman of the 32 Battalion Veterans' Association, Stefanus van der Walt, delivers the opening address

The Tree of Honour at 2 SA Infantry Battalion base in Zeerust. After the disbandment of 32 Battalion in March 1993, the unit's name was changed to 2 SA Infantry Battalion. The Tree of Honour was originally on the parade ground at Pomfret base, but with the relocation of 2 SAI Battalion to Zeerust, the monument was moved as well

President of the Veterans' Association lays a wreath

The Pica Pau school choir

Savate Day, Kabul, Afghanistan, 2008

The security situation in Kabul improved, allowing the 2008 and all subsequent ceremonies to be held at the British cemetery. The South African Roll of Honour plaque was mounted in the cemetery

Kobus Human lays a wreath

Former 32 Battalion Portuguese-speaking member Joao Tjiviva lays a wreath

Savate Day, Delville Wood, France, 2008

Wreath laid by Kim Zocher

Left to right: Kim Zocher (Germany) George Coetzee (Netherlands), Jean Louis Maximillian Winand (Belgium) and Charles Evans (UK)

Savate Day, Warner Beach, KwaZulu-Natal, 2009

Left to right: Barry Roper, Eddie Viljoen, Gert Nel and Peter Williams

Peter Williams reads the Roll of Honour, flanked by Graham Marais and Corrie du Plessis

Savate Day, Kabul, Afghanistan, 2009

Former 32 Battalion men

Front, left to right: Simin Vorojak and William Schickerling. Back, left to right: Gerhard Potgieter, François Heyns, Johannes Groenewaldt, Lubbe Heroldt and Villiers de Vos

Savate Day, Voortrekker Monument, Pretoria, 2010

The occasion included a formal dinner on the Friday evening, followed by the 32 Battalion Veterans' Association annual general meeting on the Saturday and the memorial service on the Sunday morning

At the formal dinner: Conrad Stolts, Peter Williams and Sam Heap

Former 32 Battalion men at the memorial

Savate Day, Kabul, Afghanistan, 2010

ed Wilke, former SA Special orces

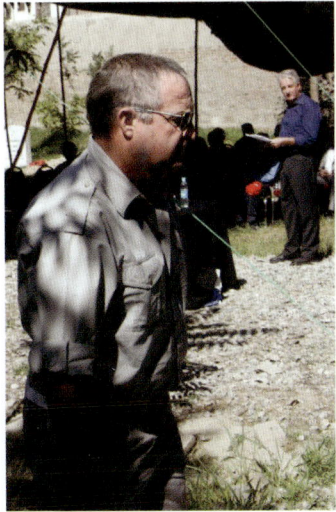

The legendary gunship pilot, Neil Ellis

A representative from the security contractors lays a wreath

Savate Day, Port Elizabeth, 2011

This was the first occasion on which a memorial cross was displayed

Barry Roper reads the Roll of Honour

Savate Day, Kabul, Afghanistan, 2011

Former chief of the SADF General Jannie Geldenhuys is the guest of honour

Former 32 Battalion men who attended the ceremony

Savate Day, Ypres, Belgium, 2011

Wreath laid by Kim Zocher

Ceremony programme

George Coetzee, Charles Evans, Kim Zocher and Maximillian Jean Louis Winand

Battlefield tour and memorial service, Savate Day, Angola, 2012

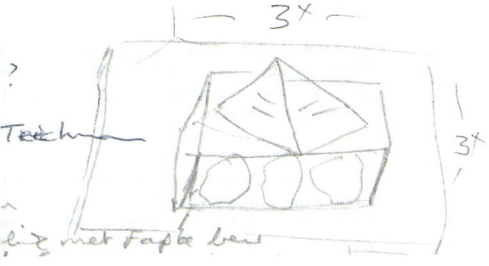

The early stages of the monument design, showing the original rough sketch (above) and a computer-generated model (right)

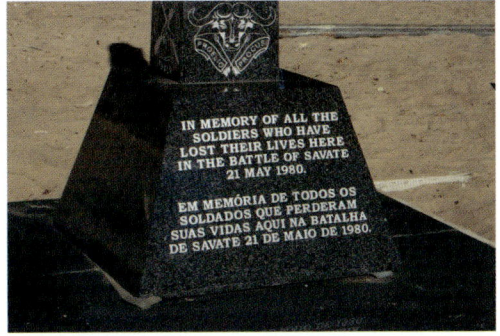

The finished Savate monument, with close-ups showing the three components being commemorated: the SADF and 32 Battalion (top); the Angolan population (middle); and the Angolan military (bottom)

The tour group at the entrance to the old Buffalo base

Justin Taylor in the internet container

The Savate welcoming party. Seated in the middle is Gert Nel, and standing behind him are Stefanus van der Walt and Koos Moorcroft

Justin Taylor relives his experience. Seated are Anton Roets and Leon Grobler, with Stefanus van der Walt on the right

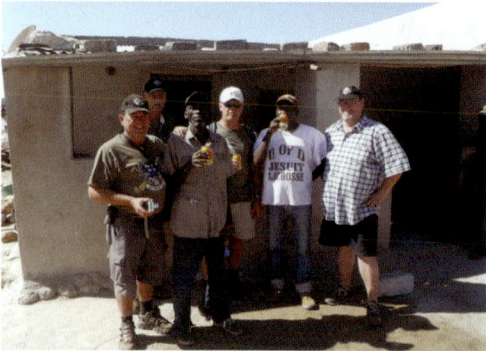
At the cuca shop. Left to right: Leon Grobler, Hannes Greyling, their guide, Gert Kotze, an unidentified man and Kim Zocher

Justin Taylor at what is left of the amphibious pontoon

Unexploded ammunition and ammunition parts on the battlefield

Leon Grobler, Stefanus van der Walt and Gert Nel listen to the sermon

The tour group listen to the prayer delivered by Reverend George Hugo

The six Battle of Savate veterans. Left to right: Nico Groenewaldt, Peter Lipman, Leon Grobler, Justin Taylor, Rick Lobb and Mike Kiley

Left: The Savate monument after the ceremony and before it was dismantled and stored in the administrator's office

Savate Day, Pretoria, 2012

The founding farther, Colonel Jan Breytenbach, and his wife. Behind them is Savate veteran Nico Groenewaldt

Kim Zocher reads the Roll of Honour, flanked by Peter Williams and Johan Stander

Savate Day, Kabul, Afghanistan, 2012

Most of the former 32 Battalion men had left Afghanistan, but the few men who remained did not forget the fallen

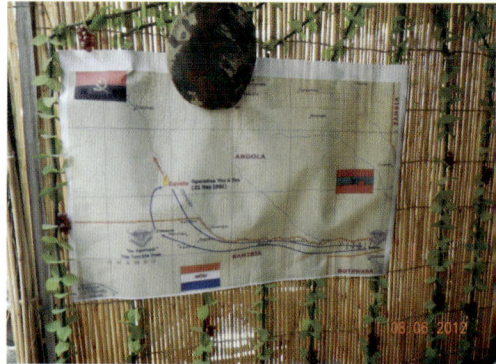

Savate Day, Ypres, Belgium, 2012

George Coetzee (Netherlands), Jean Louis Maximillian Winand (Belguim) Yvonne van Solms (Germany), Charles Evans (UK) and Fred van Solms (Germany)

Yvonne and Fred van Solms with the bugler players

Savate Day, Pretoria, 2013

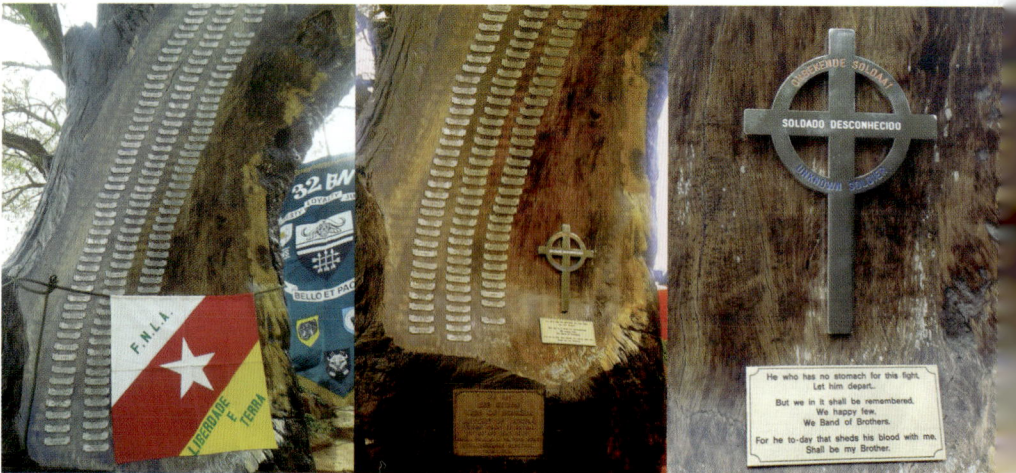

Bravo Group, which later became 32 Battalion, lost an unknown number of FNLA soldiers killed in action during Operation Savannah in 1975/76. A symbol to remember these men was added to the Tree of Honour (the spelling on the plaque later corrected)

Former 32 Battalion men after the ceremony

A representative from the Airborne Riders Motorcycle Club (Gauteng) lays a wreath

Noël Viljoen reads the Roll of Honour

Hannes Greyling and Gavin Jarman

avate Day, Ypres, Belgium, 2013

m Zocher, Jean Louis Maximillian Winand, Yvonne
n Solms, George Coetzee, Abie Slaber (Germany),
ed van Solms and an unidentified gentleman from
ance

The display at the base of the monument. The figurine is part of The Terrible Ones Collection

Savate Day, Pretoria, Durban and Cape Town, 2014

A few men from KwaZulu-Natal unable to attend the ceremony in Pretoria held a small gathering at the Mills Bomb Shellhole at Warner Beach. A much bigger group gathered in Cape Town, w here they were joined by representatives from the Russian Consulate, who read their own Roll of Honour containing the 79 names of Soviets who died in Angola during the Border War era

Reverend Ernst Endres delivers the sermon in Pretoria

Stefanus van der Walt delivers his address in Pretoria. Peter Williams stands to his left

Former 32 Battalion men and representatives from the Russian Consulate gather in Cape Town

At Mills Bomb Shellhole, left to right: Ashleigh Patrick (31 Battalion), Barry Roper, Eddie Viljoen and Peter McRae

Savate Day, Mol, Belgium, 2014

Left to right: Abie Slabber, Kim Zocher, George Coetzee, Jean Louis Maximillian Winand and Mark Craig (UK)

Former 32 Battalion men with representatives from the City of Mol fire brigade

11

32 years later

The year 2012 marked 32 years since the Battle of Savate. What better place to commemorate the battle than at Savate itself? It was the chairman of the 32 Battalion Veterans' Association, Stefanus van der Walt's, unique vision to one day commemorate Savate Day at Savate. In 2005 he put forward his idea at the association's annual general meeting:

It was also my expressed ideal, in future, to commemorate Savate Day at Savate itself, and for this I had 2010 in mind. In 2010, however, the translocation of the Tree of Honour from Zeerust to the Voortrekker Monument took precedence. Brigadier General Gert Nel then, after hearing about Koos Moorcroft's battlefield tours in Angola, tried to give impetus to the idea by asking Koos to arrange a Savate tour. The cost of R15 000 per person, at the time, was probably the reason why nobody responded. After our 2010 ceremony, Kim Zocher from Germany drew our attention to the fact that 2012 would be exactly 32 years after the Battle of Savate, and that we should plan something special around it. We agreed.

Van der Walt again tested the idea of a trip to Savate at the 2011 Savate Day service in Port Elizabeth, where it was well received. The vision even grew to include erecting a memorial at the battle site. The date of 20 May 2012 was set for the service at Savate, when the memorial would be unveiled. It would happen at exactly the same time as the annual Savate Day service at the Tree of Honour in South Africa. A television crew would relay the ceremony in Savate to the one in Pretoria.

Planning

South Africans require a visa to enter Angola, which at times is difficult to obtain because one needs an invitation from a local sponsor. Driving a vehicle in southern Angola is just as difficult, as the roads are in a bad state of repair as a result of almost four decades of civil war. The trip had the potential to be a logistical nightmare.

Since 2007, John 'Koos' Moorcroft, a former Special Forces operator and Sergeant Major of the South African Army, and owner of African Bushcraft & Survival Adventures, had been taking battlefield tours to Angola annually, stopping at some of the more important SADF/PLAN/FAPLA battle sites, including Savate. It was obvious that Moorcroft should be involved in planning the trip, given his experience. Van der Walt asked him when on his next battlefield tour to test the feeling of the Savate residents regarding their former enemy visiting the site and erecting a memorial. In late 2011, Moorcroft returned from an Angolan tour with a verbal invitation from the administrator of Savate, José Cambuande, to visit the battlefield. The task of organising the visit fell to Van der Walt and Gert Nel, president of the 32 Battalion Veterans' Association. Nel asked Moorcroft to plan a less expensive tour for those who did not want to drive to Savate on their own.

Van der Walt had to speak to Cambuande to coordinate the visit, but had difficulty contacting him. After speaking to Moorcroft, Van der Walt found a solution by using a middleman. He remembers:

> Koos mentioned to me that he had noticed that [former Springbok rugby captain] Gary Teichmann's construction company was involved in building a tar road in the vicinity of Savate. I sent Gary an email, but never got a reply. Then Peter Lipman [former 32 Battalion Recce

Wing member] mentioned that his friend, Mike van Reenen from Nelspruit, was doing the laboratory work for this road project. Eventually, I managed to have a letter delivered at Savate via the erratic internet of Hendrik Strydom [Teichmann's foreman] at the construction site. But not a word came in reply.

Van der Walt planned to accompany Van Reenen to Savate, but could not get a visa in time. It was then decided that Nel and Leon Grobler, who was also involved in the planning, would go to Savate to do the liaising. This idea was scrapped, however, when they discovered that Moorcroft was taking another battlefield tour to Angola. They asked him instead to deliver a letter to Cambuande, take some photographs at Savate, look for a suitable place to erect the memorial and find a good camping place. Moorcroft did as asked but it was not to be the end of Van der Walt's communication headache:

We were welcome to come and erect the memorial, and he [Moorcroft] even brought me a cellular phone number for Cambuande. However, I was to learn the frustrating way that there was no reception at Savate, and that Cambuande could not manage SMSs.

At this time, I started doing security work at the Smokey Hills Platinum mine near Steelpoort. Although isolated, I made enough time for the project. I got hold of one of the guards, John Daniel, to act as interpreter with Cambuande. This proved to be just the right choice, for it soon transpired that Cambuande was his uncle. Matters then flowed quite well, and we learned that the FAPLA commander, as well as the Governor of the Cuando-Cubango Province, intended to attend the occasion.

Meanwhile, Moorcroft put together a more affordable tour at R8 500 per person and worked out a nine-day tour itinerary, which allowed for a visit to the Buffalo base at the start. The Savate tour would take place at the same time as a 61 Mechanised Veterans' Association tour of the Angolan battlefields. The following is the tour itinerary, as supplied by Moorcroft:

Savate Day tour: itinerary

Day minus 1 – 15th May. Meet at De Wildt Campsite, Pretoria, and discuss the exciting adventure that we are about to begin to Angola while sitting around the braai fire. (Members of the group travelling from Cape Town and Bloemfontein can board the Overlander either in Cape Town or Bloemfontein en route to Pretoria and on the return journey to their respective destinations free of charge.)

Day 1 – 16th May. Depart from De Wildt, cross the border into Botswana at Skilpadshek en route to the Kalahari Rest Camp.

Day 2 – 17th May. Further north past Ghanzi we cross the border into Namibia at Mohembo Border Post and camp at Ngepi, a campsite situated opposite Buffalo.

Day 3 – 18th May. A visit to Buffalo Base and then we continue to Sarasungu Lodge on the Kuvango River at Rundu.

Day 4 – 19th May. Depart from Sarasungu Lodge and cross the border into Angola at Katwitwi. After completing the border formalities we proceed to Savate and set up camp next to the Okavango River and relax around the fire. The 61 Mech VA battlefields tour group arrives from Cuito Cuanavale via Menongue to share 2 days with their 32 Bn comrades and partake in the Savate Day Memorial Service.

Day 5 – 20th May. 32 Bn Veterans Savate Day Memorial Remembrance Service will be attended by Angolan Military Veterans.

Day 6 – 21st May. Depart from Savate and overnight at Sarasungu Lodge, Rundu.

Day 7 – 22nd May. Cross the border into Botswana and camp at Sepupa next to the Okavango River where the river splits into the delta.

Day 8 – 23rd May. Follow the Southern Cross southwards to Kang and camp at the Kalahari Rest camp.

Day 9 – 24th May. The group proceeds further south, crossing the border back into RSA en route to De Wildt where the tour ends. The group from Cape Town and Bloemfontein will spend the last evening at De Wildt before returning to their respective destinations on the last leg of their journey.

Satisfied that there was an invitation to visit Savate and erect a memorial, Van der Walt began to focus on the memorial itself. Many years ago, when they had visited the Magersfontein battlefield, Leon Maartens, then a major, had pointed out to Van der Walt the Scandinavian tradition of erecting two memorials: one for their own fallen and one for their fallen enemy. Van der Walt consulted with Nel, who agreed to a memorial that honoured the 32 Battalion fallen and also acknowledged the enemy. Van der Walt also felt an obligation to recognise in some way the unasked-for suffering of the Angolan civilian population, and so it was agreed to add them as a third element to the memorial.

Nel approved that the 32 Battalion Trust should carry the costs for the memorial, as it was fully consistent with its deed of foundation. The memorial would take the form of a needle, with the names of the 32 Battalion fallen on one side. To honour FAPLA and the Savate civilians, it was argued that the needle should have three sides. Freek Kruger, a former 32 Battalion platoon commander, made some sketches and generated a computer graphic of the needle. After consultation with Johan Fourie of Metro Granite in Brits, a four-sided needle was settled on and Fourie's quotation of R18 500 was accepted.

The next problem was how to transport the memorial to Savate and have it erected. Van der Walt had already arranged with Hendrik Strydom that Gary Teichmann's construction workers would cast the concrete slab on which the needle would be mounted. Moorcroft put Van der Walt in

contact with his friend Kierie Bouwer in Tsumeb, Namibia, who introduced Van der Walt to two young men who were willing to transport the
memorial to Savate.

Orphans of war

Many years after the Battle of Savate, I was one of those on an email distri-
bution list from Louis Bothma, a former 32 Battalion platoon commander.
Bothma had received a letter from a young South African named Louis
Eduard Engelbrecht, then serving in the British Army. Engelbrecht
wrote that his father, whom he never knew, was killed while serving with
32 Battalion and that he was looking for more information. Fifteen years
after his birth and just days before his mother, Yvonne, passed away from
cancer on 6 June 1996, Louis was told that his real father was Corporal
Eduard Coetzee Engelbrecht. His mother had kept this information from
him because she was afraid that he would want to enrol in the military if
he knew his father had served.

I had met Corporal Engelbrecht only once and therefore could not help.
A few men who knew him responded, but their information was scant
because Engelbrecht had served in the battalion for only six months before
he was killed. Eventually, through his own research, Bothma was able to
reunite Louis Engelbrecht with Frieda Siebert, his father's sister, and later
with other relatives. In his book *Anderkant Cuito: 'n Reisverhaal van die
Grensoorlog*, published in 2011, Bothma recounts an Angolan battlefields
tour in 2010 with 61 Mechanised Infantry Battalion veterans. Sitting
around a campfire in Savate, Bothma had read from Louis Engelbrecht's
original letter to the tour members:

> She only had one photo of him but he was very young in it. This was
> before he was sent to the border. This is all I have of him today, only
> the pain and lies. After my mother passed away, I started searching for
> my father's past. All I ask, which is fair, is to have something from him

to fill the empty space in my heart. Then at least I would have both my parents in my heart.

When I read Bothma's book in early 2013, I recalled and found the email he had circulated with Louis's plea. At the same time I received a message from the Department of Defence Documentation Centre saying that the final Savate documents, for which authority to declassify had been previously denied, were now declassified and available. With Louis's letter in mind, I decided to research the background and military career not only of his father, but of all the 32 Battalion men killed at Savate. In the end I was able to compile a comprehensive file on each man.

In December 2013 I made contact with Louis Engelbrecht via Van der Walt to tell him about my book, *The Terrible Ones*. From our correspondence, I learnt that he had still not found closure and was still looking for information about his father. I offered him the file I had compiled on Corporal Eduard Engelbrecht, which included a copy of his military identity document, to help him in the healing process. I received a respectful reply:

Please, I want the file. I do not want anybody to think that I am only looking for a man who was in the defence force, no – but I was looking for the truth, for my father, because I could see what pain it caused for both my mother and father. Now many might not give me the opportunity, but after everything my mother went through, there is no reason that she would lie to me on her death bed. This is that door which was never opened or closed, which I want to open and close, not only for me but for my children and their children.

Louis's mother had had a hard time. After her marriage at the age of 17, she lost her first baby when it was 11 months old. Her husband, who loved alcohol more than he loved her, regularly assaulted her. Eventually Yvonne and a Portuguese girlfriend of hers left South Africa for South West Africa, where they stayed in Otjiwarongo with the friend's relatives. There, in November 1979, she met Eduard Engelbrecht shortly before he left to join 32 Battalion. They corresponded by letter and she saw him again in February 1980, when he visited home. They were young and, fearing the time and space between them, they slept together.

When Yvonne eventually found out she was pregnant, she wrote to Eduard, telling him about the situation. She went to live with her grandmother on a farm and started to make arrangements for a divorce. Then she received the news of Eduard's death at Savate. Her grandmother persuaded her not to tell the Engelbrecht family about her relationship and the pregnancy – there was enough sorrow in losing a son and brother, and they would think she was a bad woman, 19 years old, married and pregnant with another man's child.

Five months after Eduard's death, on 16 October 1980, his son was born. He was christened after his great-grandfather and named Rudolph Heindrich Ludwich Fredrich Gray-Browne, but later his name was changed to Rudolph Louis Gray-Browne. Six years later Yvonne tried to commit suicide and was then diagnosed with cancer. Louis was first sent to stay with family, but was later taken away by welfare and placed in an orphanage. He was 12 years old when his mother got custody of him. Then she met and married Fanie Engelbrecht, motivated by two important factors. In his letter to me, Louis wrote:

Firstly, she dearly wanted me to be an Engelbrecht because I was truly an Engelbrecht from Eduard, and secondly so that I could have a father. My surname was changed. But Fanie was a 'joller' [partyer] and had no time for me. I went to boarding school in Middelburg and we relocated to Groblersdal. My mother then fell seriously ill, again with throat and lung cancer, and Fanie left her for somebody else.

My mother, in the last few days on her death bed, told me everything. Who my father was and why the family did not like me. Why my grandmother always called me a bastard child. My mother was 35 years old and I was 15 when she passed away on 6 June 1996.

The years that followed were just as hard for young Louis. He stayed with his grandmother, but after running away from home several times and being brought back by the police, she put him up for adoption, saying to Uncle Freek, 'Look, this child is a disgrace and only a problem for the family, nobody wants him. I ask you, please sign the papers and take him because he is not welcome here. He is a bastard child.'

Life with his new family was just as difficult. By 2002 Louis was work-ing in the mines, saving money. When the opportunity arose, he went to Scotland: 'I ran away from South Africa, away from Uncle Freek and all the pain. My mother told me that her great-grandfather was Scottish and a soldier in the Royal Regiment of Scotland in Edinburgh. That is where I went.'

After a successful seven years in the British Army, circumstances forced Louis to resign. While in the army he had married an American girl. They have two boys and now live in the United States.

After I sent him his father's file, Louis wrote to me on 11 December 2013:

At the end of the day I can sit down, smile and say, 'We eventually found each other.' My father and mother are in heaven and together serve Jesus. I live in America and am blessed with a loving family, which Jesus gave me. We are in a life of love and peace. The information in the file will never be hidden, but together with the other things of my military life will be framed and it will go to my children and theirs so that they can know who their grandfather was.

In vastly different circumstances, Joachim Matamba was also born shortly after his father was killed at Savate. Before Rifleman Joaquim Matamba left on Operation Tiro-Tiro, he knew that his wife, Markita Augusta, was expecting a baby. Although he, too, would never know his biological father, unlike Louis Engelbrecht, Joachim grew up in a poor but happy family. His mother remarried another 32 Battalion soldier, Francisco Luciano. When the battalion relocated to Pomfret in South Africa in 1989, Joachim's family decided to stay behind in South West Africa and settled in Rundu. Joachim, however, chose to relocate with his teacher, Private M.I. de Oliveira, and his family to Pomfret. A few years ago, Joachim changed his surname to De Oliveira.

Van der Walt and Nel were determined that both young men should be invited on the trip to Savate. Speaking about Engelbrecht, Van der Walt said: 'For me, it was just imperative that this son, Louis, should go to Savate along with us.' An emotional Engelbrecht accepted the invitation, but did not have the necessary funds. Nel came to the rescue, however, and offered to have the 32 Battalion Trust pay his costs. All Engelbrecht had to do was arrange for his own visa. Matamba's reaction was less enthusiastic, and he soon lost interest in the planned trip and did not end up going.

The road to Savate

Van der Walt was coordinating the project from Steelpoort when the contract Teichmann had to build the road was suddenly terminated and his equipment confiscated. When the two men who were to transport the memorial heard about this, they immediately withdrew, leaving Van der Walt in the lurch at the last moment. Metro Granite was put on hold and Van der Walt contacted Marmerwerke Karibib in Namibia to see if they could make the memorial, an alternative that would ease the transport problem. Their quotation, however, was almost double Fourie's and they could not supply the solid base block. Van der Walt then heard about Johan Boshoff from Ondangwa, Namibia, whose truck made weekly trips to Brits to load tombstones. Van der Walt contacted Boshoff, who agreed to transport and erect the memorial at Savate on 19 May for R8 500.

On 20 April, Van der Walt contacted Cambuande to confirm the arrangements. The news was not good:

[Cambuande] got vague and asked me at this late point in time to send the governor of the province a letter informing him about our visit. The very next day, I sent a hastily translated (by the mother of Manuel Ferreira who is in Portugal) email to Governor Eusebio Teixeira in Menongue, but got no reply.

Time was running out. William Mutlow, a former 32 Battalion platoon commander, suggested that Van der Walt call the former South African ambassador to Angola, Roger Ballard-Tremeer. Although willing to help, there was nothing much the official could do. He explained that it was election time in Angola, and everyone was cautious about making any commitments. Van der Walt even called Governor Teixeira's son, a businessman who was in Menongue at the time, but to no avail. By now the memorial was already in Ondangwa, but under the circumstances nobody could tell Boshoff when to erect it.

During all of this, Louis Engelbrecht was battling to get a visa out of the Angolan embassy in the US. As a last resort, Van der Walt offered to try to get it in South Africa. With only a week to go, Engelbrecht sent his passport by express mail to South Africa, but the post-office workers at O.R. Tambo International Airport in Johannesburg were on strike and his passport did not make it. The group was forced to leave without Louis. (His passport eventually reached Van der Walt a month after they returned.)

It was now time to decide if the tour should go ahead at all. In the end, 19 men elected to go to Angola as ordinary tourists. Moorcroft's wife, Issie, who normally arranged Angolan visas for the battlefield tours, dealt with the complicated visa process. Moorcroft would meet the group at the Mahango border post, where they entered Namibia from Botswana, and Justin Taylor would fly to Rundu in his own Cessna 210 light aircraft and join the group there. Former 32 Battalion NCO Jim Freeman, a radio and television journalist, and Peter Voigt, a photographer for *National Geographic*, Associated Press and television, would accompany them to handle the media aspects. On the evening of 15 May, the tour group gathered at the De Wildt resort near Hartbeespoort Dam for a hearty reunion. But there were still more hurdles to overcome. Says Van der Walt:

> Earlier that day, I went to a funeral parlour in Brits to buy a wreath and here encountered Trompie Theron's father arranging for his wife's funeral. He offered to sponsor the wreath.
>
> Now, at this late hour, we learned that the two members supposed to handle the media aspects had to cancel. Because we were still in the dark regarding the monument, I asked Jay Nel and Noel Viljoen to make us a cross of steel as a possible substitute. This impossible challenge they met in one day, and later that evening brought it over to put on some last minute paint and deliver it.

At the same time, they received news that the 61 Mechanised tour had been cancelled. Unrelated to that, a decision was made to postpone the Pretoria Savate Day service so that the tour group could also attend.

The next morning, the group left in a well-equipped Overlander with former Special Forces reverend, George Hugo, as tour leader and Anna, an efficient Afrikaans-speaking Herero woman from Namibia, as cook. Following a route through Botswana, they would make use of camping facilities along the way.

They met Moorcroft, as arranged, and arrived at Ngepi Camp in the Caprivi in the late afternoon of 17 May. Van der Walt recalls:

> Early on the third morning, the first high point is experienced from Ngepi Camp on the bank of the Kavango, as an awed group stares wordlessly across the river as first light gently reveals the outline of our Buffalo

base. Gradually well-known points of reference are recognised: the old parade ground, the Swamp house [later renamed the Recce house], overgrown but filled with memories. The long silence speaks for itself.

Later that day, we cross over the Bagani Bridge on our way to Buffalo. At the gate, we pose for a group photo, flanked by the two still intact stone guardhouses. Then, with permission of the nature conservation officials, we continue past the parade ground and derelict kimbo to where the cemetery must be. Koos Moorcroft, who has joined us at the Kavango border, leads the way in his Hilux pick-up. The bush is fast reclaiming its own, but eventually we recognise the area. Still, it takes some reconnaissance to find the first graves in the overgrown bush. Large trees and many shrubs have taken up the neat spaces between the graves, and elephants have played havoc with the crosses and the graves. It becomes a search to redefine the layout of the cemetery, with everyone wandering about, making his own private discoveries. We congregate on the riverbank, from where the training area is visible, and naturally stories about incidents with lions, buffalo and eccentric training personnel come out of the great treasure chest of memories.

Then, back to Buffalo base. Walking down the still recognisable road leads one to the overgrown ruins of what once was the throbbing heart of Buffalo – past the remnants of the admin building, ops tent, signallers, medics and mess to the once magnificent officers' bar on the bank of the river, now destroyed and reverting to the bush. Everyone has his own memories, and cannot escape the truth that a memorable era has really ended.

In the meantime, Taylor's arrival at Rundu Airport was quite eventful, as he explains:

It was the first time I had been back since 1980, so it was a very nostalgic moment touching down on the old military strip. I had to wait a while for the black Namibian customs guys to show up and it took even longer for them to fire up their X-ray machine, even after I had mentioned that they were welcome to search through my luggage.

My bags were reversed backwards and forwards a few times, accompanied by a lot of muttering and pointing at the screen before they asked if they could open up my belongings. To this, I readily complied, knowing there was nothing of any concern in there. The chap doing the search was happily rooting through my clothes when he suddenly recoiled as if he had seen a deadly snake ... he had just discovered my 32 Battalion beret. His response marked him as clearly of the Border War era, and he then made a comical effort at looking cool, trying to pretend he hadn't seen it.

A few hasty, furtive cellphone calls followed and a vehicle soon arrived in a cloud of dust, from which two authoritative looking black Namibian guys alighted, trying to pretend they hadn't been in a hurry. I greeted them cheerfully and started chatting to them, while they politely scrutinised my documentation. The older of the two had a bad limp and when I pressed him about it he mentioned that he had been a SWAPO cadre during the war, but was vague on any further details. He, in turn, asked me what my intentions were while in Namibia, to which I replied that I was joining a tour group at a lodge just outside Rundu, and would return in a few days to fly back to South Africa. I left out the 'minor detail' about our planned excursion into Angola and on to Savate, as this would certainly have complicated things. I am sure he would not have been particularly enamoured with the fact that I was returning to Angola to commemorate a battle in which our battalion had routed a brigade-strength Angolan army unit. In addition, I would have been particularly hard pressed to explain all of this to him when he would have known that we had not been officially at war with the Angolans at the time!

Just as my explanations might have got a bit tricky with further questioning, the owner of the lodge arrived to collect me. And so, with a friendly wave, they let us go on our way.

That evening, at the Sarasungu River Lodge, near Rundu, Taylor spotted the old airport customs official:

I spotted the ex-SWAPO cadre sitting alone in a corner of the bar. Delighted at the opportunity to buy him a drink and learn more about his exploits as a guerrilla fighter during the war, I went over to greet him. He was very happy to accept the offer of a beer and I found it very strange that he seemed ill at ease, if not a bit embarrassed that I had noticed him. It was almost as if I was not supposed to have recognised him. Needless to say, the conversation was short and sweet before he disappeared ... clutching the unopened beer I had bought for him!

On the morning of 19 May, the group headed for the Katwitwi border post with Angola, the final leg of the journey to Savate. To Van der Walt's dismay, at Katwitwi they were joined by the work team from Ondangwa, with the still un-erected memorial stones in their trailer. The men explained that they were not allowed to cross the border without the necessary paperwork for the memorial.

With great difficulty, they managed to get the memorial past Namibian customs, but hit further opposition on the Angolan side. There was no sign of Cambuande, who had promised to meet them at the border, and no paperwork for the cargo, which made it difficult to pay the 50 per cent tax the Angolan authorities were demanding. Taylor offered to get the documentation over email, only to discover that the data links on the South Africans' cellphones and laptops were inoperative at the remote border post. Taylor remembers:

That's when we discovered Monica's Internet Café, in a sweltering metal container back along the road approaching the border. At the time, I thought the border control officers were being unnecessarily pedantic ... and it was only on leaving Namibia a few days later that

I was to discover that there had been a sinister motive behind the whole delay.

After five hours of struggling and walking back and forth between the Angolan border post and the internet container, while the rest of the group waited patiently, Van der Walt and Taylor managed to make arrangements for the necessary paperwork to be faxed through. The group at last continued to Savate, leaving the workers behind with the memorial to wait for the fax the next morning. A decision was made to postpone the memorial service by one day and, just after sunset, the group made camp next to the Cubango River behind Savate.

The following morning, 20 May, Van der Walt had to unexpectedly travel to Cuangar. He explains:

Sunday morning, through the mists hanging over the Cubango River, a gentle sun welcomes us at the goal of our efforts, Savate. A welcoming committee soon comes to greet us, and to explain that although we are most welcome, we won't be allowed to erect the memorial – unless we can come to an agreement with the administrator at Cuangar. [Savate falls in the Cuangar municipality district.]

We make arrangements for our group to visit the battlefield, to be guided around the still present land mines by local FAPLA veterans of the same battle, while I will have to go and meet with the administrator. Then, we gather next to the Overlander for a briefing on the battle itself. Koos has brought along an enlarged satellite image of the battle area to serve as reference. After an introduction by Gert Nel, outlining the major strategic considerations around the battle, each of the six members who had actually participated in the battle itself would have an opportunity to take us back into the battle as experienced by them.

What a great, historical moment this is – the very participants at the very location where this great battle took place telling us how it happened! Leon Grobler, Peter Lipman, Nico Groenewaldt, Justin Taylor, Rick Lobb and Mike Kiley each get an opportunity to bring their angle to the story. Soon, we are all captivated by their accounts. This done, the group moves off to explore the main battlefield and trenches on foot, while I reluctantly leave them for the nearly 100 kilometre drive with the local ambulance to see the administrator in Cuangar.

The road is bad, and the driver, the vice-administrator of Savate, is in a hurry, and I am once again impressed with the tenacity of a Land Cruiser. We cross the Cubango on a long pontoon bridge, pass various small villages, and eventually enter Cuangar. At his home, I am introduced to Daniel Rufino, the administrator of the district. The conversation is in Portuguese and soon I learn that he was actually involved in the Savate battle – as acting commanding officer! The CO of FAPLA's brigade at the time was nobody less than the present governor of the Cuando Cubango Province, whom I was so desperately trying to contact, General Eusebio Teixeira. On the day of the attack, he was not present and Daniel Rufino was left in charge of the garrison.

I tell him that unfortunately Deon Ferreira has passed away, but that Brigadier General Gert Nel came along, and he expresses his regret that he won't be able to attend. He arranges to meet us on our way back across the river at Nkuru Nkuru. As two mutual soldiers, we then tackle the problem of our planned parade and erection of the memorial. On his cellphone, he calls General Teixeira in Menongue, and after a long discussion, we come to a solution. We can continue with our parade tomorrow morning, and even put up the memorial, but please, we must dismantle it afterwards. Much relieved, I greet him and rush back in the late Sunday afternoon. Along the way, I phone ahead to tell the workers to start with the concrete base for the memorial, and when, well after dark, we reach Savate, I find them casting concrete in the headlights of their bakkie. But the day was saved.

221

Back at the camp, I detect an atmosphere of contentment. Led around still present mines by guides who actually partook in the battle, the guys had a rewarding day on the old battle grounds among trenches, wrecks, spent bullets and even pieces of rocket. For six of them, it must have been very personal. Leon has clearly also understood my feelings about missing out on this opportunity, and brings me an R1 rifle magazine with a bullet hole through it. When he tells me he picked it up near the place where the body of Corporal Engelbrecht was found, I quietly decide that it must go to his son in America.

After breakfast on 21 May, the group broke camp and moved over to the village centre for the memorial parade. The heavy granite stones were manhandled into position while the villagers gathered under the trees. Cambuande arrived just in time to see the tour group formed up, dressed in their camouflage berets and black 32 Battalion Veterans' Association shirts.

It was now 09:00 in Angola, 32 years to the hour since the Battle of Savate began. In his welcoming speech, with the help of an interpreter, Cambuande asked the group's pardon for the hassles with arrangements. After Van der Walt's opening remarks, Reverend Hugo delivered a fitting sermon and then Nel addressed the parade, pointing out to the crowd the significance of the three emblems on the memorial and laying the wreath.

Afterwards, the needle and its base were dismantled, and stored in an administration building. The group said farewell and boarded the vehicle for the return trip. They spent the night at the Sarasungu River Lodge, where a benefactor sponsored a great dinner – it was a pleasant end to a historic day.

On the morning of 22 May, the group departed southwards. When the lodge owner dropped Taylor at the airport, the same customs official was waiting for him:

The 'customs officer' with the limp was there to meet me at the customs office back at Rundu's old military airfield. It was clear that he had made a point of being there to make sure I did leave when I said I would; he looked very pleased with himself and was clearly relieved to see me. It was after my friendly greeting that I managed to break through his polite yet reserved demeanour, and visibly relaxing, he told me the whole story of what had been going on in the background.

He was, in fact, the local military intelligence officer and on receiving the call from the customs officer telling him that there was a guy entering the country with a 32 Battalion beret in his baggage, he dispatched himself with alacrity to the customs office. From that point on, I was shadowed, being followed to the lodge and then our whole group was tailed all the way to the Angolan border post the next day. His devilish plan to surreptitiously join us at the bar that night was obviously an effort to pick up some intelligence about our real intentions … and no doubt he was duly alarmed at discovering that there was not only one ex 32 guy there, but a group of nearly twenty of us. Having confirmed that we were of the legendary old war era 'Os Terríveis' or 'Terrible Ones', he must have been foxed by the contrast of our amiable, relaxed and happy demeanour that certainly did not match the reputation. So, a lot of things must have been adding up that didn't make sense, merely adding to his suspicions. On top of which was his embarrassment at nearly having had his cover blown when I rushed up to buy him a beer. All in all, not a good evening for a covert intelligence operative!

The following day, our limping intelligence officer was far more furtive as he successfully kept to the shadows … we did not so much as sense his presence. I am sure he engineered the delay at the border post. This would have allowed enough time for his team to warn the Angolan officials that a group of ex 32 guys was about to enter their country.

223

I can just imagine the phone calls flashing between the Angolans and Namibians and would have given my eyeteeth to know what was discussed: 'Look out! There are twenty ex 32 guys who appear to be unarmed and amiable ... but they might just be up to something ... we need to be very, very careful ... the erecting of a monument could merely be a cover for something more sinister', etc. In hindsight, I am surprised that we were allowed across the border at all. Full credit certainly goes to the guys who had organised the tour on our side, as well as to the Angolans who ended up welcoming our visit and treating us with such hospitality and respect.

Savate then and now: Reflections by Leon Grobler

'We woke up in Savate on 20 May 2012. It was also my 52nd birthday. It was ominous waking up and seeing a lot of mist hanging over the Cubango River. It was also quiet and spooky. I have only bad memories from Savate and the weather added to the strange feeling. However, as the sun rose, it cleared up.

'We shaved, bathed, brushed teeth, etc. in the river where the locals bathe and fetch water for the day. It was Sunday and the church bell rang, much like any normal town in South Africa. The mayor and his sidekick visited Koos Moorcroft, Gert Nel and Stefanus van der Walt to discuss the parade where we would unveil the monument to commemorate the Battle of Savate.

'We indicated that we would like to tour the trenches, and Koos arranged for a guide. A few of us (Rick Lobb, Anton Roets, Nico Groenewaldt, Mike Kiley, Kim Zocher, Hannes Greyling and I) decided to walk up into the town and wait there for the guide. We passed the church, which was not a building but a big tree, under which the locals were having a service. The padre was standing behind a small table, the choir was singing (with gusto), and the women and children were sitting apart from the men, who were standing. Everybody was neatly dressed for the occasion. It made us feel a bit uncomfortable, because we were not attending church and were dressed informally.

'When entering the town, we saw a policeman standing next to the police station. We had heard a few bad things about them, like they threw people in jail for nothing and gave visitors a lot of hassles. I indicated to him that we would like to take a few photographs. He agreed, so we snapped away. He then walked away. Koos drove up and told us to move away from the police station because we might encounter problems. He looked quite anxious, so we started walking away. However, the policeman returned with a stern-looking man in civilian clothes. The animosity was thick in the air and, in Portuguese, the newcomer introduced himself as the police *comandante* (commander) of Savate. He rather coldly asked us what we were doing there and if we had been to Savate before. There was a lot of tension. Another old and skinny civilian joined the group.

'In my best Portuguese, I explained that we were visiting Savate as tourists, and that we had been there before, 32 years ago. Suddenly, the hostility vanished and they started smiling and talking in a friendly manner. We told them about the monument (celebrating the battle, 32 Battalion, FAPLA and the *povo*, the local people) and the parade and introduced ourselves. The fact that we planned to commemorate FAPLA and the *povo* went down well.

'The skinny civilian introduced himself as a *tenente* (lieutenant) who had actually fought against us during the Battle of Savate. So we started calling him *tenente*, which made him smile. He was to be our guide. The *comandante* asked him about his plans. He was obviously concerned about our safety and instructed the *tenente* to be careful where he took us. He also mentioned minefields and areas to avoid. Eventually, the *comandante* decided to join the tour, walking in front with the *tenente* while the policeman trailed the group. This arrangement made us feel safe.

'They took us to the airstrip, pointing out trenches and gun placements. There were lots of them. I then understood why Sam Heap decided to pull the two Charlie platoons back. It was plain suicide and obviously had been the correct decision at the time. What amazed me was the number of trenches north of the runway. We had missed the bulk of the base in 1980. As we walked south of the runway, I was sad because this was the ground where we, as Alpha 1, had fought exactly 32 years ago. I was thinking about my troops, Corporal Kaumba and Rifleman Caliango, who had lost their lives that day.

'The base was now obviously dilapidated: the roofs of the bunkers had collapsed, the trenches were half-filled, and trees grew on the airstrip. Nature has a way of reclaiming land. Mike Kiley smiled broadly when we saw the remains of vehicles in the car park, the legacy of Willem Ratte and his team. Mike told us what happened, how they had managed to create a lot of havoc. It was impressive. He and Rick Lobb described the enormous amount of noise when the battle started. I learnt a lot about the operation that morning from the others who had been present: the recces, the signal lieutenant and Nico Groenewaldt the driver. During a battle, you only experience your specific area and do not have a bird's-eye view.

'We found a lot of exploded bombs and 14.5, AK-47, R1 and PKM bullets on one particular patch of ground. The *tenente* recalled a white soldier who had passed away in that exact spot. Since Alpha 3 did not lose a white soldier, it must have been someone from Foxtrot. This made us sad and we had a quiet moment. Charl Muller and Tim Patrick were lost north of this point, a bit further towards the airstrip.

'I then detailed the battle from my perspective: that we heard Charl say over the radio "All stations forward!" and we stood up and advanced. He died soon afterwards. We did not stop because no one told us to. The fighting was extremely heavy then and we were running out of ammunition. I remember how the troops picked up AK ammo and gave it to the guys carrying AKs. We reached the river and turned back to sweep the base. Dave Hodgson was on my left experiencing a vastly different scenario, his battle being on a knife edge.

'Now, in 2012, we joked about why Nico had the nickname "Tripod" when he was younger, and his ability to break nuts without the help of tools. The *tenente* had a good sense of humour and really enjoyed our jokes. Even the policemen were friendly, laughing and chatting with us. They were impressed that we had found the defenders of Savate a competent force and a tough nut to crack.

'Afterwards, we went to a cuca shop for a few local beers with the *comandante*, the *tenente* and the policeman. The latter actually traded his beers for pencils and notebook paper. When I asked him why, he explained that he was on duty and could not drink. His family was also poor, and he said he would rather get these things for his kids who were at school. Now that was integrity.

'The bar lady showed us her scars from the Battle of Savate. She was four years old at the time and was caught in the crossfire fleeing across the floodplain. Her friendliness amazed me. We named her "Senora de Savate" (Savate Lady), which put a big smile on her and the other Angolans' faces.

'For us, Savate is also a metaphor. We all have our "Savate". Savate was our shared battle, one in which we won the day, but lost a lot of good men. We each carry a lot of memories from Savate. It is a battle we remember with tears in our eyes as we watch the sun set.

'This visit to Savate was markedly different from our previous experience of the place. Now the locals knew who we were, and they welcomed us with friendly faces. Their ability to forgive and to build new friendships taught me much. This is a very different Savate and I now have fonder memories.'

Postscript

At the time of writing in 2014, the memorial is still in the Angolan administration office. After the 2012 elections, the governor of the Cuando Cubango Province, the administrator of the Cuangar district and the administrator of Savate were all replaced. The 32 Battalion Veterans' Association contacted the new Savate administrator, who was reluctant to erect the monument. He then passed away and the acting administrator advised the 32 Battalion Veterans' Association to get permission directly from the Angolan government. The Heritage Foundation's Ebo Trust, which managed, after years of hard work, to repatriate the bodies of South African soldiers killed in Operation Savannah in 1975, is now involved in trying to get authority to erect the monument. All efforts, so far, have been fruitless.

In late 2011, I had argued that erecting a monument at Savate was not necessary. When would any former 32 Battalion soldier visit it? It is difficult for South Africans to travel to Angola and, surely, with increasing public awareness of the battle, others besides former 32 Battalion men might want to visit the memorial where it is more accessible. The Brigadier Gert Nel Hall in the Ditsong Museum of Military History in Johannesburg, which hosts the 32 Battalion display, was officially opened in May 2014. In my opinion, it is a far better place for the monument, since at least the South Africans involved in the battle and the general public can view it there and pay their respects not only to the 32 Battalion men who fought and died, but also to the Angolan soldiers and civilians.

Appendix
Operation Tiro-Tiro nominal roll: rank-wearing members

Headquarters	Alpha Company	Charlie Company	Echo Company	Foxtrot Company	Support Company	Recce Wing
Cmdt D. Ferreira	Lt C. de J. Muller	Lt S. Heap	2Lt D. Thompson	Lt J. Ross	**Assault Pioneer**	Lt W. Ratte
WO1 L. Uekermann	2Lt T. Patrick	Lt M. Barnard	2Lt I. Blume	2Lt H. Muller	2Lt C. Nolte	2Lt E. Swanepoel
Capt A. Erasmus	2Lt D. Hodgson	2Lt A. Olivier	Sgt B. Faul	2Lt S. O'Reily	WO2 J.D. Lourenco	2Lt W. Botha
2Lt J. Taylor	2Lt H. Heimstadt	2Lt A. Kruger	Sgt R. Organ	2Lt J. Roberts		2Lt P. Garret
Medic	2Lt B. Still	2Lt A. Theron	Sgt A. Buengu	Sgt E. Burger	**Mortar**	2Lt S. Naude
Lt S. Bouwer (dr)	Sgt P. Horn	Sgt I. Lindungo	Sgt F. Luciano	Sgt J. Ninge	2Lt C.B. Brown	2Lt E. Buameister
Lt R. van Zyl (dr)	Sgt P. Gomes	Sgt S. Santos	Cpl G. Everlett	Sgt A. Joao	Cpl J. Anderson	2Lt S. Opperman
Lt Dunlop (dr)	Sgt A. Mande	Cpl A.F. Mendes	Cpl B. Muller	Cpl E. Engelbrecht	Cpl A.J. Vambi	2Lt A. Botes
Cpl G. Hatley	Cpl D.V. Chikate	Cpl M. Coetzee	Cpl D. Stephane	Cpl T. Edwards	Cpl A. Dala	2Lt T. Marais
Omauni Ops	Cpl L. Grobler	Cpl D. Shelly	Cpl B. Calipe	Cpl Wessels	Cpl P.D. Lourenco	Sgt P. van Eeden
Maj E. Viljoen	Cpl R. Howden	Cpl C. Nell	Cpl M. Gomes	Cpl C. Meyer	Cpl H.C. Esequil	Sgt C. Maree
	Cpl D. Cline	Cpl P. Isobelle		Cpl P. Smit		Sgt J. Botha
Echelon	Cpl H. Labitzke	Cpl M.A. Vuti		Cpl A. Falcus		Sgt K. Sydow
Capt J. Louw	Cpl A. Roestof	Cpl P. Alfredo		Cpl L. Santos		Sgt K. Fitzgerhald
2Lt R. Heiser	Cpl J. Simpson	Cpl M.A. Oliveira		Cpl E. Colino		Sgt D. Laubsher
S Sgt R. Gregory	Cpl J. Cahiata	Cpl J. Manuel		Cpl D. Antonio		Sgt M. Kiley
Sgt P. Nortje	Cpl J. Francisco	Cpl S. Jorge		Cpl S. de Oliveira		Sgt K. Veenstra
	Cpl C.R. das Pedro	Cpl C. Ernesto		Cpl F. Paulo		Sgt A. Pedro
CSI	Cpl Z. Julio	Cpl J. Dianvumbi		Cpl C. Augusto		Sgt A. de Abreu
Cmdt M Oelschig	Cpl J. Franco	Cpl G.J. Marais		Cpl D. Estima		Sgt T.T. de Abreu
Maj J. Schutte	Cpl J. Freeman			Cpl A. Stolz		Cpl R. Lobb
Maj J. de Oliveira						Cpl M. Hongola
						Cpl A.F. Mendez
						Cpl C. Paulo

Key: 2Lt: Second Lieutenant; Capt: Captain; Cmdt: Commandant; Cpl: Corporal; Lt: Lieutenant; Maj: Major; Sgt: Sergeant; S Sgt: Staff Sergeant; WO1 Warrant Officer Class 1; WO2: Warrant Officer Class 2

Abbreviations and acronyms

AA: anti-aircraft
ANC: African National Congress
BRIL: brigadas de infantaria ligeira (light infantry brigades)
BRIM: brigadas de infantaria motorizada (motorised infantry brigades)
CSI: Chief Staff Intelligence
ELNA: Exército de Libertação Nacional de Angola; National Liberation Army of Angola; FNLA's military wing
F-AJMC: Forward Angolan Joint Management Centre
FALA: Forças Armadas de Libertação de Angola; Armed Forces for the Liberation of Angola; UNITA's military wing
FAPLA: Forças Armadas Populares de Libertação de Angola; People's Armed Forces for the Liberation of Angola; MPLA's military wing
FNLA: Frente Nacional para a Libertação de Angola; National Front for the Liberation of Angola
GOC: general officer commanding
HE: high explosive
HF: high frequency
MAOT: Mobile Air Operations Team
MI: Military Intelligence
MID: Military Intelligence Division
MPLA: Movimento Popular de Libertação de Angola; Popular Movement for the Liberation of Angola
NCO: non-commissioned officer
OC: officer commanding
ODP: Organização de Defesa Popular; People's Defence Organisation

PLAN: People's Liberation Army of Namibia; SWAPO's military wing

RSM: regimental sergeant major

SAAF: South African Air Force

SADF: South African Defence Force

SAMS: South African Medical Service

SDU: Self Defence Unit

SWA: South West Africa

SWAPO: South West Africa People's Organisation

SWATF: South West African Territorial Force

UNITA: União Nacional para a Independência Total de Angola; National Union for the Total Independence of Angola

VHF: very high frequency

WP: white phosphorus

Glossary

Military terminology and slang

AK: generally refers to the AK-47, a selective-fire, gas-operated assault rifle, first developed in the Soviet Union by Mikhail Kalashnikov

alferes: (Portuguese) ensign or second lieutenant

Alou: Alouette light-utility helicopter

ammo: ammunition

avançar: (Portuguese) advance/attack

avtur: A1 jet/helicopter fuel

bang gat: Afrikaans slang for someone who is afraid

battalion: military unit consisting of three rifle companies, a support company and a battalion headquarters; normally about 700 men

beacon: concrete marker built every 10 kilometres to identify position along the 420-kilometre cut line stretching from the Cunene River in the west to the Cubango River in the east, and designating the border between Angola and Ovamboland. Beacon 16 was therefore 160 kilometres east of the Cunene River. *See also cut line*

big pack: canvas backpack containing everything a soldier needs on patrol

bivvie: shelter constructed out of a groundsheet

'black is beautiful': common name for the camouflage cream used by white troops in the bush

boere/boers: Afrikaans word for white farmers, used as a derogatory term by SWAPO, the Angolans and South Africa's black population to describe the South African/SWATF security forces

buddies: two soldiers working together on an operation, mutually supporting each other

Buffalo: 32 Battalion base camp in the western Caprivi

bundu-bash: drive off-road through rough terrain

bunker: entrenched bombproof shelter

cadre: member of an insurgent rank and file

camos: camouflage clothing

casevac: casualty evacuation, usually by helicopter, of wounded soldiers for medical treatment

chana/oshana: opening in the bush where water is usually found and where locals engage in subsistence farming

chest webbing: ammunition pouches attached to a harness worn across a soldier's chest

comandante: (Portuguese) commander

commandant: pre-1994 South African military rank equivalent to lieutenant colonel

comms: radio communication

company: military unit consisting of three platoons and a company headquarters; normally about 120 men

contact: any form of encounter with the enemy, other than a mere sighting

cuca shops: similar to South African shebeens; small shops in Ovamboland and southern Angola that sell a limited stock of canned food and beer. Cuca is a Portuguese brand of beer, mostly available in Angola

cut line: demarcation line or border between South West Africa and Angola. *See also* beacon

dog biscuit: unappetising but nutritious biscuit found in a ration pack

echelon: combat-element logistical and support vehicles

first-line ammunition: ammunition for personnel and support weapons carried by each soldier at the start of a deployment

foxhole: hole dug in the ground and used for cover

gunship: Alouette helicopter armed with a machine gun

haak-en-steek: common Afrikaans name for the umbrella thorn acacia

inimigo: (Portuguese) enemy

kimbo: (Portuguese) village

Kwê: shortened form of Kwêvoël, a South African–manufactured, six-wheel-drive, 10-ton, mine-resistant cargo vehicle

laager: (Afrikaans) encirclement manoeuvre done by vehicles for overnight protection

lay-up place: safe hiding place in the bush where troops can wait for optimum operational conditions

mixed veg: tasteless tinned cubed mixed vegetables

mochila: (Portuguese) backpack

mort: SADF abbreviation for mortar

platoon: military unit consisting of three sections of 10 men each, plus a platoon headquarters (comprising a platoon commander, platoon sergeant, radio operator, medical orderly and two mortarmen); normally about 40 men

povo: (Portuguese) local population or civilians

pula: Portuguese nickname for a white person

rat pack: 24-hour ration pack

recce: reconnaissance; highly trained reconnaissance soldier

rooikat: (Afrikaans) caracal

section: military unit consisting of 10 men (eight riflemen, a section leader and a second in command)

sit-rep: situation report

space blanket: light-weight, low-bulk blanket made of thin, heat-reflective plastic sheeting; design reduces heat loss in a person's body, which would otherwise occur due to thermal radiation, water evaporation or convection

SPs: black Portuguese soldiers; the letters 'SP' (Special Project) appeared after their force number

spoor: tracks, scent or broken foliage, usually left by an animal in the wild

States: nickname for Republic of South Africa

stick: military term for a group of three or four men

stopper group: cut-off group preventing an enemy escape

tenente: (Portuguese) lieutenant

trommel: (Afrikaans) steel trunk

webbing: battle harness in which ammunition, rations and water are carried

when-we's: name given to former Rhodesian military servicemen, who were constantly referring to their service and experience in the Rhodesian Army ('When we were in Rhodesia ...')

white phos: hand grenade or shell containing white phosphorus

Weapons, vehicles, aircraft and equipment used at the Battle of Savate

Weapons

AK-47: Avtomat Kalashnikova 47, a Soviet-made 7.62 × 39-millimetre automatic rifle

AKM: folding-butt variant of the AK-47

B10: Bezotkatnojie orudie-10, a Soviet-made 82-millimetre recoilless rifle

Browning: light machine gun with old three-inch cartridge modified to take 7.62 × 51-millimetre cartridges. Or a heavy machine gun with old 0.5-inch cartridge modified to 12.7 × 107-millimetre-calibre, also known as Five-O-Browning

G3: 7.62 × 51-millimetre NATO battle rifle developed in the 1950s by German armament manufacturer Heckler & Koch in collaboration with Spanish state-owned design and development agency Centro de Estudios Técnicos de Materiales Especiales (CETME)

Grad-P: single-tube, light portable 122-millimetre-calibre Soviet rocket launcher. Mounted on a tripod, it could fire a 46-kilogram rocket with an 18.3-kilogram warhead a maximum distance of 11 kilometres. *See also* mono-Katyusha

H-hour: the time of day at which an attack, landing or other military operation is scheduled to begin

hand grenades: Soviet F1, RGD 5, RG 4, RG 5 and RG 42; South African M26

HK21: Heckler & Kock, model 21; German 7.62 × 51-millimetre general-purpose light-machine gun, developed in 1961 by small-arms manufacturer Heckler & Koch

LMG: light machine gun

M72: portable, one-shot, 66-millimetre unguided light anti-tank weapon; also known as the M72 LAW

M79: 40-millimetre US grenade launcher

MAG: Mitrailleuse d'Appui Général, a Belgian general-purpose 7.62 × 51-millimetre machine gun manufactured by Fabrique Nationale d'Herstal (FN)

mono-Katyusha: single rocket launcher tube from the BM-21 Katyusha rocket launcher. *See also* Grad-P

mortars: 60, 81, 82 and 120-millimetre calibres

PKM: variant of the Soviet Pulemyot Kalashnikova (PK) 7.62 x 54-millimetre machine gun

R1: South African–made 7.62 x 51-millimetre-calibre automatic rifle, similar to the British SLR and Belgian FN, and replaced by the R4 rifle

RPD: Ruchnoy Pulemyot Degtyaryova, Soviet-made light machine gun with drum magazine, 7.62 x 39-millimetre calibre

RPG7: variant of the Reaktivniy Protivotankovyi Granatomet, an anti-tank, tube-launched grenade of Soviet origin, with a maximum effective range of 500 metres and an explosive warhead weighing 2.4 kilograms

RPK: Ruchnoy Pulemyot Kalashnikova, AK-47 with a longer and heavier barrel mounted on a bipod and equipped with a drum or 40-round magazine

ZPU-1: single-barrelled anti-aircraft gun based on the Soviet 14.5-millimetre Krupnokaliberniy Pulemyot Vladimirova (KPV) heavy machine gun

Vehicles

BRDM: Boyevaya Razvedyvatelnaya Dozornaya Mashina, a Soviet-made light armoured car. Eight-wheeled and amphibious, it carries 14.5 x 114-millimetre and 7.62 x 54-millimetre machine guns

BTR-152: acronym for *bronetransporter*, translated from Russian as 'armoured transporter', model 152; non-amphibious Soviet armoured personnel carrier that entered service in 1950; replaced in the infantry vehicle role in the early 1970s by the BTR-60

Buffel: South African–manufactured mine-protected vehicle mounted on a Unimog chassis capable of transporting a section, and with a V-shaped hull designed to deflect the blast and debris of exploding mines

GAZ-66: Gorkovsky Avtomobilny Zavod, a Soviet-manufactured 4 x 4 military truck

GSP amphibious ferry: Gusenichniy Samokhodniy Parom, a Soviet heavy amphibious ferry, introduced in 1959. Standard heavy amphibious ferry of the former Warsaw Pact armed forces

IFA: Industrieverband Fahrzeugbau, East German–manufactured 4 x 4 military truck

Kwêvoël: South African–manufactured, six-wheel-drive, 10-ton, mine-resistant cargo vehicle, also referred to as a Kwê. The name derives from the truck's engine noise, which is similar to the distinct call of the grey loerie, also known as the grey go-away-bird (Afrikaans: *kwêvoël*)

STAR: Polish-manufactured, 3.5-ton military truck

Aircraft

Alouette III: single-engine light helicopter of French origin, used in a trooper role to carry a crew of two plus four soldiers, or in a casualty-evacuation role to carry a crew of two plus two stretchers, or in an offensive role as a gunship to carry a 20-millimetre cannon firing out of the port side

Cessna 185: single-engine, four-seat light aircraft

Impala: single-engine, light jet ground-attack aircraft, armed with 68-millimetre rockets, bombs and a 30-millimetre cannon

Puma: French-built twin-engine transport helicopter that carried a crew of three plus 16 lightly armed or 12 fully armed troops

Telstar: aircraft flown at medium altitude to relay VHF radio messages from aircraft on low-flying operational missions

Other equipment, mines and ammunition

A52: very-high-frequency radio

A72: ultra-high-frequency radio

B22: high-frequency radio

Claymore: anti-personnel mine that directs shrapnel at a predetermined area

HEAT: 82-millimetre recoilless high-explosive anti-tank ammunition for the B10 recoilless rifle

Klepper Aerius kayak: collapsible two-man canoe made of canvas and vinyl mounted on a lightweight wooden frame

PE4: plastic explosives

TA grenade: terephthalic acid smoke grenade

TM46: large, circular, metal-cased Soviet anti-tank landmine

TMM: *Tyazhelo Mekhniznrovanny Most*; Soviet-manufactured vehicle-launched bridge, developed to allow forces to traverse small gaps and gaps wider than a single bridge but that do not require a pontoon

238

Index

By the same author

32 Battalion

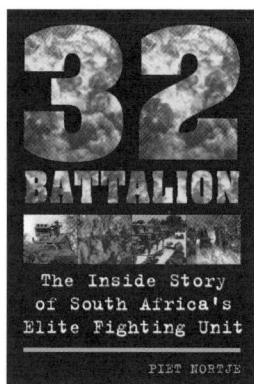

Every war has at least one – a unit so different, so daring, that it becomes the stuff of which legends are made and heroes are born. Among the South African forces fighting in Angola from 1975 to 1989, that unit was 32 Battalion.

Founded in utmost secrecy from the vanquished remnants of a foreign rebel movement, undefeated in 12 years of front-line battle, feared by enemies that included both conventional Cuban armies and Namibian guerrilla fighters, the Buffalo Soldiers became the South African army's best combat unit since World War II, with no fewer than 13 members winning the highest decoration for bravery under fire.

But when peace broke out in southern Africa, the victors of Savate became the victims of sophistry. Their fate and future determined by politicians who understood little and cared less about this truly unique fraternity, 32 Battalion ceased to exist in 1993, its short history and long list of battle honours known only to those whose enemies called them Os Terriveis – the Terrible Ones.

Now, for the first time, the story of 32 Battalion can be told in full, with neither adornment nor apology, by one of its longest-serving members.

The book draws from top secret documents, revealing information that has never been made public before. Also included are rare photographs that evoke the colourful, and often controversial, history of 32 Battalion, as well as detailed maps depicting specific operations and deployments.

ISBN: 978 1 86872 914 2 (print)
ISBN: 978 1 77020 143 9 (ePub)
ISBN: 978 1 77020 144 6 (PDF)

The Terrible Ones

The military history publishing event of the decade.
Two hardcover volumes, contained in a slipcase.
1380 pages. 80 maps. 600 photographs.
Based on 10 000 pages of previously classified documents.
Draws from over 200 interviews with former 32 Battalion members
as well as Portuguese, SWAPO, Angolan, Cuban and Russian soldiers.
A must for collectors.

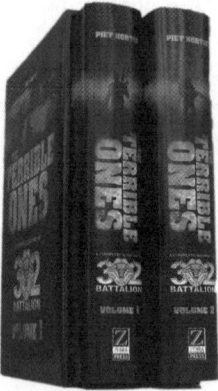

The soldiers of 32 Battalion were so feared by their enemies that they were called '*Os Terriveis*' – 'The Terrible Ones'. Founded in utmost secrecy from the vanquished remnants of an Angolan rebel movement, they were forged into an effective fighting machine that took on guerrilla forces and conventional armies alike. Undefeated in 12 years of frontline battle, the 'Buffalo Soldiers' became the South African Army's best combat unit since World War II.

This comprehensive two-volume work chronicles the unit's explosive history. Starting in the early 1960s, it covers events in Angola that would eventually result in the formation of 32 Battalion, and it ends in the 2000s, when the soldiers of the unit unknowingly betrayed themselves. It describes in detail the 117 documented military operations that 32 Battalion took part in from 1976 to 1993, explaining how they were planned and executed, and illustrating them with maps. It also provides personal recollections from former 32 Battalion members and their allies and enemies, vividly recreating the experience of what happened on the ground.

The Terrible Ones provides a complete picture with new insights, drawing from thousands of pages of documents in the Department of Defence Documentation Centre that have only recently been declassified. Definitive and magisterial, this is one of the most impressive military histories ever written.

ISBN: 978 1 77022 397 4

Do you have any comments, suggestions or
feedback about this book or any other Zebra Press titles?
Contact us at **talkback@zebrapress.co.za**

*

Visit **www.randomstruik.co.za** and subscribe
to our newsletter for monthly updates and news